John Walkenbach's Favorite Excel® Tips & Tricks

John Walkenbach

WILEY

Wiley Publishing, Inc.

John Walkenbach's Favorite Excel® Tips & Tricks

Published by
Wiley Publishing, Inc.
111 River Street
Hoboken, NJ 07030-5774
www.wiley.com

Copyright © 2005 by Wiley Publishing, Inc., Indianapolis, Indiana

Published by Wiley Publishing, Inc., Indianapolis, Indiana

Published simultaneously in Canada

For general information on our other products and services, please contact our Customer Care Department within the U.S. at 800-762-2974, outside the U.S. at 317-572-3993, or fax 317-572-4002.

For technical support, please visit www.wiley.com/techsupport.

Wiley also publishes its books in a variety of electronic formats. Some content that appears in print may not be available in electronic books.

Library of Congress Control Number: 2005924606

ISBN-13: 978-0-7645-9816-6

ISBN-10: 0-7645-9816-3

Manufactured in the United States of America

10 9 8 7 6 5

1B/SU/QW/QV/IN

WILEY

About the Author

John Walkenbach is a leading authority on spreadsheet software, and principal of J-Walk and Associates Inc., an Arizona–based consulting firm that specializes in spreadsheet application development. John is the author of about 40 spreadsheet books, and has written more than 300 articles and reviews for a variety of publications, including *PC World*, *InfoWorld*, *PC Magazine*, *Windows*, and *PC/Computing*. He also maintains a popular Internet Web site (*The Spreadsheet Page*, www.j-walk.com/ss), and is the developer of the Power Utility Pak, an award-winning add-in for Microsoft Excel. John graduated from the University of Missouri, and earned a Masters and PhD from the University of Montana.

Acknowledgments

Writing a book that contains Excel tips was much more difficult than I originally thought it would be. The challenge is deciding upon what exactly constitutes a tip. If I present a technique that you didn't know about, you may consider it to be a valuable tip. But if you're already familiar with the technique, it's *not* a tip.

I decided to select my tips based on a specific Excel user — a person who really exists, but who will remain nameless. This person uses Excel on a regular basis, but she has never bothered to take the time to dig in and learn how to work more efficiently. I think this target reader has a lot in common with millions of other Excel users. If that's the case, most of them will find this book to be very useful. So thanks to my anonymous target reader.

Thanks are also due to the people behind the scenes who converted my Microsoft Word files into a tangible book. First, thanks to Greg Croy, my acquisitions editor. This book was Greg's idea, and I'm glad that he chose me to be the author. I also appreciate the help and guidance of Mark Enochs, my project editor. He kept me on schedule and made lots of helpful suggestions. Finally, thanks to Allen Wyatt, my very capable technical editor. He corrected quite a few errors, made some very useful suggestions, and taught me a few things in the process.

Credits

Project Editor
Mark Enochs

Executive Editor
Greg Croy

Copy Editor
Jean Rogers

Technical Editor
Allen Wyatt

Editorial Manager
Kevin Kirschner

Editorial Assistant
Amanda Foxworth

Special Help
Andy Hollandbeck
Beth Taylor

Media Development Manager
Laura VanWinkle

Media Development Supervisor
Richard Graves

Vice President and Executive Group Publisher
Richard Swadley

Vice President and Publisher
Andy Cummings

Executive Acquisitions Director
Mary Bednarek

Editorial Director
Mary C. Corder

Book Designer
Kathie S. Rickard

Project Coordinator
Nancee Reeves

Layout and Graphics
Carrie A. Foster
Lauren Goddard
Denny Hager
Jennifer Heleine
Lynsey Osborn

Proofreader
Laura L. Bowman

Indexer
Steve Rath

Quality Control Technicians
Laura Albert
Leeann Harney

Vice President of Production Services
Gerry Fahey

Director of Composition Services
Debbie Stailey

Contents at a Glance

Introduction   1

Part I: Basic Excel Usage   7

Part II: Data Entry   67

Part III: Formatting   103

Part IV: Basic Formulas and Functions   157

Part V: Useful Formula Examples   207

Part VI: Charts and Graphics   271

Part VII: Data Analysis and Lists   313

Part VIII: Working with Files   351

Part IX: Printing   377

Part X: Customizing Toolbars and Menus   405

Part XI: Spotting, Fixing, and Preventing Errors   423

Part XII: Basic VBA and Macros   443

Part XIII: Conversions and Mathematical Calculations   483

Part XIV: Sources for Excel Information   511

Index   521

Table of Contents

Introduction   1

  What You Should Know   1
  What You Should Have   2
  Conventions in This Book   2
  Entering VBA Code   4
  How This Book Is Organized   5
  How to Use This Book   5
  About the Power Utility Pak Offer   6
  Reach Out   6

Part I: Basic Excel Usage   7

  Understanding Excel Versions   9
  Maximizing Menu Efficiency   11
  Selecting Cells Efficiently   13
  Making "Special" Range Selections   17
  Undoing, Redoing, and Repeating   21
  Changing the Number of Undo Levels   23
  Discovering Some Useful Shortcut Keys   25
  Navigating Sheets in a Workbook   27
  Resetting the Used Area of a Worksheet   29
  Understanding Workbooks versus Windows   31
  Avoiding the Task Pane When Using Excel 2003 Help   33
  Customizing the Default Workbook   35
  Changing the Sheet Tab Appearance   37
  Hiding User Interface Elements   39
  Hiding Columns or Rows   41
  Hiding Cell Contents   43
  Performing Inexact Searches   45
  Replacing Formatting   47
  Increasing the Number of Rows and Columns   49
  Limiting the Usable Area in a Worksheet   51
  Using an Alternative to Cell Comments   55
  Changing the Text Size in Excel's Help Window   57
  Making a Worksheet "Very Hidden"   59
  Troubleshooting Common Setup Problems   61

Part II: Data Entry   67

  Understanding the Types of Data   69
  Moving the Cell Pointer after Entering Data   73
  Selecting a Range of Input Cells before Entering Data   75

Using AutoComplete to Automate Data Entry   77
Keeping Titles in View by Freezing Panes   79
Automatically Filling a Range with a Series   81
Working with Fractions   85
Proofing Your Data with Audio   87
Controlling Automatic Hyperlinks   89
Entering Credit Card Numbers   91
Using Excel's Built-In Data Entry Form   93
Customizing and Sharing AutoCorrect Entries   95
Restricting Cursor Movement to Input Cells   97
Controlling the Office Clipboard   99
Creating a Drop-Down List in a Cell   101

Part III: Formatting   103

Quick Number Formatting   105
Using "Tear Off" Toolbars   107
Creating Custom Number Formats   109
Using Custom Number Formats to Scale Values   113
Using Custom Date Formatting   117
Some Useful Custom Number Formats   119
Showing Text and a Value in a Cell   123
Merging Cells   125
Formatting Individual Characters in a Cell   127
Displaying Times That Exceed 24 Hours   129
Fixing Non-Numeric Numbers   131
Using AutoFormats   133
Dealing with Gridlines, Borders, and Underlines   135
Creating 3D Formatting Effects   137
Wrapping Text in a Cell   139
Seeing All Characters in a Font   141
Entering Special Characters   143
Using Named Styles   145
Understanding How Excel Handles Color   147
Setting Up Alternate Row Shading   151
Adding a Background Image to a Worksheet   155

Part IV: Basic Formulas and Functions   157

When to Use Absolute References   159
When to Use Mixed References   161
Changing the Type of a Cell Reference   163
AutoSum Tricks   165
Using the Status Bar Selection Statistics Feature   167
Converting Formulas to Values   169

Transforming Data without Using Formulas   171
Transforming Data by Using Formulas   173
Deleting Values While Keeping Formulas   175
Dealing with Function Arguments   177
Annotating a Formula without Using a Comment   179
Making an Exact Copy of a Range of Formulas   181
Monitoring Formula Cells from Any Location   183
Displaying and Printing Formulas   185
Avoiding Error Displays in Formulas   187
Using Goal Seeking   189
Understanding the Secret about Names   191
Using Named Constants   193
Using Functions in Names   195
Editing Name References   197
Using Dynamic Names   199
Creating Worksheet-Level Names   201
Working with Pre-1900 Dates   203
Working with Negative Time Values   205

Part V: Useful Formula Examples   207

Calculating Holidays   209
Calculating a Weighted Average   213
Calculating a Person's Age   215
Ranking Values with an Array Formula   217
Counting Characters in a Cell   219
Expressing a Number as an Ordinal   221
Extracting Words from a String   223
Parsing Names   225
Removing Titles from Names   227
Generating a Series of Dates   229
Determining Specific Dates   231
Displaying a Calendar in a Range   235
Various Methods of Rounding Numbers   237
Rounding Time Values   241
Returning the Last Nonblank Cell in a Column or Row   243
Using the COUNTIF Function   245
Counting Cells That Meet Multiple Criteria   247
Counting Distinct Entries in a Range   251
Calculating Single-Criterion Conditional Sums   253
Calculating Multiple-Criterion Conditional Sums   255
Looking Up an Exact Value   257
Performing a Two-Way Lookup   259
Performing a Two-Column Lookup   261
Performing a Lookup Using an Array   263
Using the INDIRECT Function   265
Creating Megaformulas   267

Part VI: Charts and Graphics   271

Creating a Text Chart Directly in a Range   273
Annotating a Chart   275
Creating a Self-Expanding Chart   277
Creating Combination Charts   281
Dealing with Missing Data in a Line Chart   283
Creating a Gantt Chart   285
Creating a Thermometer-Style Chart   287
Creating a Picture Chart   291
Plotting Single-Variable Mathematical Functions   293
Plotting Two-Variable Mathematical Functions   295
Creating a Semi-Transparent Chart Series   297
Saving a Chart as a Graphics File   299
Making Charts the Same Size   301
Displaying Multiple Charts on a Chart Sheet   303
Freezing a Chart   305
Adding a Watermark to a Worksheet   307
Changing the Shape of a Cell Comment   309
Inserting a Graphic into a Cell Comment   311

Part VII: Data Analysis and Lists   313

Using the List Feature in Excel 2003   315
Sorting on More Than Three Columns   319
Using Custom Views with AutoFiltering   321
Putting Advanced Filter Results on a Different Sheet   323
Comparing Two Ranges with Conditional Formatting   325
Randomizing a List   329
Filling the Gaps in a Report   331
Creating a List from a Summary Table   333
Finding Duplicates by Using Conditional Formatting   337
Preventing Row or Column Insertions within a Range   339
Creating a Quick Frequency Tabulation   341
Controlling References to Cells within a PivotTable   343
Grouping Items by Date in a PivotTable   345
Hiding the Field Buttons in a PivotChart   349

Part VIII: Working with Files   351

Importing a Text File into a Worksheet Range   353
Getting Data from a Web Page   355
Displaying a Workbook's Full Path   359
Saving a Preview of Your Workbook   361

Using Document Properties 363

Learning Who Opened a File Last 365

Finding the Missing No To All Button When Closing Files 367

Getting a List of Filenames 369

Understanding Excel's Passwords 371

Using Workspace Files 373

Reducing the Size of a Workbook 375

Part IX: Printing 377

Controlling What Gets Printed 379

Displaying Repeating Rows or Columns on a Printout 381

Printing Noncontiguous Ranges on a Single Page 383

Preventing Objects from Printing 385

Page Numbering Tips 387

Previewing Page Breaks 389

Adding and Removing Page Breaks 391

Printing to a PDF File 393

Avoiding Printing Specific Rows 395

Making Your Printout Fit on One Page 397

Printing Formulas 399

Copying Page Setup Settings Across Sheets 401

Using Custom Views for Printing 403

Part X: Customizing Toolbars and Menus 405

Finding the Multifunctional Toolbar Buttons 407

Finding the Hidden Menu Commands 409

Customizing Menus and Toolbars 411

Creating a Custom Toolbar 413

Taming Pop-Up Toolbars 417

Attaching Toolbars to Worksheets 419

Backing Up Your Customized Toolbars and Menus 421

Part XI: Spotting, Fixing, and Preventing Errors 423

Using Excel's Error-Checking Features 425

Identifying Formula Cells 427

Dealing with Floating-Point Number Problems 429

Creating a Table of Cell and Range Names 431

Viewing Names Graphically 433

Locating Phantom Links 435

Understanding Displayed versus Actual Values 437

Tracing Cell Relationships 439

Part XII: Basic VBA and Macros   443

Learning about Macros and VBA   445
Recording a Macro   447
Understanding Security Issues Related to Macros   451
Using a Personal Macro Workbook   453
Understanding Functions versus Subs   455
Displaying Pop-Up Messages   457
Getting Information from the User   461
Running a Macro When a Workbook Is Opened   463
Creating Simple Worksheet Functions   467
Making Excel Talk   471
Understanding Custom Function Limitations   473
Executing a Menu Item with a Macro   475
Storing Custom Functions in an Add-In   477
Displaying a Pop-Up Linked Calendar   479
Using Add-Ins   481

Part XIII: Conversions and Mathematical Calculations   483

Converting Between Measurement Systems   485
Converting Temperatures   493
Solving Right Triangles   495
Calculating Area, Surface, Circumference, and Volume   497
Solving Simultaneous Equations   501
Generating Unique Random Integers   503
Generating Random Numbers   505
Calculating Roots and a Remainder   507
Calculating a Conditional Average   509

Part XIV: Sources for Excel Information   511

Using Excel's Help System   513
Searching the Internet for Help   515
Using Excel Newsgroups   517
Browsing Excel-Related Web Sites   519

Index   521

Introduction

Excel is a very popular program. Millions of people throughout the world use it on a regular basis. But it's a safe bet that the vast majority of users have yet to discover some of the amazing things this product can do. If I've done my job, you'll find enough useful information in this book to help you use Excel on a new level.

What You Should Know

This is not a beginner's guide to Excel. Rather, it's a book for those who already use Excel but realize that they have a lot more to learn. This book is filled with tips and tricks that I've learned over the years, and I'm certain that about 99 percent of all Excel users will find something new and useful in these pages.

If you have absolutely no experience with Excel, this may not be the best book for you. To get the most out of this book, you should have some background using Excel. Specifically, I assume that you know how to accomplish the following with Excel:

- Create workbooks, insert sheets, save files, and other basic tasks
- Navigate through a workbook
- Use Excel's menus, toolbars, and dialog boxes
- Use basic Windows features, such as file management and copy-and-paste techniques

What You Should Have

To make the best use of this book, you need a copy of Microsoft Excel. I wrote this book based on Excel 2003 (which is part of Microsoft Office 2003). With a few exceptions (noted in the text), the material in this book also applies to all earlier versions of Excel that are still in use.

NOTE

I use Excel for Windows exclusively, and I do not own a Macintosh. Therefore, I can't guarantee that all of the examples in this book will work with Excel for Macintosh. Excel's cross-platform compatibility is pretty good, but it's definitely not perfect.

As far as hardware goes for the computer you use to run Excel, the faster the better. And, of course, the more memory in your system, the happier you'll be. Finally, I strongly recommend that you use a high-resolution video mode: at least 1024 x 768.

Conventions in This Book

Take a minute to skim this section and learn some of the typographic conventions used throughout this book.

NOTE

You need to use the keyboard to enter formulas. In addition, you can work with menus and dialog boxes directly from the keyboard — a method you may find easier if your hands are already positioned over the keys.

Formula Listings

Formulas usually appear on a separate line in `monospace` font. For example, I may list the following formula:

```
=VLOOKUP(StockNumber,PriceList,2,False)
```

Excel supports a special type of formula known as an *array formula*. When you enter an array formula, press Ctrl+Shift+Enter (not just Enter). Excel encloses an array formula in curly braces in order to remind you that it's an array formula.

NOTE

Do not type the curly braces for an array formula. Excel will put them in automatically.

VBA Code Listings

This book also contains examples of VBA code. Each listing appears in a `monospace` `font`; each line of code occupies a separate line. To make the code easier to read, I usually use indentation on specific lines. Indentation is optional, but it does help to delineate statements that go together.

If a line of code doesn't fit on a single line in this book, I use the standard VBA line continuation sequence: a space followed by an underscore character. This indicates that the line of code extends to the next line. For example, the following two lines comprise a single VBA statement:

```
If Right(cell.Value, 1) = "!" Then cell.Value _
   = Left(cell.Value, Len(cell.Value) - 1)
```

You can enter this code either exactly as shown on two lines, or on a single line without the trailing underscore character.

Key Names

Names of keys on the keyboard appear in normal type, for example Alt, Home, PgDn, and Ctrl. When you should press two or more keys simultaneously, the keys are connected with a plus sign: "Press Ctrl+G to display the Go To dialog box."

Menus

When you need to select a command by using menus, I use a shorthand for the menu choice like this: "Select Edit⇨Copy." This translates to "Select Edit from the menu bar, and then click Copy on the menu."

Functions, Procedures, and Named Ranges

The names of Excel's worksheet functions appear in all uppercase, like so: "Use the SUM function to add the values in column A."

Macro and VBA procedure names appear in normal type: "Execute the InsertTotals procedure." I often use mixed upper- and lowercase to make these names easier to read. Named ranges appear in italic: "Select the *InputArea* range."

Unless you're dealing with text inside of quotation marks, Excel is not sensitive to case. In other words, both of the following formulas produce the same result:

```
=SUM(A1:A50)
=sum(a1:a50)
```

Excel, however, will convert the characters in the second formula to uppercase.

Mouse Conventions

The mouse terminology in this book is all standard fare: pointing, clicking, right-clicking, dragging, and so on. You know the drill.

What the Icons Mean

Throughout the book, icons appear in the left margin to call your attention to points that are particularly important.

NOTE

I use Note icons to tell you that something is important — perhaps a concept that may help you master the task at hand or something fundamental for understanding subsequent material.

WARNING

I use Warning icons when the operation that I'm describing can cause problems if you're not careful.

CROSS-REFERENCE

I use the Cross-Reference icon to refer you to other tips that have more to say on a particular topic.

Entering VBA Code

Some of these tips and tricks involve VBA (Visual Basic for Applications). VBA is a programming language built into Excel. Following is the basic procedure that you use to enter a VBA procedure into a workbook:

1. Press Alt+F11 to activate the VBA editor window.

2. Click your workbook's name in the Project window. If the Project window is not visible, press Ctrl+R to display it.

3. Choose Insert⇨Module to add a VBA module to the project. A code window will appear.

4. Type the code in the code window.

When your workbook contains VBA code, you may receive a warning when you open the workbook. This warning depends on your security settings. Choose Tools⇨Macro⇨Security to view or change your security settings. I recommend the Medium security setting. When this setting is in effect, you will have the option to enable or disable macros in every workbook you open.

How This Book Is Organized

In order to provide some semblance of order, I grouped these tips and tricks into 14 parts:

- Part I: Basic Excel Usage
- Part II: Data Entry
- Part III: Formatting
- Part IV: Basic Formulas and Functions
- Part V: Useful Formula Examples
- Part VI: Charts and Graphics
- Part VII: Data Analysis and Lists
- Part VIII: Working with Files
- Part IX: Printing
- Part X: Customizing Toolbars and Menus
- Part XI: Spotting, Fixing, and Preventing Errors
- Part XII: Basic VBA and Macros
- Part XIII: Conversions and Mathematical Calculations
- Part XIV: Sources for Excel Information

How to Use This Book

This book really isn't intended to be read cover-to-cover, as you would read a novel — but I'm sure some people will do so. More likely, you'll want to use it as a reference book and consult it when necessary. If you're faced with a challenging task, you may want to check the index first to see whether the book specifically addresses your problem. The order of the parts and tips is arbitrary. Most readers will probably skip around, picking up useful tidbits here and there.

About the Power Utility Pak Offer

Toward the back of the book, you'll find a coupon that you can redeem for a discounted copy of my award-winning Power Utility Pak — a collection of useful Excel utilities, plus many new worksheet functions. I developed this package using VBA exclusively.

You can also use this coupon to purchase the complete VBA source code for a nominal fee. Studying the code is an excellent way to pick up some useful programming techniques. You can take the product for a test drive by downloading the trial version from my Web site at www.j-walk.com/ss.

 NOTE
Power Utility Pak requires Excel 2000 for Windows or later.

Reach Out

I'm always interested in getting feedback on my books. The best way to provide this feedback is via e-mail. Send your comments and suggestions to author@j-walk.com.

Unfortunately, I'm not able to reply to specific questions. Posting your question to one of the Excel newsgroups is, by far, the best way to get such assistance. See Part XIII for more information.

Also, when you're out surfing the Web, don't overlook my Web site ("The Spreadsheet Page") at www.j-walk.com/ss.

Now, without further ado, it's time to turn the page and expand your horizons.

Part I

Basic Excel Usage

In this part, you'll find tips and tricks covering some of the fundamental uses of Excel, from how to select cells and navigate sheets in a workbook, to hiding rows and columns, as well as troubleshooting common setup problems.

Tips and Where to Find Them

Tip 1 Understanding Excel Versions 9

Tip 2 Maximizing Menu Efficiency 11

Tip 3 Selecting Cells Efficiently 13

Tip 4 Making "Special" Range Selections 17

Tip 5 Undoing, Redoing, and Repeating 21

Tip 6 Changing the Number of Undo Levels 23

Tip 7 Discovering Some Useful Shortcut Keys 25

Tip 8 Navigating Sheets in a Workbook 27

Tip 9 Resetting the Used Area of a Worksheet 29

Tip 10 Understanding Workbooks versus Windows 31

Tip 11 Avoiding the Task Pane When Using Excel 2003 Help 33

Tip 12 Customizing the Default Workbook 35

Tip 13 Changing the Sheet Tab Appearance 37

Tip 14 Hiding User Interface Elements 39

Tip 15 Hiding Columns or Rows 41

Tip 16 Hiding Cell Contents 43

Tip 17 Performing Inexact Searches 45

Tip 18 Replacing Formatting 47

Tip 19 Increasing the Number of Rows and Columns 49

Tip 20 Limiting the Usable Area in a Worksheet 51

Tip 21 Using an Alternative to Cell Comments 55

Tip 22 Changing the Text Size in Excel's Help Window 57

Tip 23 Making a Worksheet "Very Hidden" 59

Tip 24 Troubleshooting Common Setup Problems 61

Understanding Excel Versions

What version of Excel do you use? Chances are, you don't even know. To find out, select Help⇨About Microsoft Excel. Figure 1-1 shows that I'm currently using version 11, also known (officially) as Microsoft Office Excel 2003. Most people just call it Excel 2003. Notice the decimal places after the version number? That represents the *build* of the product. In my case, I'm using build 5612. I don't know what the other numbers represent.

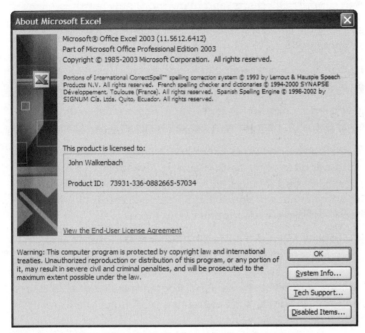

Figure 1-1: This dialog box displays the Excel version.

So who cares what version of Excel you use? Most of the time, nobody cares. As long as your version does what you want it to do, the version makes no difference at all. But if you share your workbooks with other users, the version *may* be important. For example, suppose you use Excel 2003, and you give a co-worker (who uses Excel 97) a copy of a workbook. If you happened to make use of a feature that was introduced in Excel 2000, Excel 2002, or Excel 2003, it's possible that your co-worker may not be able to work with your file. He or she will still be able to open the file, but some functionality may be missing.

Fortunately (or unfortunately, for power users), Excel's basic feature set has not changed much since Excel 2000. Therefore, version compatibility problems are not much of a problem.

For the record, the following table shows the major version numbers of Excel.

Part I

Version	Released	Comments
1	1985	The first version of Excel was for the Apple Macintosh.
2	1987	The first Windows version was labeled "2" to correspond to the Macintosh version. Because Windows was not widely used, this version included a run-time version of Windows.
3	1990	This version included toolbars, drawing capabilities, outlining, add-in support, 3D charts, and many more new features.
4	1992	The first "popular" version of Excel. It included quite a few usability features.
5	1993	Excel 5 was a major upgrade. It included multisheet workbooks and support for VBA.
7*	1995	This version was known as Excel 95. It was the first major 32-bit version of Excel. Feature-wise, it was very similar to Excel 5.
8	1997	This version was known as Excel 97. This was the first version to support conditional formatting and data validation. It also incorporated new menus and toolbars. VBA programmers found quite a few enhancements, including a completely new VBA editor, UserForms, class modules, and more.
9	1999	This version was known as Excel 2000. It could use HTML as a native file format, and (for the first time) supported COM add-ins. It also featured a "self-repair" capability, enhanced Clipboard, and pivot charts. VBA programmers were able to use modeless UserForms, and several new VBA functions were introduced.
10	2001	Known as Excel 2002, this version was part of Office XP. It has a long list of new features, but most of them will probably be of little value to the majority of users. Perhaps the most significant feature is the ability to recover your work when Excel crashes.
11	2003	As I write this, it's the current version, officially known as Microsoft Office Excel 2003. The new features in this version are: (a) improved support for XML, (b) a new "list range" feature, (c) Smart Tag enhancements, and (d) corrected statistical functions.

There is no Excel 6. Beginning with Excel 7, the version numbering was changed so all of the Microsoft Office applications had the same version number.

Hardly anyone uses a version of Excel prior to Excel 97, but if you must share a workbook with someone using Excel 5 or Excel 95, you'll need to save your file in an older format. Select File⇨Save As, and then choose Microsoft Excel 5.0/95 Workbook (*.xls) from the Save As Type drop-down list.

Maximizing Menu Efficiency

Just about every Windows program has menus, and most users know how to use them. But most users don't know how to use menus *efficiently*. If your goal is to maximize your efficiency when using Excel, it's worth your while to learn a few menu usage tips.

Make Sure That Excel Always Displays Full Menus

Perhaps one of the dumbest decisions ever to come out of Microsoft is the so-called "adaptive menus." If you choose this option, Excel's menus adapt to show the most commonly used commands at the top, and some menu items only appear after a delay. On the surface, this may seem like a good idea, but there's definitely a lot to be said for having menus in which the items always appear in the same order. For example, it doesn't take long to learn that Filter is the second menu item on the Data menu. If that item can move around, it will take you longer to find it.

To make sure that your copy of Excel is set up to always display full menus, choose View⇨ Toolbars⇨Customize. In the Customize dialog box, click the Options tab. Make sure that the Always Show Full Menus option is enabled. This setting, by the way, will transfer to all of your other Microsoft Office applications.

Use the Keyboard as Much as Possible

Most people think that menus are designed for use with a mouse. That may be true, but if you want to improve your productivity, forget the mouse and access the menus using your keyboard. Notice that every menu and menu item has an underlined letter. Access the top-level menus by pressing Alt along with the underlined letter. For example, Alt+O displays the Format menu. Then you can press another underlined letter on the submenu to execute the command. Or you may prefer to use the arrow keys to select a menu item, and then execute it by pressing Enter.

For example, to clear the formatting in the selected range of cells, press Alt+EAA (which stands for Edit⇨Clear⇨All).

Many of Excel's menu items lead to a dialog box (those menu items display with three dots at the end). You can also navigate the dialog boxes using only the keyboard. Use the Tab key to move among the options, or press an underlined letter to change an option. When a check box is selected, use the spacebar to toggle between checked and unchecked. Press Enter to simulate clicking the OK button (or press the Esc key to cancel the dialog box).

For example, suppose you have a range of formulas and you'd like to convert those formulas to values. Here's how to do it using only the keyboard:

1. Select the range that contains the formula cells.
2. Press Ctrl+C (the keyboard shortcut for Edit⇨Copy).
3. Press Alt+ES (for Edit⇨Paste Special).

4. In the Paste Special dialog box, press V (the underlined letter for the Values option).

5. Press Enter.

Repeat this a few times and it becomes second nature — almost like a single command. Bottom line? Every time you move your hand from the keyboard to your mouse, it takes time. Practice accessing the menus using the keyboard, and you'll eventually find that your productivity increases.

Learn the Menu Shortcuts

You may have noticed that some menu items display a keyboard shortcut. For example, the Cells menu item (displayed when you choose Format⇨Cells) shows Ctrl+1 next to it. This means, of course, that you can press Ctrl+1 to go directly to the Format Cells dialog box.

Examine the Excel menu items and memorize the menu shortcuts for commands that you use frequently. Then get in the habit of using them.

Use the Right-Click Menus

One nice thing about Excel is the convenience of its shortcut menus. You can right-click just about anything on-screen to get a context-sensitive shortcut menu.

And if you're trying to decrease your mouse dependence, you can also press Shift+F10 to display the shortcut menu for the selected item (cell, range, chart element, and so on).

Selecting Cells Efficiently

Many Excel users think that the only way to select a range of cells is to drag over the cells with the mouse. Although selecting cells with a mouse works, it's rarely the most efficient way to accomplish the task. The answer, of course, is to use your keyboard to select ranges.

Selecting a Range Using the Shift and Arrow Keys

The simplest way to select a range is to press (and hold) Shift, and then use the arrow keys to highlight the cells. For larger selections, you can use PgDn or PgUp while pressing Shift to move in larger increments.

You can also use the End key to quickly extend a selection to the last nonempty cell in a row or column. To select the range B3:B8 (see Figure 3-1) using the keyboard, move the cell pointer to B3, and then press the Shift key while you press End, followed by the down arrow key. Similarly, to select B3:D3, press the Shift key while you press End, followed by the right-arrow key.

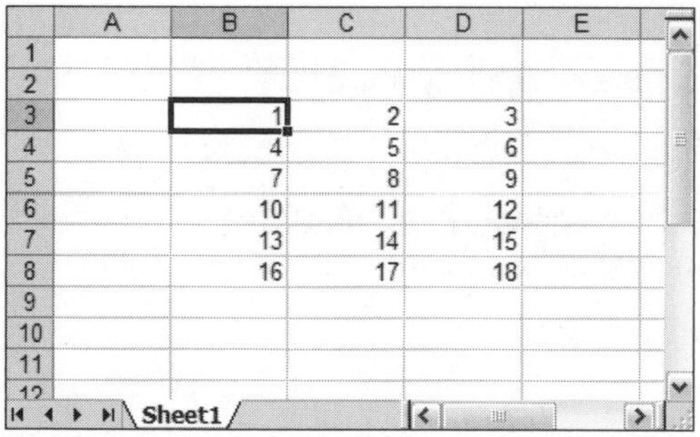

Figure 3-1: A range of cells.

Selecting the Current Region

Often, you'll need to select a large rectangular selection of cells — the current region. To select the entire block of cells, move the cell pointer anywhere within the range and press Ctrl+Shift+8.

Selecting a Range by Shift+Clicking

In the case of a very large range, using the mouse may be the most efficient method — but dragging is not required. Select the upper-left cell in the range. Then scroll to the lower-right corner of the range, press Shift, and click the lower-right cell.

Selecting Noncontiguous Ranges

Most of the time, your range selections are probably simple rectangular ranges. In some cases, you may need to make a multiple selection — a selection that includes nonadjacent cells or ranges. For example, you may want to apply formatting to cells in different areas of your worksheet. If you make a multiple selection, you can apply the formatting in one step to all of the selected ranges. Figure 3-2 shows an example of a multiple selection.

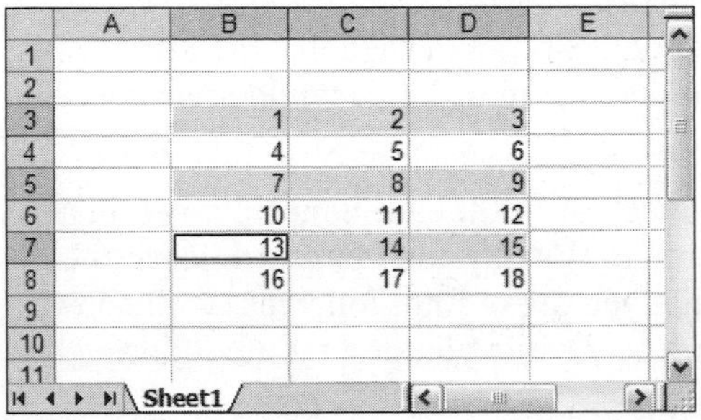

Figure 3-2: A multiple selection that consists of noncontiguous ranges.

You can select a noncontiguous range using your mouse or the keyboard.

Press Ctrl as you click and drag the mouse to highlight the individual cells or ranges.

From the keyboard, select a range as described previously (using the Shift key). Then press Shift+F8 to select another range without canceling the previous range selection. Repeat this as many times as needed.

Selecting Entire Rows

To select a single row, click in the row heading. Or select any cell in the row and press Shift+spacebar.

To select multiple adjacent rows, click and drag in the row headings. Or select any cell in the first (or last) row, press Shift+spacebar, and use the arrow keys to extend the selection down (or up).

To select multiple nonadjacent rows, press Ctrl while you click the borders for the rows you want to include.

Selecting Entire Columns

To select a single column, click in the column heading. Or select any cell in the column and press Ctrl+spacebar.

To select multiple adjacent columns, click and drag in the column headings. Or select any cell in the first (or last) column, press Ctrl+spacebar, and use the arrow keys to extend the selection to the right (or to the left).

To select multiple nonadjacent columns, press Ctrl while you click the borders for the rows you want to include.

Selecting Multisheet Ranges

In addition to two-dimensional ranges on a single worksheet, ranges can extend across multiple worksheets to be three-dimensional ranges.

Figure 3-3 shows a simple example of a multisheet workbook. The workbook has four sheets, named Totals, Marketing, Operations, and Manufacturing. The sheets are laid out identically.

	A	B	C	D	E	F	G
1	Budget Summary						
2							
3		Q1	Q2	Q3	Q4	Year Total	
4	Salaries	286,500.00	286,500.00	286,500.00	290,500.00	1,150,000.00	
5	Travel	40,500.00	42,525.00	44,651.25	46,883.81	174,560.06	
6	Supplies	59,500.00	62,475.00	65,598.75	68,878.69	256,452.44	
7	Facility	144,000.00	144,000.00	144,000.00	144,000.00	576,000.00	
8	Total	530,500.00	535,500.00	540,750.00	550,262.50	2,157,012.50	
9							

budget.xls — Totals / Marketing / Operations / Manufacturing /

Figure 3-3: Each worksheet in this workbook is laid out identically.

Assume that you want to apply the same formatting to all the sheets — for example, you want to make the column headings bold with background shading. Selecting a multisheet range is the best approach. When the ranges are selected, the formatting is applied to all sheets.

In general, selecting a multisheet range is a simple two-step process:

1. Select the range in one sheet.

2. Select the worksheets to include in the range.

NOTE

To select a group of contiguous worksheets, press Shift and click the sheet tab of the last worksheet that you want to include in the selection. To select individual worksheets, press Ctrl and click the sheet tab of each worksheet that you want to select. When you make the selection, the sheet tabs of the selected sheets appear as reverse video, and Excel displays [Group] in the title bar.

When you're finished working with the multisheet range, click any sheet tab to get out of Group mode.

Making "Special" Range Selections

As you use Excel, you'll probably find yourself wondering how you can locate specific types of cells in your worksheets. For example, wouldn't it be handy to be able to locate every cell that contains a formula, or perhaps all of the cells whose values depend on the current cell?

Excel provides an easy way to locate these and many other special types of cells. You do this by choosing Edit⇨Go To (or pressing F5) to display the Go To dialog box, and then clicking the Special button to display the Go To Special dialog box, as shown in Figure 4-1.

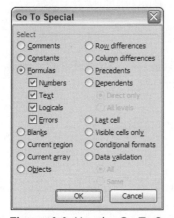

Figure 4-1: Use the Go To Special dialog box to select specific types of cells.

After you make your choice in the dialog box, Excel selects the qualifying subset of cells in the current selection. Usually, this results in a multiple selection. If no cells qualify, Excel lets you know with the message *No cells were found*.

NOTE

If you bring up the Go To Special dialog box with only one cell selected, Excel bases its selection on the entire active area of the worksheet. Otherwise, the selection is based on the selected range.

Table 4-1 summarizes the options available in the Go To Special dialog box.

TABLE 4-1 GO TO SPECIAL OPTIONS

Option	What It Does
Comments	Selects only the cells that contain cell comments.
Constants	Selects all nonempty cells that don't contain formulas. This option is useful if you have a model set up and you want to clear out all input cells and enter new values. The formulas remain intact. Use the check boxes under the Formulas option to choose which cells to include.
Formulas	Selects cells that contain formulas. Qualify this by selecting the check box for the type of result: Numbers, Text, Logicals (the logical values TRUE or FALSE), or Errors.
Blanks	Selects all empty cells.
Current Region	Selects a rectangular range of cells around the active cell. This range is determined by surrounding blank rows and columns. You can also use the Ctrl+Shift+8 shortcut key combination.
Current Array	Selects the entire array (used for multicell array formulas).
Objects	Selects all graphic objects on the worksheet.
Row Differences	Analyzes the selection and selects cells that are different from other cells in each row.
Column Differences	Analyzes the selection and selects the cells that are different from other cells in each column.
Precedents	Selects cells that are referred to in the formulas in the active cell or selection (limited to the active sheet). You can select either direct precedents or precedents at any level.
Dependents	Selects cells with formulas that refer to the active cell or selection (limited to the active sheet). You can select either direct dependents or dependents at any level.
Last Cell	Selects the bottom-right cell in the worksheet that contains data or formatting.
Visible Cells Only	Selects only visible cells in the selection. This option is useful when dealing with outlines or a filtered list.
Conditional Formats	Selects cells that have a conditional format applied (using the Format⇨ Conditional Formatting command).
Data Validation	Selects cells that are set up for data entry validation (using the Data⇨ Validation command). The All option selects all such cells. The Same option selects only the cells that have the same validation rules as the active cell.

NOTE

When you select an option in the Go To Special dialog box, be sure to note which sub-options become available. For example, when you select the Constants option, the sub-options under Formulas become available to help you further refine the results. Likewise, the suboptions under Dependents also apply to Precedents, and those under Data Validation also apply to Conditional formats.

Undoing, Redoing, and Repeating

This tip describes three procedures that every Excel user needs to understand. These procedures help you recover from mistakes and improve your editing efficiency.

Undoing

Just about every command in Excel can be reversed by using the Edit⇨Undo command. Select Edit⇨Undo after issuing a command in error, and it's as if you never issued the command. You can reverse the effects of the last 16 commands that you executed by selecting Edit⇨Undo multiple times.

Rather than use Edit⇨Undo, you may prefer to click the Undo button on the Standard toolbar. If you click the arrow on the right side of the button, you can see a description of the commands that can be reversed (see Figure 5-1). But the most efficient way to undo an operation is to press Ctrl+Z.

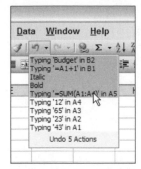

Figure 5-1: The Undo button displays a list of the actions that can be undone.

NOTE

Although undoing an operation is useful, keep in mind that two operations will wipe out the undo information: Saving your workbook and running a macro. After performing either of these operations, you won't be able to undo previous operations.

Redoing

The Redo command essentially undoes the Undo command. If you undo too much, you can select Edit⇨Redo (or press Ctrl+Y) to repeat commands that have been undone.

Repeating

One of the most useful Excel commands is Edit⇨Repeat (or its shortcut key combination, Ctrl+Y). This command simply repeats the last action.

Here's an example of how useful it can be. Assume that you have a workbook and you need to insert 25 new worksheets. You could use the Insert⇨Worksheet command 25 times. Or you could use that command one time, and then press Ctrl+Y 24 times. It's even more useful if the action to be repeated involves a dialog box. For example, you may apply lots of formatting to a cell using the Format Cells dialog box. After doing so, it's a snap to apply that same formatting to other cells or ranges by pressing Ctrl+Y.

NOTE

Excel provides only one level of repeating, so if you perform another action, you can't repeat the previous action.

Changing the Number of Undo Levels

By default, Excel lets you undo the previous 16 commands. If you would like to increase or decrease the number of levels of undo, you can do so by editing the Windows registry.

You can use the Registry Editor (`regedit.exe`, included with Windows) to edit the registry. To open the Registry Editor, click the Windows Start button, select Run, type **regedit** in the Run dialog box, and click OK. Figure 6-1 shows the Registry Editor.

WARNING

Modifying the Windows registry can potentially cause serious damage to your system. Make sure you back up the registry before making any changes. To back up the registry key that you're about to modify in the Registry Editor, right-click the key and choose Export. For more information, choose Help⇨Help Topics in the Registry Editor.

When the Registry Editor is open, locate this key (for Excel 2003):

```
HKEY_CURRENT_USER\Software\Microsoft\Office\11.0\Excel\Options
```

Create a new DWORD value named UndoHistory and set it to the number of undo levels desired. Valid values range from 0 (no undo) to 100.

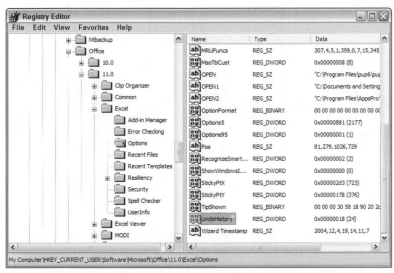

Figure 6-1: Using the Registry Editor to edit the Windows registry.

Keep in mind that increasing the number of undo levels also increases the amount of memory that's allocated for Excel. If you specify too many levels of undo, your system performance may be affected.

Discovering Some Useful Shortcut Keys

Excel has no shortage of shortcut keys. Your productivity is sure to increase if you take the time to learn the shortcut keys for commands that you use frequently. In the following table, I list some of the most useful shortcut keys. This is certainly not an exhaustive list — just those that I find most useful.

Shortcut	What It Does
F11	Creates a new chart (on a separate chart sheet) from the selected data
F5	Displays the Go To dialog box
Shift+F2	Enables you to edit the comment in the active cell
Shift+F10	Displays the shortcut menu for the selected item
Ctrl+F6	Activates the next window
Shift+F6	Activates the previous windows
Ctrl+B	Makes the selected cells bold
Ctrl+C	Copies the selected cells
Ctrl+D	Fills down
Ctrl+F	Displays the Find dialog box
Ctrl+H	Displays the Replace dialog box
Ctrl+I	Makes the selected cells italic
Ctrl+N	Creates a new default workbook
Ctrl+R	Fills to the right
Ctrl+V	Pastes a copied or cut item in the selected cell
Ctrl+X	Cuts the selected cells
Ctrl+Y	Repeats the last command
Ctrl+Z	Undoes the last action

Part I

Navigating Sheets in a Workbook

As you know, a single workbook can contain multiple worksheets. The sheet tabs at the bottom of Excel's window identify the worksheets. All Excel users know that they can acti-vate a different sheet by clicking its sheet tab. If the tab for the sheet you want isn't visi-ble, you can use the "CD player" controls to the left of the first sheet tab to scroll the tabs left or right (see Figure 8-1).

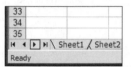

Figure 8-1: Use these controls to scroll the sheet tabs left or right.

You can also change the width of the horizontal scroll bar to reveal more sheet tabs. Just click the vertical bar on the left side of the scroll bar and drag it to the right.

Another way to activate a sheet is to right-click on the CD player controls. This displays a pop-up list of sheet names (see Figure 8-2). Just click a name, and you're there. If all of the sheet names aren't listed, click the More Sheets item at the bottom, and a dialog box that lists the sheet names appears. Just double-click a sheet name to activate that sheet.

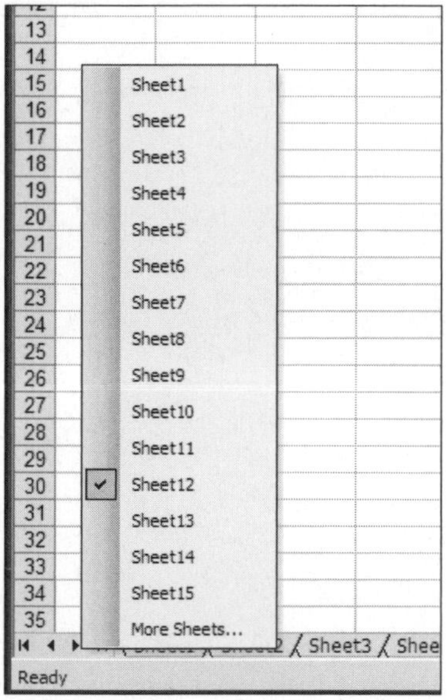

Figure 8-2: Right-clicking the CD player controls displays a list of sheet names.

Part I

In many cases, the most efficient way to activate a different sheet is to avoid the mouse and use the keyboard. Surprisingly, many users don't know about two useful keyboard commands:

- **Ctrl+PgDn:** Activates the next sheet
- **Ctrl+PgUp:** Activates the previous sheet

I use these keys 90 percent of the time — but then again, I avoid using a mouse whenever I can.

Resetting the Used Area of a Worksheet

When you press Ctrl+End, Excel activates the lower-right cell in the worksheet. In some cases, you will find that the lower-right cell in the worksheet is an empty cell — not the *real* last cell. In other words, Excel sometimes loses track of the used area of your worksheet.

First, try saving the workbook. After the workbook is saved, Excel may correctly identify the last cell. If Excel still doesn't identify the last cell, it's probably because you've deleted data but left the formatting in the cells. In order to force Excel to identify the real used area, you need to delete the columns to the right of your actual data, and then delete the rows below your actual data.

For example, assume that the real last cell in your workbook is H25, but pressing Ctrl+End actually takes you to some other cell, say M50.

To delete those formatted cells, follow these steps:

1. Select columns I:IV (activate any cell in column I, and then press Ctrl+spacebar, followed by Shift+End, right-arrow key).

2. Select Edit⇨Delete.

3. Select rows 26:65536 (activate any cell in row 26, and then press Shift+spacebar, followed by Ctrl+End, down-arrow key).

4. Select Edit⇨Delete.

5. Save your workbook.

You'll find that pressing Ctrl+End now takes you to the *real* last cell.

Understanding Workbooks versus Windows

One of the most common questions asked in the Excel newsgroups is "Why is Excel displaying two copies of my workbook?" Then the Excel users go on to describe the symptoms: The filename is followed by a colon and a number (for example, `budget.xls:2`).

Normally, a workbook displays in a single window within Excel. However, it's possible to create multiple windows for a single workbook by using the Window⇨New Window command.

Most of the people who ask this question in the newsgroups have probably issued the Window⇨New Window command by accident. What they're really asking is for a way to close the additional window(s). That's an easy one: Just click the X in the title bar of the unwanted window(s). By the way, the multiple window configuration is saved with the workbook, so when you open the file later, the multiple windows will still display.

Although many people are confused about multiple windows, there are at least two good reasons why you might want your workbook to display in two or more windows:

- You can view two worksheets in the same workbook simultaneously. For example, you can display Sheet1 in the first window, Sheet2 in the second window, and then tile the two windows so that both are visible. The Window⇨Arrange command is useful for tiling windows.

- You can view cells and their formulas at the same time. Create a second window, and then press Ctrl+` to display the formulas. Tile the two windows so you can view the formulas and their results side-by-side (see Figure 10-1).

NOTE

Excel 2003 introduced a new feature: Compare Side By Side, accessible via the Window⇨Compare Side By Side With command. This makes it easier to compare two worksheets because Excel automatically scrolls the second window to keep them both synchronized. In order to use this feature with a single workbook, you need to first create a second window by using the Window⇨New Window command.

Part I

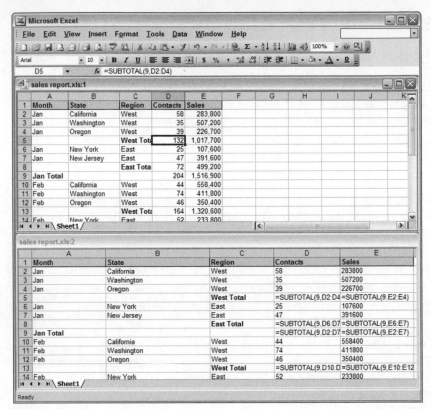

Figure 10-1: Displaying two windows for a workbook lets you view the cells and their formulas.

Avoiding the Task Pane When Using Excel 2003 Help

The Excel designers are always coming up with new ideas that will make life easier for Excel users. But, depending on your perspective, some of these new ideas may be more annoying than helpful.

In particular, I dislike how the Excel 2003 Help system works. In fact, I absolutely hate the fact that the annoying task pane displays the help topics, and the actual Help appears in a separate window. When searching for help on a particular topic, the user is forced to jump back and forth between the task pane and the Help window.

My solution is to execute the Help file directly. First you need to find it. Use Windows Explorer and go to:

```
C:\Program Files\Microsoft Office\Office11\1033
```

Then look for a file named XLMAIN11.CHM. This is a compiled HTML Help file. Double-click that file, and you'll get a more traditional-looking Help window — complete with a Contents tab and a Search tab (see Figure 11-1).

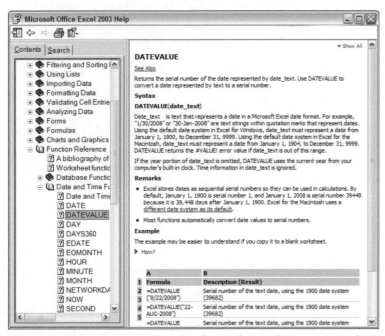

Figure 11-1: Displaying an Excel Help window with Contents and a Search tab.

Part I

NOTE

The 1033 part of the path varies, depending on the language version of Excel. Also, the rest of the path may vary, depending on how Office was installed. If you can't locate the XLMAIN11.CHM file manually, use the Windows Search feature to find it.

To make this Help file more accessible, you can create a shortcut on your desktop, or even create a hyperlink to it in a worksheet.

One potential disadvantage is that this Help file will not search the Microsoft.com Web site for newer content. But for me, this is a minor point.

Customizing the Default Workbook

When you create a new Excel workbook, you get a standard default workbook. But what if you don't like that workbook? For example, you may prefer a workbook with only one worksheet. Or maybe you don't like the default font or font size. Perhaps you prefer to have the gridlines hidden in your worksheets. Or maybe you have a standard header that you always use on printed pages.

As it turns out, Excel gives you quite a bit of control in this area. It's relatively simple to create an entirely different default workbook. The trick is creating a template file named `book.xlt`, and then saving that file to the proper location on your hard drive.

 NOTE

If all you care about is changing the number of worksheets in a new workbook, that change is very easy and a template is not required. Select Tools⇨Options. Click the General tab and specify the desired number of sheets in the Sheets in New Workbook setting. I always keep this set to 1 (after all, it's easy enough to add more by choosing Insert⇨Worksheet).

To create a new default workbook template, all you need to do is customize a blank workbook exactly as you like it. Here's a list of some of the items that you can change:

- **Number of sheets:** Add or delete sheets as you like. You can also change their names.

- **Font and font size:** Choose Format⇨Style. In the Style dialog box, select Normal from the Style Name drop-down list, and then click the Modify button and make your changes. Notice that you can change other things here, including the default number format.

- **Print settings:** Choose File⇨Page Setup to specify print settings. For example, you can include header or footer information, adjust the margins, and so on.

- **Change column widths:** If you don't like the default column widths, change them.

- **Add a graphic:** You can even insert a graphic object or two — for example, your company logo or a picture of your cat.

When the new default workbook is set up to your specifications, choose File⇨Save As. In the Save As dialog box

1. Select Template (*.xlt) in the Save As Type drop-down list.

2. Name the file `book.xlt`.

3. Make sure the file is saved to your XLStart directory.

Part I

NOTE

If you're using Office 2003, the XLStart directory is probably `C:\Program Files\Microsoft Office\Office11\XLStart`. If you can't locate the directory, search your hard drive for *XLStart*.

After you save the file, you can close it. Now, every time you start Excel, the blank workbook that's displayed will be based on the template you created. In addition, when you click the New button (or press Ctrl+N), the new workbook will be created from your template.

If you ever need to bypass your new default workbook and start with one of Excel's default workbooks, choose File⇨New to display the New Workbook task pane. Then click the Blank workbook item.

NOTE

If you're using Excel on a network, the XLStart directory may actually be on a network drive. In this case, you'll need the proper permission to save a file in this location. As an alternative, you can create a startup directory on your own system and store `book.xlt` in this new directory.

The directory name you choose doesn't matter, but you will need to tell Excel where it is. To do so, choose Tools⇨Options, and then click the General tab. In the At Startup, Open All Files In field, enter the complete path to your new directory.

Changing the Sheet Tab Appearance

Many users don't realize it, but it's possible to change the appearance of the sheet tabs displayed in a workbook. This tip describes how to change the size of the text and the color of the sheet tabs.

Changing the Sheet Tab Color

If your workbook has many sheets, you may find it helpful to color-code the sheet tabs. For example, you might use red tabs for sheets that need to be checked and green tabs for sheets that have already been checked.

To change the color of a sheet tab, right-click on a sheet tab, and then select Tab Color from the shortcut menu. You can then pick a background color from the palette. To change the color of multiple sheet tabs at once, press Ctrl while you click the sheet tabs. Then right-click and change the color.

 NOTE

The ability to change sheet tab color is limited to Excel 2002 and later. If a workbook with colored sheet tabs is opened with an earlier version of Excel, the colors are not displayed. But, interestingly, the sheet tab information remains in the workbook, even if the file is saved by an earlier version of Excel.

When the colored tab sheet is active, the text appears underlined with that color. When the sheet is not active, the entire background of the sheet tab is displayed in that color.

Changing the Sheet Tab Text Size

If you find that the text displayed in your sheet tabs is too small (or too large), you can change the size of the text — but you'll have to make a systemwide change.

The text size in Excel's sheets tabs is determined by a Windows systemwide setting. To change it, access the Windows Display Properties dialog box. The easiest way to do this is to right-click on your desktop and select Properties from the shortcut menu. In the Display Properties dialog box that appears, follow these steps (which assume you're using Windows XP):

1. Click the Appearance tab in the Display Properties dialog box.
2. Click the Advanced button to display the Advanced Appearance dialog box (see Figure 13-1).
3. Choose Scrollbar from the Item drop-down list.
4. Adjust the Size setting, and then click OK.

Be aware that this setting affects the scroll bars in all your applications.

Figure 13-1: Use the Advanced Appearance dialog box to change the text size in Excel's sheet tabs.

Hiding User Interface Elements

Many parts of Excel's user interface can be hidden. This tip is a handy summary of all of the elements that you can hide.

Hiding Toolbars

Right-click any toolbar, and you'll see a list of toolbars. A check mark indicates that the toolbar is visible. Click the toolbar name to remove the check mark (and hide the toolbar).

Not all toolbars appear in the list when you right-click a toolbar. If the toolbar that you want to hide is not on the list, select View⇨Toolbars⇨Customize. In the Customize dialog box, click the Toolbars tab. Remove the check mark from the toolbar(s) that you wish to hide. Notice that one of the "toolbars" is named Worksheet Menu Bar. This represents Excel's main menu — which can also be hidden.

Hiding User Interface Elements

The View tab of the Options dialog box enables you to hide quite a few elements. To display this dialog box, select Tools⇨Options (see Figure 14-1).

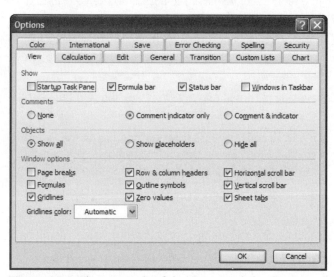

Figure 14-1: The View tab of the Options dialog box is a good place to go when you need to hide things.

You can hide (or show) any of the following items:

- **Startup Task Pane:** I find the task pane very annoying, and I always keep it turned off.

- **Formula Bar:** This item is located just below the top toolbars, and it displays the contents of the selected cell.

- **Status Bar:** This is the bar at the bottom of Excel's window that displays a variety of information. I like to keep this turned on.

- **Windows in Taskbar:** When this option is turned on, each workbook appears as a separate icon in the Windows taskbar. It's too much clutter for my tastes, so I keep it turned off.

- **Comments:** If you use cell comments, you can choose to display a comment indicator (or not), or display the comment and indicator. I use the second option, Comment Indicator Only.

- **Objects:** This setting refers to graphic objects embedded in your sheets (including charts). You might want to hide these objects if you have many of them and your system performance is suffering.

- **Page Breaks:** You can turn off the dotted line page break display if you like.

- **Formulas:** When this setting is in effect, Excel displays the actual text of your formula cells (not their calculated result). I never use this option.

- **Gridlines:** When checked, cell gridlines are visible. I turn off this option for about half of the worksheets I create. If you format ranges using cell borders, turning off the gridlines makes the borders more prominent.

- **Row & Column Headers:** If this setting is turned off, you won't see the row (numbers) and column (letters) headers.

- **Outline Symbols:** Relevant only if you've added a worksheet outline (using the Data➪ Group and Outline command). If you don't like seeing the outline symbols, you can turn them off. Or you can press Ctrl+8 to toggle the display of the outline symbols.

- **Zero Values:** If this setting is unchecked, zero values in cells are not displayed — the cell appears blank.

- **Horizontal Scroll Bar:** Uncheck this setting to hide the horizontal worksheet scroll bar.

- **Vertical Scroll Bar:** Uncheck this setting to hide the vertical worksheet scroll bar.

- **Sheet Tabs:** If you don't like seeing the sheet tabs, turn them off by unchecking this setting.

Hiding Columns or Rows

If you have data in a column or row that you don't want to see, you can hide the column or row. Doing this is often useful if you have formulas that provide intermediate calculations, and you don't want them to appear in a report. Formulas that refer to data in hidden rows or columns will continue to function normally (hidden data is not ignored by formulas).

To hide one or more columns, select a cell in the column(s) to be hidden. Then choose Format⇨Column⇨Hide. Alternatively, right-click a column header and choose Hide from the shortcut menu.

To hide one or more rows, select a cell in the row(s) to be hidden. Then choose Format⇨Row⇨Hide. Alternatively, right-click a row header and choose Hide from the shortcut menu.

Part I

Hiding Cell Contents

Excel doesn't provide a direct way to hide the contents of cells, but there are a few ways to fake it:

- Use a special custom number format. Select the cell(s) to be hidden, choose Format⇨ Cells, and click the Number tab in the Format Cells dialog box. Select Custom in the Category list, and then in the Type field, enter ;;; (three semicolons).
- Make the font color the same as the background color.
- Add a rectangle shape to your worksheet and position it over the cell or cells to be hidden.

All of these methods have a problem: The cell's contents will still be displayed in the formula bar when the cell is selected. If you don't want to see the cell contents in the formula bar, you can either hide the formula bar or perform these additional steps:

1. Select the cells.
2. Choose Format⇨Cells, and then click the Protection tab in the Format Cells dialog box.
3. Select the Hidden check box and click OK.
4. Select Tools⇨Protection⇨Protect Sheet.
5. In the Protect Sheet dialog box, add a password if desired, and click OK.

Keep in mind that when a sheet is protected, you won't be able to change any cells unless they are not locked. And, by default, all cells are locked. You change the locked status of a cell using the Protection tab in the Format Cells dialog box.

Performing Inexact Searches

If you have a large worksheet with lots of data, locating what you're looking for can be difficult. Excel's Find and Replace dialog box is a useful tool for locating information, and it has a few features that many users overlook.

Access the Find and Replace dialog box by using the Edit⇨Find command (or Ctrl+F). If you'll be replacing information, you can use Edit⇨Replace (or Ctrl+H). The only difference is which of the two tabs is displayed in the dialog box (see Figure 17-1).

Figure 17-1: The Find and Replace dialog box.

In many cases, you'll want to locate "approximate" text. For example, suppose that you're trying to find data for a customer named Stephen R. Rosencrantz. You could, of course, search for the exact text: *Stephen R. Rosencrantz*. However, there's a reasonably good chance that the search will fail. It's possible that the name was entered differently, maybe as Steve Rosencrantz or S.R. Rosencrantz. It's even possible that the name was misspelled Rosentcrantz.

The most efficient search for this name is to use a wildcard character and search for *st*rosen** and click the Find All button. In addition to reducing the amount of text that you enter, this search is practically guaranteed to locate the customer, if the record is in your worksheet.

The Find and Replace dialog box supports two wildcard characters:

- ? matches any single character
- * matches any number of characters

Wildcard characters also work with values. For example, searching for *3** locates all cells that contain a value that begins with 3. Searching for *1?9* locates all three-digit values that begin with 1 and end with 9.

NOTE

To actually search for a question mark or an asterisk, precede the character with a tilde character (~). For example, the following search string will find the text *NONE*:

~*NONE~*

If you need to search for the tilde character, use two tildes.

If your searches don't seem to be working correctly, double-check these three options:

- **Match Case:** If this check box is selected, the case of the text must match exactly. For example, searching for *smith* will not locate *Smith*.

- **Match Entire Cell Contents:** If this check box is selected, a match will occur if the cell contains only the search string (and nothing else). For example, searching for *Excel* will not locate a cell that contains *Microsoft Excel*.

- **Look In:** This drop-down list has three options: Values, Formulas, and Comments. If, for example, Values is selected, searching for *900* will not find a cell that contains 900 if that value is generated by a formula.

Remember that searching works with the selected range of cells. If you want to search the entire worksheet, select only one cell.

Also, remember that searches do not include numeric formatting. For example, if you have a value that uses currency formatting so it appears as $54.00, searching for *$5** will not locate that value.

Working with dates can be a bit tricky because Excel offers many ways to format dates. If you search for a date using the default date format, Excel will locate the dates even if they are formatted differently. For example, if your system uses the m/d/y date format, the search string *10/*/2005* finds all dates in October 2005, regardless of how the dates are formatted.

You can also use an empty Replace With field. For example, to quickly delete all asterisks from your worksheet, enter ~* in the Find What field and leave the Replace With field blank. When you click the Replace All button, Excel will find all the asterisks and replace them with nothing.

Replacing Formatting

One of the most useful features introduced in Excel 2002 is the ability to search for (and replace) cell formatting. For example, if you have cells that use the 14-point Arial font, it's a simple matter to change the formatting in all of those cells to something else.

The process isn't as intuitive as it could be, so I'll walk you through the steps. Assume that your worksheet contains many cells that are formatted as follows: yellow background, 14-point Arial in bold. Furthermore, assume that these cells are scattered throughout the workbook. The goal is to change all of those cells so they display with 16-point Times New Roman in bold, white text with a black background.

To change the formatting by searching and replacing, follow these steps:

1. Click on any single cell, and select Edit⇨Replace (or press Ctrl+H) to display the Find and Replace dialog box. If you want to limit the searching to a particular range, select the range rather than a single cell.

2. In the Find and Replace dialog box, make sure that the Find What and the Replace With fields are blank.

3. Click the upper Format button (the one beside the Find What field) to display the Find Format dialog box.

4. You can use the Find Format dialog box to specify the formatting that you're looking for, but it's much easier to click the Choose Format from Cell button and then click on a cell that already has that formatting.

5. Click the lower Format button (the one beside the Replace With field) to display the Find Format dialog box again.

6. Use the tabs in the Find Format dialog box to specify the desired formatting. In this example, click the Font tab and select Times New Roman, size 16, bold style, and white color. On the Patterns tab, choose black as the cell shading color. At this point, the dialog box should resemble Figure 18-1.

7. In the Find and Replace dialog box, click the Replace All button.

NOTE

If you use the Choose Format from Cell button in Step 4, you may find that not all occurrences of the formatting are replaced. Usually, this is because one or more aspects of the formatting do not match. For example, if you clicked on a cell that had General number formatting, it won't replace cells that have Date number formatting. The solution is to click the Format button to display the Find Format dialog box, and then click the Clear button in each dialog box tab in which the formatting is not relevant.

Part I

Figure 18-1: The Replace tab of the Find and Replace dialog box.

In some cases, you may prefer to simply select the cells with a particular format. To do so, perform Steps 1–4 in the preceding list. Then click the Find All button. The dialog box expands to display information about the qualifying cells (see Figure 18-2). Click on the bottom part of the dialog box, and then press Ctrl+A to select all of the qualifying cells.

When these cells are selected, you can then format them any way you like.

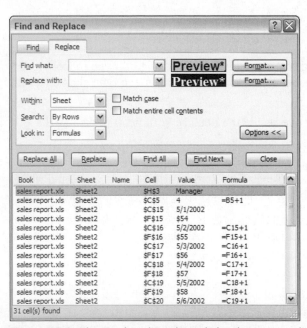

Figure 18-2: The Find and Replace dialog box expands to display a list of all matching cells.

Increasing the Number of Rows and Columns

Perhaps the most common question about using Excel is "How can I increase the number of rows and columns?"

The answer is short (but not so sweet): You can't.

Users often encounter the 256-column limitation when they want to set up a spreadsheet that contains data for each day in a year. If they store the data horizontally, they run out of columns in mid-September. For this problem, the solution is to arrange the data vertically rather than horizontally. In some cases, you may be able to use multiple worksheets — but doing so makes it impossible to work with your data as a single table.

Yet another option, suggested by Technical Editor Alan Wyatt, is to change the alignment of the information in your cells so it appears at a 90-degree angle (use the Alignment tab of the Format Cells dialog box to do this). Then change the height and width of the cells, and print your data in landscape mode. See Figure 19-1 for an example. This trick doesn't actually change the number of dimensions, but it does provide the *illusion* of more columns. It will take quite a bit of work to get things set up properly, and you may never get used to the fact that your data starts at the bottom of the worksheet rather than the top.

Part I

	Product 1	Product 2	Product 3	Product 4	Product 5	Product 6	Product 7	Product 8	Product 9	Product 10	Product 11	Product 12	Product 13	Product 14	Product 15	Product 16	Product 17	Total
1/3/2005	214,688	261,074	248,411	266,091	141,934	289,393	88,289	74,164	84,273	278,986	388,473	362,244	143,015	423,683	280,620	177,747	344,306	4,067,391
1/2/2005	465,839	410,780	450,517	113,943	233,635	468,945	9,280	237,064	399,643	145,077	351,335	439,816	369,908	293,670	62,072	221,940	8,368	4,681,832
1/1/2005	476,486	154,982	430,106	338,277	452,671	306,184	447,934	140,393	181,139	57,924	433,655	274,000	143,354	39,668	319,929	268,410	141,783	4,606,895

Sheet1 \ Sheet2

Figure 19-1: If you care to work sideways, this worksheet provides you with 65,536 "columns" and 256 "rows."

The reason for the 256-column limitation is probably due to the fact that, by software standards, Excel is very old, and it contains lots of code that would be "broken" if the number of columns was increased.

Sorry, I truly wish that I had a miraculous tip to offer here.

Limiting the Usable Area in a Worksheet

Have you ever wanted to restrict access to a certain range within a worksheet? For example, you might want to set up a worksheet so that only cells in a particular range can be activated or modified. This tip describes two ways to accomplish this task: by using the ScrollArea property, and by using worksheet protection.

Setting the ScrollArea Property

The trick is to change the worksheet's ScrollArea property. Figure 20-1 shows a worksheet. The instructions that follow will restrict the usable area of the worksheet to the range D5:E16.

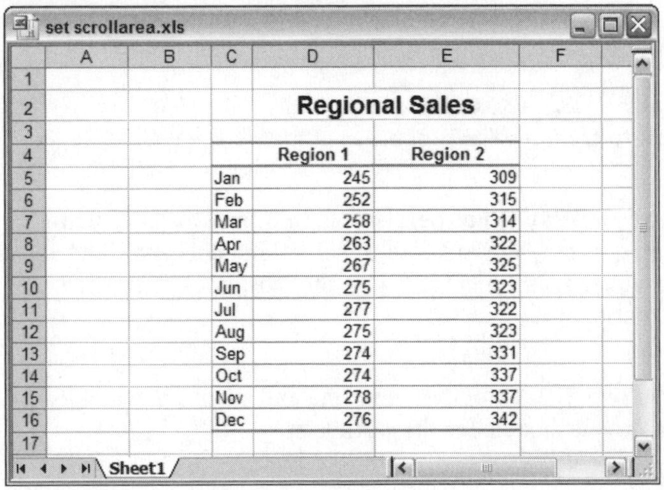

Figure 20-1: It's possible to restrict the usable area of a worksheet to a particular range.

Here's how to do it:

1. Right-click on any toolbar and select Control Toolbox.

2. On the Control Toolbox toolbar, click the Properties button to display the Properties window (see Figure 20-2).

3. In the Properties window, enter D5:E16 in the ScrollArea field and press Enter. You can't point to the range; you must enter the range address manually.

After performing these steps, you'll find that it's not possible to activate any cell outside of the specified range. Note that the scroll area is limited to a single contiguous range of cells.

Part I

Figure 20-2: Use the Properties window to control some properties of the worksheet.

But there's a problem: The ScrollArea property is not persistent. In other words, if you save your file, close it, and then open it again, you are free to select any cell you like. One solution is to write a simple VBA macro that is executed when the workbook is opened. To add such a macro, follow these instructions:

1. Right-click the Excel icon directly to the left of the File menu and choose View Code. This displays the ThisWorkbook code module for the workbook.

2. Enter the following VBA code in the ThisWorkbook code module:

```
Private Sub Workbook_Open()
    Worksheets("Sheet1").ScrollArea = "D5:E16"
End Sub
```

3. Press Alt+F11 to return to Excel.

4. Save the workbook, close it, and reopen it.

The Workbook_Open procedure is executed automatically, and the ScrollArea property is set.

WARNING

This is by no means a foolproof method to prevent users from accessing parts of a workbook. When the workbook is opened, the user can choose to disable macros for the workbook. In such a case, the ScrollArea property is not set.

Using Worksheet Protection

The second method of limiting the usable area of a worksheet is more flexible, but it's limited to Excel 2002 and later. This method relies on unlocking cells and protecting the workbook:

1. Select all of the cells that you want to be accessible. These can be single cells, or any number of ranges.

2. Select Format⇨Cells (or press Ctrl+1) to display the Format Cells dialog box.

3. In the Format Cells dialog box, click the Protection tab and remove the check mark from the Locked check box.

4. Select Tools⇨Protection⇨Protect Sheet to display the Protect Sheet dialog box.

5. In the Protect Sheet dialog box, remove the check mark from the Select Locked Cells check box (see Figure 20-3).

6. If desired, specify a password that will be required in order to unprotect the sheet, and then click OK.

After performing these steps, only the unlocked cells (those you selected in Step 1) are accessible.

Figure 20-3: Use the Protect Sheet dialog box to prevent the user from selecting locked cells.

 WARNING

Worksheet passwords are not at all secure. In fact, it's a trivial matter to crack such a password. Therefore, worksheet protection is more of a convenience feature than a security feature.

Part I

Using an Alternative to Cell Comments

As you probably know, you can attach a comment to any cell by using the Insert⇨Comment command. The View tab in the Options dialog box determines how comments are displayed. You have three choices: None, Comment Indicator Only, or Comment & Indicator. So, depending on the setting, it's possible that your comments will never be seen.

This tip describes how to use Excel's Data Validation feature to display a pop-up message whenever a cell is activated. Follow these steps to add a message to a cell:

1. Activate the cell that you want to display the pop-up message.

2. Select Data⇨Validation to display the Data Validation dialog box.

3. In the Data Validation dialog box, click the Input Message tab.

4. (Optional) In the Title field, enter a title for your message.

5. Enter the message itself in the Input Message box.

After performing these steps, the message will appear whenever the cell is activated (see Figure 21-1 for an example). You can also click and drag the message to a different location if it's in your way.

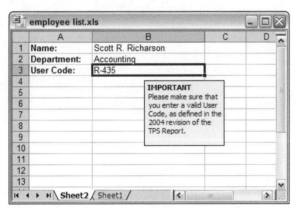

Figure 21-1: This message was created using Excel's Data Validation command.

Changing the Text Size in Excel's Help Window

If your eyesight isn't what it used to be, you may find that the text in Excel's Help window is too small to read comfortably. If you use a mouse with a scroll wheel (and you definitely *should* use a wheel mouse), the solution is simple: Activate the Help window, and then press the Ctrl key and roll the mouse wheel. (Rolling up displays smaller text, and rolling down displays larger text.)

This change will also affect the size of the text displayed in Internet Explorer.

If you don't use a wheel mouse, the process is a bit more involved:

1. Close the Excel Help window if it's open.

2. Launch the Internet Explorer Web browser.

3. Select View⇨Text Size, and then choose a size: Largest, Larger, Medium, Smaller, Smallest.

The next time you display Excel Help, it will be in the text size you selected in Internet Explorer. This setting, of course, also determines how the text will appear in all of the Web pages you view in the browser.

Part I

Making a Worksheet "Very Hidden"

You probably already know how to hide a worksheet: Just activate the sheet and choose Format⇨Sheet⇨Hide. A potential problem is that it's also very easy to unhide the sheet: Just select Format⇨Sheet⇨Unhide.

If you would like to make it more difficult for the casual user to unhide a hidden sheet, you need to make the worksheet "very hidden." Here's how to do it:

1. Activate the sheet you want to hide.

2. Right-click on any toolbar and choose Control Toolbox to display the Control Toolbox toolbar.

3. Click the Properties button on the Control Toolbox toolbar to display the Properties window (see Figure 23-1).

4. In the Properties window, click the Visible property to display a down-arrow button; click the button to display a drop-down list and select 2 -xlSheetVeryHidden.

After performing these steps, you'll find that it's not possible to unhide the sheet by using the Format⇨Sheet⇨Unhide command. In fact, it's not even possible to unhide it by using the Properties window.

Figure 23-1: Use the Properties window to make a worksheet very hidden.

So does that mean the sheet is hidden forever? Nope. In order to make the very hidden sheet visible again, you need to use a simple VBA macro. The macro listed here unhides Sheet2 of the active workbook (change the sheet name as appropriate):

```
Sub UnhideSheet()
    Worksheets("Sheet2").Visible = True
End Sub
```

WARNING

Making a worksheet very hidden is not a security feature. Anyone who really wants to know what resides on a very hidden sheet can easily find out by using the UnhideSheet macro.

Troubleshooting Common Setup Problems

Excel is a pretty good program, but sometimes things can go a bit haywire. This tip describes a baker's dozen of common problems and shows you how to solve them.

Symptom: Excel Crashes When It Starts

When Excel is launched, it opens an *.xlb file, which contains your menu and toolbar customizations. If this file is damaged, it may cause Excel to crash when it is started. Also, this file may (for some reason) be very large. In such a case, this may also cause Excel to crash. Typically, your *.xlb file should be 500K or smaller.

If Excel crashes when it is started, try deleting your *.xlb file. Follow these steps to do so:

1. Close Excel.

2. Use the Windows Search feature (choose Start⇨Search) to search your hard drive for *.xlb. The filename and location will vary.

3. Create a backup copy of this file and then delete the file.

4. Restart Excel. Hopefully, Excel will now start up normally.

NOTE
Deleting your *.xlb file will also delete any toolbar or menu customizations you have made in Excel.

Symptom: Many Documents Open Automatically at Start Up

If Excel automatically opens lots of files when it starts up, here are two things to check:

- **Your XLStart directory:** Files stored in your XLStart directory are opened automatically when Excel starts. Move the files in this folder to a different folder.

- **Your Alternate Startup directory:** Select Tools⇨Options. In the Options dialog box, click the General tab. Locate the setting called At Startup, Open All Files In. If this field is not empty, delete its contents or specify a different directory.

Symptom: Excel's Menus Are Messed Up

If your menus change, or if there is a delay before all menu items are listed, you need to make a change. Follow these steps to make Excel show the entire menu:

1. Select View⇨Toolbars⇨Customize. Alternatively, right-click on any toolbar or menu item and select Customize from the shortcut menu.

2. In the Customize dialog box, click the Options tab.

3. Place a check mark next to the Always Show Full Menus check box and click OK.

Symptom: Commands Are Missing from the Menu

If the steps in the preceding section don't solve the problem, you can reset Excel's menu bar as follows:

1. Select View⇨Toolbars⇨Customize. Alternatively, right-click on any toolbar or menu item and select Customize from the shortcut menu.

2. In the Customize dialog box, click the Toolbars tab.

3. Scroll down the Toolbars list and select Worksheet Menu Bar.

4. Click the Reset button.

5. If your Chart menu is also messed up, repeat this procedure using the Chart Menu Bar option in Step 3.

 NOTE
These steps will return Excel's menu to its default state, which will destroy any menu customizations that you have done.

Symptom: Excel Displays Extraneous Menu Commands

Another common problem is extraneous menu items. For example, you may have used an add-in that added a new menu item to the Tools menu. And, for whatever reason, that menu item was not removed when you uninstalled the add-in.

To remove the extraneous menu item, follow these steps:

1. Select View⇨Toolbars⇨Customize.

2. When the Customize dialog box is displayed, click the extraneous menu item and "drag it away" — that is, drag it away from the menu and release the mouse button. That will delete the menu item.

3. Click OK to close the Customize dialog box.

Symptom: Double-Clicking an Excel File Does Not Work

Normally, double-clicking an XLS workbook file starts Excel (if it's not already open) and opens that file. If this doesn't work for you, you'll need to reregister Excel. To do so:

1. Close Excel.

2. Choose Start⇨Run to display the Run dialog box.

3. Type the following in the Open field, and then click OK:

```
excel /regserver
```

4. You'll see a message box that displays the progress of the registration. When the message box closes, Excel should be back to normal.

Symptom: When Excel Starts, You Get an Error Message: "Compile Error in Hidden Module"

The most likely cause of this error is an add-in that contains a programming error. You can track down the erroneous add-in by removing them all, and then loading them back in one by one. Follow these steps to remove all of your add-ins:

1. Select Tools⇨Add-Ins to display the Add-Ins dialog box.

2. Make note of which add-ins are currently loaded (those with a check mark next to them).

3. Remove all of the check marks, and then click OK to close the Add-Ins dialog box.

After you've removed the add-ins, reinstall them one at a time by using the Add-Ins dialog box and selecting the add-in's check box. Close the Add-In dialog box and the newly selected add-in is opened. Repeat this until you've reinstalled all of the add-ins. If you see the error message, you'll know which add-in is the culprit.

Part I

Symptom: You Get a Macro Warning When No Macros Exist

When you open a workbook, you may be prompted to enable or disable macros — even though no macros exist in the workbook.

Press Alt+F11 to activate the Visual Basic Editor. Locate your workbook in the projects window. If the workbook contains any VBA modules (for example, Module1), delete the module. Even an empty VBA module will trigger the macro warning.

Examine the code modules to ThisWorkbook and the code module for each sheet (for example, Sheet1). Make sure that these modules do not contain any macro code. You cannot delete these code modules, but they must be empty to avoid the macro warning dialog box.

Symptom: You Get an Erroneous "File Is Being Edited By" Message

When you open a file that somebody else on your network is already working on, you get a message that tells you the file must be opened in read-only mode. In some cases, you may get this message even though the file is definitely not in use. This can be caused by an Excel crash, in which the file was not released (that is, it wasn't properly saved and closed). The only way around this problem is to restart Windows.

Symptom: Numbers Are Entered with the Wrong Number of Decimal Places

You may notice that numbers in cells do not appear as you typed them. For example, you type **154** in a cell, but it appears as 1.54. The problem here is that somehow Excel's fixed-decimal mode was turned on. Follow these steps to return to normal:

1. Select Tools⇨Options to display the Options dialog box.
2. Click the Edit tab.
3. Remove the check mark from the Fixed Decimal option and click OK.

Of course, this feature can be useful when you're entering some types of data, but most of the time, you'll want to keep the fixed-decimal mode turned off.

Symptom: A Workbook Opens with More Than One Window

What happened in this case is that you probably issued the Window⇨New Window command by accident. Each workbook can appear in any number of different windows, and each window is labeled with the filename followed by the window number (for example, budget.xls:2).

To close unwanted workbook window(s), just click the X in the title bar of the unwanted window(s).

Symptom: Numbers, Not Letters, Appear in the Column Header

Normally, Excel columns are labeled with letters. If they actually appear as numbers, you can change them back to the default as follows:

1. Select Tools⇨Options to display the Options dialog box.
2. Click the General tab.
3. Remove the check mark from the R1C1 Reference Style option and click OK.

Symptom: Excel Just Isn't Working Right

If things are really messed up, select Help⇨Detect and Repair. Microsoft Office will attempt to locate the problem and fix it.

 NOTE

Detect and Repair is available only in the more recent versions of Excel. If your version does not have this command, try uninstalling and then reinstalling Excel (or Office).

Part I

Part II

Data Entry

In this part, you'll find tips related to entering data into an Excel workbook. Entering data into an Excel worksheet is easy, but there's an excellent chance that the tips here will improve your overall efficiency.

Tips and Where to Find Them

Tip 25 Understanding the
Types of Data   69

Tip 26 Moving the Cell Pointer after
Entering Data   73

Tip 27 Selecting a Range of Input Cells
before Entering Data   75

Tip 28 Using AutoComplete to Automate
Data Entry   77

Tip 29 Keeping Titles in View by
Freezing Panes   79

Tip 30 Automatically Filling a Range
with a Series   81

Tip 31 Working with Fractions   85

Tip 32 Proofing Your Data with Audio   87

Tip 33 Controlling Automatic
Hyperlinks   89

Tip 34 Entering Credit Card Numbers   91

Tip 35 Using Excel's Built-In
Data Entry Form   93

Tip 36 Customizing and Sharing
AutoCorrect Entries   95

Tip 37 Restricting Cursor Movement to
Input Cells   97

Tip 38 Controlling the Office Clipboard 99

Tip 39 Creating a Drop-Down List
in a Cell   101

Understanding the Types of Data

Whenever you enter something into a cell in a worksheet, Excel goes to work and makes a decision regarding the type of data you entered. That decision will be one of the following:

- You entered a value.

- You entered a date or time.

- You entered some text.

- You entered a formula.

If you understand how Excel interprets what you enter into a cell, you can save yourself a bit of frustration when Excel's decision about what you entered isn't what you had in mind.

Entering Values

Any cell entry that consists of numerical digits is considered a value. Values can also include a few special characters:

- **Negative sign:** If a negative sign (–) precedes the value, Excel interprets it as a negative number.

- **Plus sign:** If a plus sign (+) precedes the value, Excel interprets it as a positive number (and does not display the plus sign).

- **Percent sign:** If a percent sign (%) follows the numbers, Excel interprets the value as a percentage and automatically applies percent numeric formatting.

- **Currency symbol:** If your system's currency symbol (for example, a dollar sign) precedes the numbers, Excel interprets the entry as a monetary value and automatically formats it as currency.

- **Thousands separator:** If the number includes one or more of your system's thousand separator (for example, a comma), Excel interprets the entry as a number and also applies numeric formatting to display the thousands separator symbol. Note that the thousands separator must be in the appropriate position. For example, if the comma is your system's thousands separator, Excel interprets 4,500 as a value, but it does *not* interpret 45,00 as a value.

- **Scientific notation:** If the value contains the letter E, Excel attempts to interpret it as scientific notation. For example, 3.2E5 is interpreted as 3.2×10^5.

Entering Dates and Times

Excel treats dates and times as special types of numeric values. Typically, these values are formatted so that they appear as dates or times because humans find it far easier to understand these values if they appear in the correct format.

Excel handles dates by using a serial number system. The earliest date that Excel understands is January 1, 1900. This date has a serial number of 1. January 2, 1900, has a serial number of 2, and so on. This system makes it easy to deal with dates in formulas. For example, you can enter a formula to calculate the number of days between two dates.

NOTE

The date examples in this book use the U.S. English system. Depending on your regional settings, entering a date in a format such as June 1, 2006 may be interpreted as text rather than a date. In such a case, you would need to enter the date in a format that corresponds to your regional date settings — for example, 1 June, 2006.

The following table provides a sampling of the date formats that Excel recognizes. After entering a date, you can format it to appear in a different date format by using the Number tab of the Format Cells dialog box.

Entered into a Cell	Excel's Interpretation (U.S. Settings)
6-26-06	June 26, 2006
6-26-2006	June 26, 2006
6/26/06	June 26, 2006
6/26/2006	June 26, 2006
6-26/06	June 26, 2006
June 26, 2006	June 26, 2006
Jun 26	June 26 of the current year
June 26	June 26 of the current year
6/26	June 26 of the current year
6-26	June 26 of the current year

Excel is pretty smart when it comes to recognizing dates that you enter, but it's not perfect. For example, Excel does not recognize any of the following entries as dates: June 1 2006, Jun-1 2006, and Jun-1/2006. Rather, it interprets these entries as text. If you plan to use dates in formulas, make sure that the date you enter is actually recognized as a date; otherwise, your formulas will produce incorrect results.

A common problem is that Excel interprets your entry as a date when you intended to enter a fraction. For example, if you enter the fraction 1/5, Excel interprets it as January 5. The solution is to precede your entry with an equal sign.

When you work with times, Excel simply extends its date serial number system to include decimals. In other words, Excel works with times by using fractional days. For example, the date serial number for June 1, 2006, is 38869. Noon on June 1, 2006 (halfway through the day), is represented internally as 38869.5 because the time fraction is simply added to the date serial number to get the full date/time serial number.

Again, you normally don't have to be concerned with these serial numbers (or fractional serial numbers, for times). Just enter the time into a cell in a recognized format.

The following table shows some examples of time formats that Excel recognizes.

Entered into a Cell	Excel's Interpretation
11:30:00 am	11:30 AM
11:30:00 AM	11:30 AM
11:30 pm	11:30 PM
11:30	11:30 AM
13:30	1:30 PM

The preceding samples don't have a day associated with them, so they are represented internally as a value less than 1. In other words, Excel is using the nonexistent date of January 0, 1900. You also can combine dates and times, however, as shown in the following table.

Entered into a Cell	Excel's Interpretation
6/26/06 11:30	11:30 AM on June 26, 2006
6/26/06 12:00	Noon on June 26, 2006
6/26/2005 0:00	Midnight on June 26, 2006

When you enter a time that exceeds 24 hours, the associated date for the time increments accordingly. For example, if you enter the following time into a cell, it is interpreted as 1:00 AM on January 1, 1900:

```
25:00:00
```

The day part of the entry increments because the time exceeds 24 hours. Keep in mind that a time value without a date uses January 0, 1900 as the date.

Entering Text

If Excel can't interpret your cell entry as a value, a date, a time, or a formula, then it's considered text.

A single cell can hold a massive amount of text — about 32,000 characters. However, you'll find that Excel has lots of limitations when you use large amounts of text in a cell. In fact, it can't even display all of the characters.

Entering Formulas

Normally, you signal that you're entering a formula by beginning the cell entry with an equal sign (=). However, Excel will also accept a plus sign or a minus sign. And (to accommodate old Lotus 1-2-3 users) if your formula begins with a worksheet function, Excel will also accept an ampersand (@). However, as soon as you press Enter, the ampersand is replaced with an equal sign.

Formulas can contain the following elements:

- Mathematical operators, such as + (for addition) and * (for multiplication)
- Parentheses
- Cell references (including named cells and ranges)
- Values or text
- Worksheet functions (such as SUM or AVERAGE)

If the formula you entered is not syntactically correct, Excel may propose a correction. Keep in mind that Excel's suggested corrections are not always right.

Moving the Cell Pointer after Entering Data

By default, Excel automatically moves the cell pointer to the next cell down when you press the Enter key after entering data into a cell. To change this setting, choose Tools⇨ Options and click the Edit tab (see Figure 26-1). The check box that controls this behavior is labeled Move Selection after Enter. You can also specify the direction in which the cell pointer moves (down, left, up, or right).

Your choice is completely a matter of personal preference. I prefer to keep this option turned off and use the arrow keys instead of pressing Enter. Not surprisingly, these direction keys send the cell pointer in the direction that you indicate. For example, if you're entering data in a row, press the right-arrow (→) key rather than Enter. The other arrow keys work as expected, and you can even use the PgUp and PgDn keys.

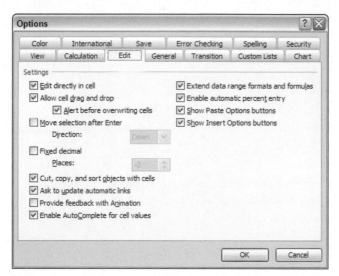

Figure 26-1: You can use the Options dialog box Edit tab to select a number of very helpful input option settings.

Selecting a Range of Input Cells before Entering Data

Here's a tip that most Excel users don't know about: When a range of cells is selected, Excel automatically moves the cell pointer to the next cell in the range when you press Enter.

The "next cell" is determined by the Direction setting in the Edit tab of the Options dialog box. For example, if the Direction setting is Down (or if the Move Selection after Enter option is not enabled), it works like this: If the selection consists of multiple rows, Excel moves down the column; when it reaches the end of the selection in the column, it moves to the first selected cell in next column. To skip a cell, just press Enter without entering anything. To go backward, press Shift+Enter. If you prefer to enter the data by rows rather than by columns, press Tab rather than Enter.

Using AutoComplete to Automate Data Entry

Excel's AutoComplete feature makes it very easy to enter the same text into multiple cells. With AutoComplete, you type the first few letters of a text entry into a cell, and Excel automatically completes the entry, based on other entries that you've already made in the column. Besides reducing typing, this feature also ensures that your entries are spelled correctly and are consistent.

Here's how it works. Suppose that you're entering product information in a column. One of your products is named Widgets. The first time that you enter **Widgets** into a cell, Excel remembers it. Later, when you start typing **Widgets** in that same column, Excel recognizes it by the first few letters and finishes typing it for you. Just press Enter and you're done. It also changes the case of letters for you automatically. If you start entering **widget** (with a lowercase *w*) in the second entry, Excel makes the *w* uppercase to be consistent with the previous entry in the column.

 NOTE
You also can access a mouse-oriented version of AutoComplete by right-clicking the cell and selecting Pick from List from the shortcut menu. Excel then displays a drop-down list that has all the entries in the current column, and you just click the one that you want.

Keep in mind that AutoComplete works only within a contiguous column of cells. If you have a blank row, for example, AutoComplete will only identify the cell contents below the blank row.

If you find the AutoComplete feature distracting, you can turn it off by choosing Tools⇨ Options and clicking the Edit tab of the Options dialog box. Remove the check mark from the Enable AutoComplete for Cell Values check box, and then click OK.

Keeping Titles in View by Freezing Panes

A common type of spreadsheet contains a table of data with descriptive headings in the first row (see Figure 29-1). As you scroll down the worksheet, the first row scrolls off the screen, so you can no longer see the column descriptions. Excel offers a handy solution to this problem: freezing panes. This keeps the headings visible while you are scrolling through the worksheet.

	A	B	C	D	E
1	**Code**	**Description**	**Location**	**Dir**	**Year**
2	670526	USNTS	SHFT	E	1967
3	640611	164501.0 USNTS	SHFT	E	1964
4	750605	181500.0 FRFAN	SHFT	N	1975
5	630208	USNTS	SHFT	E	1963
6	620425	USCHR	AIRD	E	1962
7	680528	USNTS	SHFT	E	1968
8	611107	112959.9 FRECK	TUNN	N	1961
9	620118	USNTS	SHFT	E	1962
10	840331	USNTS	SHFT	E	1984
11	630913	USNTS	SHFT	E	1963
12	661111	120000.7 USNTS	SHFT	E	1966
13	700130	USNTS	SHFT	E	1970
14	811203	USNTS	SHFT	E	1981
15	721109	USNTS	SHFT	E	1972
16	880707	USNTS	SHFT	E	1988
17	660702	153400.0 FRMUR	BARG	N	1966
18	860911	USNTS	SHFT	E	1986
19	710818	140000.0 USNTS	SHFT	E	1971
20	810529	USNTS	SHFT	E	1981
21	690515	USNTS	SHFT	E	1969

Sheet1

Figure 29-1: The column headers in Row 1 will no longer be visible when you scroll down.

To freeze the first row, for example, move the cell pointer to cell A2. Then select Window⇨ Freeze Panes. Excel inserts a dark horizontal line to indicate the frozen rows. If your column headings consist of more than one row, move the cell pointer to the cell in column A that's below the row that you want to remain visible.

In some cases, you may also want to freeze the first column. That way, when you scroll to the right, you can still see the data in column A. So, to freeze row 1 and column A, move the cell pointer to cell B2 before you issue the Window⇨Freeze Panes command.

The navigation keys operate as if the frozen rows or columns do not exist. For example, if you press Ctrl+Home while the worksheet has frozen panes, the cell selector moves to the top-left unfrozen cell. Similarly, the Home key moves to the first unfrozen cell in the current row. You can move into the frozen rows or columns by using the direction keys or your mouse.

To remove the frozen panes, select Window⇨Unfreeze Panes.

Part II

Automatically Filling a Range with a Series

If you need to fill a range with a series of values, one approach is to enter the first value, write a formula to calculate the next value, and copy the formula. For example, Figure 30-1 shows a series of consecutive numbers in column A. Cell A1 contains the value 1, and cell A2 contains this formula, which was copied down the column:

```
=A1+1
```

	A	B	C
1	1		
2	2		
3	3		
4	4		
5	5		
6	6		
7	7		
8	8		
9	9		
10	10		
11	11		
12	12		
13	13		
14			

Figure 30-1: Excel offers an easy way to generate a series of values like this.

A simpler approach is to let Excel do the work using the handy Autofill feature, as follows:

1. Enter **1** into cell A1.

2. Enter **2** into cell A2.

3. Select A1:A2.

4. Move the mouse cursor to the lower-right corner of cell A2 (that is, the cell's "fill handle." Then, when the mouse pointer turns into a black plus sign, drag down the column to fill in the cells.

NOTE

Cells do not contain a fill handle if the Allow Cell Drag and Drop option is not enabled. To change this setting, select Tools⇨Options. In the Options dialog box, click the Edit tab, and place a check mark next to Allow Cell Drag and Drop.

The data entered in Steps 1 and 2 provide Excel with the information it needs to complete the series. If you entered a 3 into cell A2, the series would then consist of odd integers: 1, 3, 5, 7, and so on. Autofill also works with dates and even a few text items — day names and month names. The following table lists a few examples of the types of data that can be autofilled.

First Value	Autofilled Values
1	2, 3, 4, etc.
Sunday	Monday, Tuesday, Wednesday, etc.
Quarter-1	Quarter-2, Quarter-3, Quarter-4, Quarter-1, etc.
Jan	Feb, Mar, Apr, etc.
January	February, March, April, etc.
Month 1	Month 2, Month 3, Month 4, etc.

You can also create your own lists of items that will be autofilled. To do so, select Tools⇨ Options. In the Options dialog box, click the Custom Lists tab, and then enter your items in the List Entries box. Then click the Add button to create the list. Figure 30-2 shows a custom list of region names.

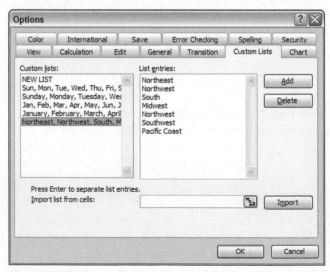

Figure 30-2: These region names will work with the Excel Autofill feature.

For more control over what happens when using Autofill, click and drag the fill handle using the right mouse button. When you release the button, you get a shortcut menu with some options (see Figure 30-3). The items available on the shortcut menu depend on the type of data selected. For example, if the first cell in the series contains a date, then the date-related options are enabled.

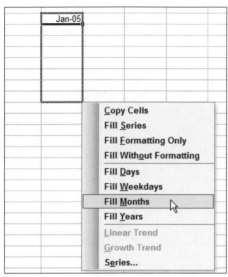

Figure 30-3: The shortcut menu for Autofill.

Working with Fractions

Although most users work with decimal values, some types of data normally display as fractions, not decimals. This tip describes how to enter noninteger values as fractions.

To enter a fraction into a cell, leave a space between the whole number and the fraction. For example, to enter 6 7/8, type **6 7/8**, and then press Enter. When you select the cell, 6.875 appears in the formula bar, and the cell entry appears as a fraction.

If you have a fraction only (for example, 1/8), you must enter a zero first, like this: **0 1/8** — otherwise, Excel will likely assume that you are entering a date. When you select the cell and look at the formula bar, you see 0.125. In the cell, you see 1/8.

If the numerator is larger than the denominator, Excel will convert it to a whole number and a fraction. For example, if you enter **0 65/8**, Excel converts it to 8 1/8.

After you enter a fraction, take a look at the number format for the cell. You'll see that Excel automatically applied one of its Fraction number formats (see Figure 31-1).

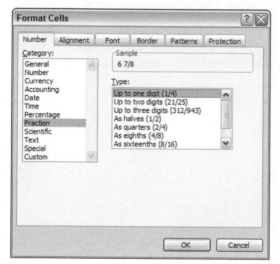

Figure 31-1: A list of Excel's built-in Fraction number formats.

Figure 31-2 shows a worksheet that displays fractional data. The values in column C are expressed in fourths, eighths, and 16ths, and the values in column D are all in 16ths.

If none of the built-in Fraction number formats meets your needs, you may be able to create a custom number format. Choose Format⇨Cells, and in the Format Cells dialog box, click the Number tab. In the Category list, click Custom, and then enter a number format string in the Type field. For example, enter the following number format string in the Type field to display a value in 32nds:

??/32

	A	B	C	D	E
1					
2		Closing Price Per Share			
3		January	14 1/8	14 2/16	
4		February	15 3/8	15 6/16	
5		March	16 1/4	16 4/16	
6		April	14 3/16	14 3/16	
7		May	11 1/4	11 4/16	
8		June	10	10	
9		July	12 1/8	12 2/16	
10		August	13 3/8	13 6/16	
11		September	15 5/16	15 5/16	
12		October	15 3/8	15 6/16	
13		November	18 7/8	18 14/16	
14		December	20 3/4	20 12/16	
15					

Sheet1

Figure 31-2: Displaying values as fractions.

The following number format string displays a value in terms of fractional dollars. For example, the value 154.87 is displayed as *154 and 87/100 Dollars*.

```
0 "and "??/100 "Dollars"
```

The following example displays the value in 16ths, with a quotation mark appended to the right. This format string is useful when you deal with inches (for example, 2/16").

```
# ??/16\"
```

Proofing Your Data with Audio

Excel 2002 introduced a feature that many users tend to overlook: Text to Speech. In other words, Excel is capable of speaking to you. You can have this feature read back a specific range of cells, or you can set it up so it reads the data as you enter it.

To enable Excel's Text to Speech feature, choose Tools⇔Speech⇔Show Text To Speech Toolbar. You'll see the toolbar shown in Figure 32-1. To read a range of cells, select the range first, and then click the Speak Cells button. You can also specify the orientation (By Rows or By Columns). To read the data as it's entered, click the Speak On Enter button.

Figure 32-1: Excel's Text To Speech toolbar.

This is one of those "hate it or love it" features. Some people (myself included) find the voice is far too annoying to use it for any extended period of time. And if you enter the data at a relatively rapid clip, the voice simply won't be able to keep up with you.

You have a small bit of control over the voice used in Excel's Text to Speech feature. To adjust the voice, access the Windows Control Panel, double-click the Speech icon, and then click the Text To Speech tab in the Speech Properties dialog box (see Figure 32-2).

You can choose a different voice and also adjust the speed. Click the Preview Voice button to help make your choices.

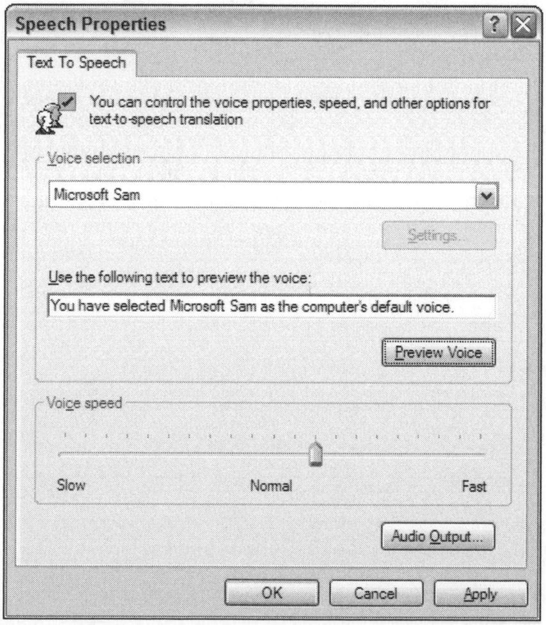

Figure 32-2: Use the Speech Properties dialog box to adjust the voice.

Part II

Controlling Automatic Hyperlinks

One of the most common Excel questions is "How can I prevent Excel from creating automatic hyperlinks?"

Normally, Excel watches what you type and if it looks anything like an e-mail address or a Web URL, it converts your entry into a hyperlink. Sometimes that's good, but sometimes it's not. For example, if you enter **Meeting@4:00 pm** into a cell, Excel erroneously considers that to be an e-mail address and dutifully creates a hyperlink.

Overriding an Automatic Hyperlink

To override a single automatic hyperlink, just press Ctrl+Z. The hyperlink goes away, but the text you entered remains intact. Another option is to precede your entry with an apostrophe so it is evaluated as plain text.

Turning Off Automatic Hyperlinks

If you use Excel 2002 or later, it's very easy to turn off the automatic hyperlink feature. Select Tools⇨AutoCorrect Options to display the AutoCorrect dialog box (see Figure 33-1). Then, click the AutoFormat As You Type tab and remove the check mark from the Internet and Network Paths with Hyperlinks check box.

If you use Excel 2000, you may be surprised to discover that there is no way to turn off automatic hyperlinks.

Figure 33-1: Use the AutoCorrect dialog box to turn off automatic hyperlinks.

Part II

Removing an Existing Hyperlink

To remove a hyperlink from a cell (but keep the cell's contents), right-click the cell and select Remove Hyperlink from the shortcut menu.

Note that the Remove Hyperlink shortcut menu item appears only when a single cell is selected. Amazingly, Excel provides no direct way to remove hyperlinks from more than one cell at a time.

Removing Multiple Hyperlinks

If you need to remove more than one hyperlink, this technique may save some time:

1. Enter the number 1 into any blank cell.

2. Select the cell and press Ctrl+C to copy it.

3. Hold down the Ctrl key as you click each hyperlink you want to remove. Note that you can't select a range. You must click each cell individually.

4. Select Edit⇨Paste Special to display the Paste Special dialog box.

5. In the Paste Special dialog box, select the Multiply option, and click OK.

All the hyperlinks are removed, but the text making up the hyperlinks remains.

Removing Hyperlinks Using VBA

To quickly remove all hyperlinks on a worksheet, you can use a simple VBA statement. The following instructions use the Immediate window, so the macro is not stored in your workbook.

1. Activate the worksheet that contains the hyperlinks to be deleted.

2. Press Alt+F11 to activate the VBA Editor.

3. In the VBA Editor, select View⇨Immediate Window (or press Ctrl+G).

4. Type this command (and then press Enter):

```
Cells.Hyperlinks.Delete
```

Entering Credit Card Numbers

If you've ever tried to enter a 16-digit credit card number into a cell, you may have discovered that Excel always changes the last digit to a zero. Why is that? It's because Excel can only handle 15 digits of numerical accuracy.

If you need to store credit card numbers in a worksheet, you have two options:

- **Precede the credit card number with an apostrophe.** Excel will then interpret the data as a text string rather than as a number.

- **Preformat the cell or range using the Text number format.** Select the range, and then choose Format⇨Cells. In the Cells dialog box, click the Number tab and choose Text in the Category list.

This tip, of course, also applies to other long numbers (such as part numbers) that are not used in numeric calculations.

Part II

Using Excel's Built-In Data Entry Form

When entering data into an Excel list, some people prefer to use a dialog box — also known as Excel's Data Entry Form. Before you can use this form, you'll need to have the column headers set up in your worksheet. You may or may not have some actual data below the column headers.

To display the Data Entry Form, activate any cell within your list and select Data⇨Form. You'll see a dialog box similar to the one shown in Figure 35-1 (the fields shown in the actual dialog box will vary, depending on your column headers).

Figure 35-1: Excel's Data Entry Form.

NOTE

If the number of columns in your list exceeds the limit of your display, the dialog box contains two columns of field names. If your list consists of more than 32 columns, however, the Data⇨Form command doesn't work. You must forgo this method of data entry and enter the information directly into the cells.

When the Data Form dialog box appears, the first record (if any) in the list is displayed. Notice the indicator in the upper-right corner of the dialog box; this indicator tells you which record is selected and the total number of records in the list.

To enter a new record, click the New button to clear the fields. Then you can enter the new information into the appropriate fields. Press Tab or Shift+Tab to move among the fields. When you click the New (or Close) button, the data that you entered is appended to the bottom of the list. You also can press Enter, which is equivalent to clicking the New button. If your list contains any formulas, these are also entered into the new record in the list for you automatically.

NOTE

If your list is named *Database*, Excel automatically extends the range definition to include the new row(s) that you add to the list using the Data Form dialog box. Note that this works only if the list has the name *Database*; no other name will work. Use the Insert⇨Name⇨Define command to name the range.

You can use the Data Form dialog box for more than just data entry. You can edit existing data in the list, view data one record at a time, delete records, and display records that meet certain criteria.

The dialog box contains a number of additional buttons, as follows:

- **Delete:** Deletes the displayed record.

- **Restore:** Restores any information that you edited. You must click this button before you click the New button.

- **Find Prev:** Displays the previous record in the list. If you entered a criterion, this button displays the previous record that matches the criterion.

- **Find Next:** Displays the next record in the list. If you entered a criterion, this button displays the next record that matches the criterion.

- **Criteria:** Clears the fields and lets you enter a criterion upon which to search for records. For example, to locate records that have a salary greater than $50,000, enter **>50000** into the Salary field. Then you can use the Find Next and Find Prev buttons to display the qualifying records.

- **Close:** Closes the dialog box (and enters the data that you were entering, if any).

Customizing and Sharing AutoCorrect Entries

Most users have encountered Excel's AutoCorrect feature — often by accident. For example, if you enter **(c)** into a cell, Excel automatically "corrects" it by substituting a copyright symbol ©. It also corrects some spelling errors, as well as other common mistakes, such as starting a word with two initial uppercase letters.

NOTE

To override an auto correction, press Ctrl+Z. For example, if you need to enter **(c)** rather than a copyright symbol, just press Ctrl+Z after Excel makes its correction.

Fortunately, the AutoCorrect feature is highly customizable, and you can turn it off completely if you find it annoying. You may find it worth the effort to spend some time and configure AutoCorrect so it works best for you. Figure 36-1 shows the AutoCorrect dialog box, which is displayed when you select Tools⇨AutoCorrect Options.

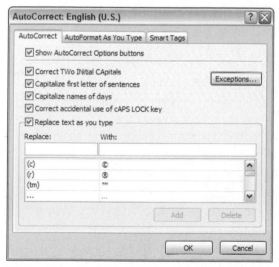

Figure 36-1: Use the AutoCorrect dialog box to customize Excel's AutoCorrect settings.

To add an AutoCorrect shortcut, just type the shortcut text in the Replace field (for example, **msft**), and type the text that it will expand to in the With field (for example, **Microsoft Corporation**). To remove an existing shortcut, just locate it in the list and click the Delete button.

Part II

The AutoCorrect shortcuts that you create in Excel are used in other Microsoft Office applications (and vice versa). The shortcut definitions are stored in an `*.acl` file. The location will vary, and the exact name depends on the language version of Office. If you use the U.S. English language version of Office, the file will be named `mso1033.acl`, and the location will probably be:

```
C:\Documents and Settings\<username>\Application Data\Microsoft\Office
```

If you create some custom AutoCorrect shortcuts that you'd like to share with a colleague, you just make a copy of your `*.acl` file and place it in his or her directory. Be aware that replacing the `*.acl` file will wipe out any custom AutoCorrect shortcuts that your colleague may have created.

Restricting Cursor Movement to Input Cells

A common type of spreadsheet uses two types of cells: input cells and formula cells. The user enters data into the input cells, and the formulas display the results.

Figure 37-1 shows a simple example. The input cells are in the range C4:C7. These cells are used by the formulas in C10:C13. To prevent the user from accidentally typing over the formula cells, it's useful to limit the cursor movement so the formula cells can't even be selected.

	A	B	C	D
1		Mortgage Loan Worksheet		
2				
3		Input Cells		
4		Purchase Price	$204,425	
5		Down Payment	20%	
6		Loan Term (months)	360	
7		Interest Rate	8.00%	
8				
9		Result Cells		
10		Loan Amount	$163,540	
11		Monthly Payment	$1,200.00	
12		Total Payments	$432,000	
13		Total Interest	$268,460	
14				
15				
16				

Figure 37-1: This spreadsheet has input cells at the top and formula cells below.

With Excel 2002 or later, setting up this sort of thing is a snap. Just unlock the input cells, and then protect the sheet. Following are specific instructions for the example shown in the figure:

1. Select C4:C7.

2. Select Format⇨Cells.

3. In the Format Cells dialog box, click the Protection tab and remove the check mark from the Locked check box. (By default, all cells are locked.) Click OK.

4. Select Tools⇨Protection⇨Protect Sheet.

5. In the Protect Sheet dialog box, remove the check mark from the Select Locked Cells option, and make sure that the Select Unlocked Cells option is checked.

6. If you like, specify a password that will be required to unprotect the sheet.

7. Click OK.

Part II

After performing these steps, only the unlocked cells can be selected. If you need to make any changes to your worksheet, you'll need to unprotect the sheet first by choosing Tools⇨ Sheet⇨Unprotect).

Although this example used a contiguous range of cells for the input, that isn't necessary for the steps to work. The input cells can be scattered throughout your worksheet.

Controlling the Office Clipboard

You are undoubtedly familiar with the Windows Clipboard. When you copy (or cut) something (such as text or a graph), it goes to the Clipboard. Then, the information can be pasted somewhere else.

In Office 2000, Microsoft introduced something called the Office Clipboard. Why another Clipboard? The simple answer is because the Office Clipboard is more versatile than the Windows Clipboard — it enables you to store up to 24 copied items. The Windows Clipboard, on the other hand, can only hold a single item — when you copy or paste something, the previous Windows Clipboard contents are wiped out. The downside to the Office Clipboard is that it only works in Microsoft Office applications (Word, Excel, PowerPoint, Access, and Outlook).

If the Office Clipboard doesn't seem to be working, you can display it by selecting Edit⇨ Office Clipboard. This shows the task pane with the Office Clipboard displayed.

Every time you copy (or cut) something, the task pane displays a portion of the information (see Figure 38-1). Newly added items replace older items, so you will only be able to access a maximum of 24 items. To paste the information, just select the paste location and click the item in the task pane.

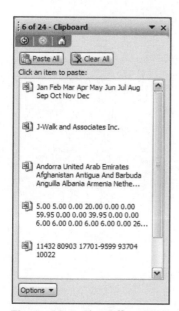

Figure 38-1: The Office Clipboard displays in the task pane.

WARNING

For Excel users, the Office Clipboard has a serious limitation: It cannot hold formulas. If you copy a range of formulas to the Office Clipboard and then paste the data elsewhere, you'll find that the formula results (not the formulas themselves) are pasted.

Part II

Although the Office Clipboard can be useful, a significant number of users find it annoying — especially those who loathe the presence of the task pane. To control some aspects of the Office Clipboard, click the Options button at the bottom of the task pane (see Figure 38-2). Normally, the Office Clipboard displays automatically when you copy two pieces of information. To prevent this from happening, remove the check mark from the Show Office Clipboard Automatically option.

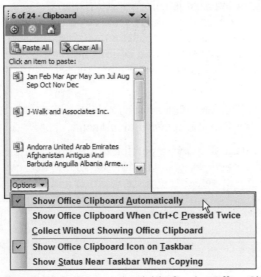

Figure 38-2: Options available for the Office Clipboard.

Creating a Drop-Down List in a Cell

I think most Excel users probably believe that some type of VBA macro is required to display a drop-down list in a cell. The fact is that it's very easy to display a drop-down list in a cell — and macros are not required.

Figure 39-1 shows an example. Cell B2, when selected, displays a down arrow. Click the arrow and you get a list of items (in this case, month names). Click an item, and it's entered into the cell.

Figure 39-1: Use Data Validation to create a drop-down list in a cell.

The trick to setting up a drop-down list is to use Data Validation. The following steps describe how to create a drop-down list of items in a cell:

1. Enter the list of items in a range. In this example, the month names are in the range E1:E12.

2. Select the cell that will contain the drop-down list.

3. Select Data⇨Validation.

4. In the Data Validation dialog box, click the Settings tab.

5. In the Allow drop-down list, select List.

6. In the Source box, specify the range that contains the items.

7. Make sure the In-Cell Dropdown option is checked (see Figure 39-2), and click OK.

If your list is short, you can avoid Step 1. Rather, just type your list items (separated by commas) in the Source box in the Data Validation dialog box.

Normally, the list of items must be on the same worksheet as the cell that contains the drop-down list. But you can get around this limitation if you provide a name for the range that contains the list. For example, you can select Insert⇨Name⇨Define to define the name MonthNames for E1:E12. Then, in the Data Validation dialog box, enter **=MonthNames** in the Source box.

Part II

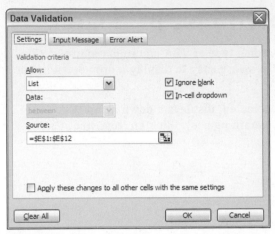

Figure 39-2: Using the Data Validation dialog box to create a drop-down list.

Part III

Formatting

Excel has lots of formatting options to make your work look good. In this part, you'll find tips that cover formatting numbers, dates, times, text, and many other aspects of Excel.

Tips and Where to Find Them

Tip 40	Quick Number Formatting	105
Tip 41	Using "Tear Off" Toolbars	107
Tip 42	Creating Custom Number Formats	109
Tip 43	Using Custom Number Formats to Scale Values	113
Tip 44	Using Custom Date Formatting	117
Tip 45	Some Useful Custom Number Formats	119
Tip 46	Showing Text and a Value in a Cell	123
Tip 47	Merging Cells	125
Tip 48	Formatting Individual Characters in a Cell	127
Tip 49	Displaying Times That Exceed 24 Hours	129
Tip 50	Fixing Non-Numeric Numbers	131
Tip 51	Using AutoFormats	133
Tip 52	Dealing with Gridlines, Borders, and Underlines	135
Tip 53	Creating 3D Formatting Effects	137
Tip 54	Wrapping Text in a Cell	139
Tip 55	Seeing All Characters in a Font	141
Tip 56	Entering Special Characters	143
Tip 57	Using Named Styles	145
Tip 58	Understanding How Excel Handles Color	147
Tip 59	Setting Up Alternate Row Shading	151
Tip 60	Adding a Background Image to a Worksheet	155

Quick Number Formatting

As you probably know, a value in a cell can be displayed in many different ways. Normally, you change a cell's number formatting by using the Number tab of the Format Cells dialog box (accessed with the Format⇨Cells command).

Many of the common number formats can be applied without using the Format Cells dialog box. If you use any of these number formats on a regular basis, you'll save some time by using the keyboard shortcuts shown in Table 40-1. Note that, on most keyboards, the third key in these Ctrl+Shift shortcuts is located on the top row of your keyboard.

TABLE 40-1   SHORTCUT KEYS TO APPLY NUMBER FORMATTING

Shortcut Keys	What the Shortcut Does
Ctrl+Shift+` (the accent/ tilde key above Tab)	Applies the General number format (removes any other number formatting).
Ctrl+Shift+1	Applies the Number format with two decimal places, thousands separator, and minus sign (–) for negative values.
Ctrl+Shift+2	Applies the Time format with the hour and minute, and AM or PM.
Ctrl+Shift+3	Applies the Date format with the day, month, and year.
Ctrl+Shift+4	Applies the Currency format with two decimal places (negative numbers are displayed in parentheses).
Ctrl+Shift+5	Applies the Percentage format with no decimal places.
Ctrl+Shift+6	Applies the Exponential Number format with two decimal places.

Using "Tear Off" Toolbars

Every Excel user takes advantage of Excel's toolbar buttons. But most users don't realize that some of these toolbar controls offer more than meets the eye. Five of Excel's toolbar controls can be "torn off" to create another free-floating mini-toolbar.

Specifically, I'm referring to five toolbar buttons that are used for formatting:

- Borders (on the Formatting toolbar)
- Fill Color (on the Formatting toolbar and on the Drawing toolbar)
- Font Color (on the Formatting toolbar and on the Drawing toolbar)
- Autoshapes (on the Drawing toolbar)
- Line Color (on the Drawing toolbar)

Each of these controls contains an arrow that, when clicked, results in a pop-up list. For example, when you click the arrow on the right side of the Fill Color button, you get a palette of options.

Here's the trick: If you click and drag at the top of that palette, you create a new mini-toolbar. You can then move this mini-toolbar to a convenient location. If you're doing a lot of color formatting, using the free-floating Fill Color and Font Color toolbars can save you a bit of time.

Figure 41-1 shows how it looks after I tore off the Fill Color palette.

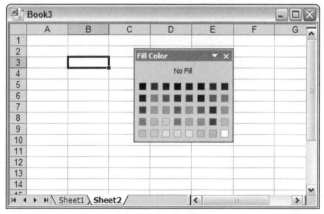

Figure 41-1: This floating palette was torn from the Fill Color toolbar control.

To get rid of a mini-toolbar, just click the X in its title bar.

Creating Custom Number Formats

Although Excel provides a good variety of built-in number formats, you may find that none of these suit your needs. In such a case, there's a pretty good chance that you'll be able to create a custom number format. You do this in the Number tab of the Format Cells dialog box (see Figure 42-1).

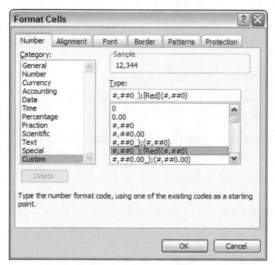

Figure 42-1: Create custom number formats in the Number tab of the Format Cells dialog box.

Many Excel users — even advanced users — avoid creating custom number formats because they think the process is too complicated. The fact is that custom number formats tend to *look* more complex than they actually are.

You construct a number format by specifying a series of codes as a number format string. To enter a custom number format, follow these steps:

1. Select Format⇨Cells to display the Format Cells dialog box.

2. Click the Number tab and select the Custom category.

3. Enter your custom number format in the Type field.

   See Tables 42-1 and 42-2 for examples of codes you can use to create your own custom number formats.

4. Click OK to close the Format Cells dialog box.

Part III

Parts of a Number Format String

A custom format string enables you to specify different format codes for four categories of values: positive numbers, negative numbers, zero values, and text. You do so by separating the codes for each category with a semicolon. The codes are arranged in the following structure:

```
Positive format; Negative format; Zero format; Text format
```

Following are general guidelines to determine how many sections you need:

- If you use only one section, the format string applies to all values.
- If you use two sections, the first section applies to positive values and zeros, and the second section applies to negative values.
- If you use three sections, the first section applies to positive values, the second section applies to negative values, and the third section applies to zeros.
- If you use all four sections, the last section applies to text stored in the cell.

The following is an example of a custom number format that specifies a different format for each of these types:

```
[Green]General; [Red]General; [Black]General; [Blue]General
```

This example takes advantage of the fact that colors have special codes. A cell formatted with this custom number format displays its contents in a different color, depending on the value. When a cell is formatted with this custom number format, a positive number is green, a negative number is red, a zero is black, and text is blue.

 NOTE
When you create a custom number format, don't overlook the Sample box in the Number tab of the Format Cells dialog box. This box displays the value in the active cell using the format string in the Type field. It's a good idea to test your custom number formats by using the following data: a positive value, a negative value, a zero value, and text. Often, creating a custom number format takes several attempts. Each time you edit a format string, it is added to the list. When you finally get the correct format string, access the Format Cells dialog box one more time and delete your previous attempts.

Custom Number Format Codes

Table 42-1 lists the formatting codes available for custom formats, along with brief descriptions.

TABLE 42-1   CODES USED TO CREATE CUSTOM NUMBER FORMATS

Code	Comments
General	Displays the number in General format
#	Digit placeholder that displays only significant digits, and does not display insignificant zeros
0 (zero)	Digit placeholder that displays insignificant zeros if a number has fewer digits than there are zeros in the format
?	Digit placeholder that adds spaces for insignificant zeros on either side of the decimal point so that decimal points align when formatted with a fixed-width font — you can also use ? for fractions that have varying numbers of digits
.	Decimal point
%	Percentage
,	Thousands separator
E- E+ e- e+	Scientific notation
$ - + / ( ) : space	Displays this character
\	Displays the next character in the format
*	Repeats the next character to fill the column width
_ (underscore)	Leaves a space equal to the width of the next character
"text"	Displays the text inside the double quotation marks
@	Text placeholder
[color]	Displays the characters in the color specified and can be any of the following text strings (not case-sensitive): Black, Blue, Cyan, Green, Magenta, Red, White, or Yellow
[COLOR n]	Displays the corresponding color in the color palette, where n is a number from 0 to 56
[condition value]	Enables you to set your own criteria for each section of a number format

Table 42-2 lists the codes used to create custom formats for dates and times.

Part III

TABLE 42-2   CODES USED IN CREATING CUSTOM FORMATS FOR DATES AND TIMES

Code	Comments
m	Displays the month as a number without leading zeros (1–12)
mm	Displays the month as a number with leading zeros (01–12)
mmm	Displays the month as an abbreviation (Jan–Dec)
mmmm	Displays the month as a full name (January–December)
mmmmm	Displays the first letter of the month (J–D)
d	Displays the day as a number without leading zeros (1–31)
dd	Displays the day as a number with leading zeros (01–31)
ddd	Displays the day as an abbreviation (Sun–Sat)
dddd	Displays the day as a full name (Sunday–Saturday)
yy or yyyy	Displays the year as a two-digit number (00–99), or as a four-digit number (1900–9999)
h or hh	Displays the hour as a number without leading zeros (0–23), or as a number with leading zeros (00–23)
m or mm	Displays the minute as a number without leading zeros (0–59), or as a number with leading zeros (00–59)
s or ss	Displays the second as a number without leading zeros (0–59), or as a number with leading zeros (00–59)
[ ]	Displays hours greater than 24, or minutes or seconds greater than 60
AM/PM	Displays the hour using a 12-hour clock; if no AM/PM indicator is used, the hour uses a 24-hour clock

Using Custom Number Formats to Scale Values

If you deal with large numbers, you may prefer to display those numbers scaled to thousands or millions instead of displaying the entire number. For example, you might want to display a number like 132,432,145 in millions — 132.4.

The way to display scaled numbers is to use a custom number format. The actual number, of course, will be used in calculations that involve that cell. The formatting affects only how the number is displayed. To enter a custom number format, select Format⇨Cells to display the Format Cells dialog box. Then click the Number tab and select the Custom category. Your custom number format goes in the Type field.

Table 43-1 shows examples of number formats that scale values in millions.

TABLE 43-1   EXAMPLES OF DISPLAYING VALUES IN MILLIONS

Value	Number Format	Display
123456789	#,###,,	123
1.23457E+11	#,###,,	123,457
1000000	#,###,,	1
5000000	#,###,,	5
–5000000	#,###,,	–5
0	#,###,,	(blank)
123456789	#,###.00,,	123.46
1.23457E+11	#,###.00,,	123,457.00
1000000	#,###.00,,	1.00
5000000	#,###.00,,	5.00
–5000000	#,###.00,,	–5.00
0	#,###.00,,	.00
123456789	#,###,,"M"	123M
1.23457E+11	#,###,,"M"	123,457M
1000000	#,###,,"M"	1M

continued

Part III

TABLE 43-1   EXAMPLES OF DISPLAYING VALUES IN MILLIONS *(continued)*

Value	Number Format	Display
–5000000	#,###,,"M"	–5M
123456789	#,###.0,,"M"_);(#,###.0,,"M)";0.0"M"_)	123.5M
1000000	#,###.0,,"M"_);(#,###.0,,"M)";0.0"M"_)	1.0M
–5000000	#,###.0,,"M"_);(#,###.0,,"M)";0.0"M"_)	(5.0M)
0	#,###.0,,"M"_);(#,###.0,,"M)";0.0"M"_)	0.0M

Table 43-2 shows examples of number formats that scale values in thousands.

TABLE 43-2   EXAMPLES OF DISPLAYING VALUES IN THOUSANDS

Value	Number Format	Display
123456	#,###,	123
1234565	#,###,	1,235
–323434	#,###,	–323
123123.123	#,###,	123
499	#,###,	(blank)
500	#,###,	1
500	#,###.00,	.50

Table 43-3 shows examples of number formats that display values in hundreds.

TABLE 43-3   EXAMPLES OF DISPLAYING VALUES IN HUNDREDS

Value	Number Format	Display
546	0"."00	5.46
100	0"."00	1.00

Value	Number Format	Display
9890	0"."00	98.90
500	0"."00	5.00
−500	0"."00	−5.00
0	0"."00	0.00

Part III

Using Custom Date Formatting

When you enter a date into a cell, Excel formats the date using the system short date format. You can change this format by opening the Windows Control Panel and selecting Regional Settings.

Excel provides many useful built-in date and time formats, accessible in the Date and Time categories in the Number tab of the Format Cells dialog box. The following table shows some other date and time formats that you may find useful. The Value column of the table shows the date/time serial number.

Value	Number Format	Display
38867	mmmm d, yyyy (dddd)	May 30, 2006 (Tuesday)
38867	"It's" dddd!	It's Tuesday!
38867	dddd, mm/dd/yyyy	Tuesday, 05/30/2006
38867	"Month: "mmm	Month: May
38867	General (m/d/yyyy)	38867 (5/30/2006)
0.345	h "Hours"	8 Hours
0.345	h:mm o'clock	8:16 o'clock
0.345	h:mm a/p"m"	8:16 am
0.345	h "hours and" m "minutes"	8 hours and 16 minutes
0.78	h:mm a/p".m."	6:43 p.m.

Part III

Some Useful Custom Number Formats

This tip provides some useful examples of custom number formats.

CROSS-REFERENCE

See Tip 42 for the steps to enter a custom number format in the Format Cells dialog box.

Hiding Zeros

In the following format string, the third element of the string is empty, which causes zero value cells to display as blank:

```
General;General;;@
```

This format string uses the General format for positive and negative values. You can, of course, substitute any other format codes.

Displaying Leading Zeros

To display leading zeros, create a custom number format that uses the 0 character. For example, if you want all numbers to display with 10 digits, use the number format string that follows. Values with fewer than 10 digits will display with leading zeros.

```
0000000000
```

In the following example, the format string uses the repeat character code (an asterisk) to apply leading zeros to fill the entire width of the cell:

```
*00
```

Two zeros are required because the first one represents the character to be repeated, and the second one represents the value to be displayed.

Formatting Percentages

Using a percent symbol (%) in a format string causes the cell to display in Percentage format. Note that the percent sign also appears in the formula bar.

The following format string formats values less than or equal to 1 in Percentage format. Values greater than 1 and text are formatted using the General format.

```
[<=1]0.00%;General
```

When you mix cells with Percentage and General formatting in a column, you may prefer to see the nonpercent values indented from the right so the values line up properly. To do so, apply the following number format to nonpercent cells. This format string uses an underscore followed by the percent symbol. The result is a space equal to the width of the percent symbol.

```
#.00_%
```

Displaying Fractions

Excel supports quite a few built-in fraction number formats (select the Fraction category from the Number tab of the Format Cells dialog box). For example, to display the value .125 as a fraction with 8 as the denominator, select As Eighths (4/8) from the Type list.

You can use a custom format string to create other Fraction formats. For example, the following format string displays a value in 50ths:

```
# ??/50
```

The following format string displays a value in terms of fractional dollars. For example, the value 154.87 is displayed as *154 and 87/100 Dollars*.

```
0 "and "??/100 "Dollars"
```

The following example displays the value in sixteenths, with a quotation mark appended to the right. This format string is useful when you deal with inches (for example, 3/16").

```
# ??/16\"
```

Repeating Text

The number format string displays the contents of the cell three times. For example, if the cell contains the text *Budget*, the cell displays *Budget Budget Budget*.

```
;;;@ @ @
```

Displaying a Negative Sign on the Right

The following format string displays negative values with the negative sign to the right of the number. Positive values have an additional space on the right, so both positive and negative numbers align properly on the right.

```
0.00_-;0.00-
```

Formatting Based on the Cell's Value

Conditional formatting refers to formatting that is applied based on the contents of a cell. Excel's Conditional Formatting feature provides the most efficient way to perform conditional formatting, but you also can use custom number formats. Keep in mind that this type of number formatting has nothing to do with Excel's Conditional Formatting feature.

 NOTE

Conditional number formatting is limited to three conditions — two of them explicit, and the third one implied (that is, everything else). The conditions are enclosed in square brackets and must be simple numeric comparisons.

The following format string uses a different format, depending on the value in the cell. This format string essentially separates the numbers into three groups: less than or equal to 4, greater than or equal to 8, and other.

```
[<=4]"Low"* 0;[>=8]"High"* 0;"Medium"* 0
```

The following number format string displays values less than 1 with a cent symbol on the right (for example, .54¢). Otherwise, values display with a dollar sign (for example, $3.54). Notice, however, that the decimal point is present when the value is displayed with a cent symbol. I'm not aware of any way to eliminate the decimal point.

```
[<1].00¢;$0.00_¢
```

The following number format is useful for telephone numbers. Values greater than 9999999 (that is, numbers with area codes) are displayed as (xxx) xxx-xxxx. Other values (numbers without area codes) are displayed as xxx-xxxx.

```
[>9999999](000) 000-0000;000-0000
```

For ZIP Codes, you might want to use the format string that follows. This displays ZIP Codes using five digits. But if the number is greater than 99999, it uses the "ZIP plus four" format (xxxxx-xxxx).

```
[>99999]00000-0000;00000
```

Coloring Values

Custom number format strings can display the cell contents in various colors. The following format string, for example, displays positive numbers in red, negative numbers in green, zero values in black, and text in blue:

```
[Red]General;[Green]General;[Black]General;[Blue]General
```

Following is another example of a format string that uses colors. Positive values are displayed normally; negative numbers and text cause *Error!* to be displayed in red.

```
General;[Red]"Error!";0;[Red]"Error!"
```

Using the following format string, values that are less than 2 are displayed in red. Values greater than 4 are displayed in green. Everything else (text, or values between 2 and 4) displays in black.

```
[Red][<2]General;[Green][>4]General;[Black]General
```

As seen in the preceding examples, Excel recognizes color names such as [Red] and [Blue]. It also can use other colors from the color palette, indexed by a number. The following format string, for example, displays the cell contents using the sixteenth color in the color palette:

```
[Color16]General
```

 NOTE
You cannot change cells that are colored using a number format string by using normal cell formatting commands.

Suppressing Certain Types of Entries

You can use number formatting to hide certain types of entries. For example, the following format string displays text, but not values:

```
;;
```

This format string displays values (with one decimal place), but not text or zeros:

```
0.0;-0.0;;
```

This format string displays everything except zeros (values display with one decimal place):

```
0.0;-0.0;;@
```

You can use the following format string to completely hide the contents of a cell:

```
;;;
```

Note that when the cell is activated, however, the cell's contents are visible on the formula bar.

Showing Text and a Value in a Cell

If you need to display a number and text in a single cell, Excel provides three options:

- Concatenation
- The TEXT function
- A custom number format

For example, assume that cell A1 contains a value, and in a cell somewhere else in your worksheet you'd like to display the word *Total:* along with that value. It would look something like this:

```
Total: 594.34
```

The sections that follow describe the three methods for accomplishing this.

Using Concatenation

The following formula concatenates the text *Total:* with the value in cell A1:

```
="Total: "&A1
```

This is the simplest solution, but it has a problem. The result of the formula is text, so that cell cannot be used in a numeric formula.

Using the TEXT Function

Another solution uses the TEXT function, which displays a value using a specified number format.

```
=TEXT(A1,"""Total: ""0.00")
```

The second argument for the TEXT function is a number format string — the same type of string that you use when you create a custom number format. Besides being a bit unwieldy (due to the extra quotation marks), this formula suffers from the same problem mentioned in the previous section: The result is not numeric.

Using a Custom Number Format

If you would like to display text and a value — and still be able to use that value in a numeric formula — the solution is to use a custom number format.

To add text, just create the number format string as usual and put the text within quotation marks. For this example, the following custom number format does the job:

```
"Total: "0.00
```

Even though the cell displays text, Excel still considers the cell contents to be a numeric value.

Merging Cells

Merging cells is a simple concept: Join two or more cells together into a single cell. To merge cells, just select them and click the Merge and Center button on the Formatting toolbar.

Merging cells is usually done as a way to enhance the appearance of a worksheet. Figure 47-1, for example, shows a worksheet with four sets of merged cells: C2:I2, J2:P2, B4:B8, and B9:B13. The merged cells in column B also use vertical text.

	A	B	C	D	E	F	G	H	I	J	K	L	M	N	O	P	
1																	
2						Week 1							Week 2				
3			1	2	3	4	5	6	7	8	9	10	11	12	13	14	
4			1	32	53	10	17	33	49	36	82	94	34	83	42	32	
5		Group 1	81	0	77	38	78	81	6	58	57	59	19	26	14	10	
6			23	3	64	66	0	45	60	13	33	93	57	2	47	13	
7			19	48	82	41	53	54	11	11	36	47	42	17	29	46	
8			40	65	10	26	41	10	72	93	11	96	94	67	16	1	
9			44	31	51	24	26	50	0	89	59	53	20	82	21	82	
10		Group 2	43	41	6	82	71	57	4	96	47	42	94	26	61	10	
11			65	75	52	76	27	85	36	8	88	36	29	91	68	17	
12			24	98	82	48	17	67	76	30	95	0	7	47	2	40	
13			44	42	45	65	94	75	35	0	67	97	67	46	77	91	
14																	

Figure 47-1: This worksheet has four sets of merged cells.

Remember that merged cells can only contain one piece of information: a single value, text, or formula. If you attempt to merge a range of cells that contains more than one nonempty cell, Excel prompts you with a warning that only the data in the upper-leftmost cell will be retained.

To unmerge cells, just select the merged area and click the Merge and Center button again.

NOTE

Excel also provides a Merge Across button, which lets you select a range and then creates multiple merged cells — one for each row in the selection. The Merge Across button is not on any of the toolbars, so if you want to use it, you'll need to add it yourself. Choose View⇨Toolbars⇨Customize, and click the Commands tab in the Customize dialog box. You'll find the Merge Across button in the Edit Category.

Part III

Formatting Individual Characters in a Cell

Excel's cell formatting isn't an all or none proposition. In some cases, you may find it helpful to be able to format individual characters within a cell.

NOTE

This technique is limited to cells that contain text. It doesn't work if the cell contains a value or a formula.

To apply formatting to characters within a text string, you need to select those characters first. You can select the characters by clicking and dragging your mouse in the formula bar. Or double-click the cell and then click and drag the mouse to select specific characters directly in the cell. A more efficient way to select individual characters is to press F2, and then use the arrow keys to move between characters, and the Shift+arrow keys to select characters.

When the characters are selected, use the toolbar controls to change the formatting. For example, you can make the selected text bold, italic, a different color, or even a different font.

Figure 48-1 shows a few examples of cells that contain individual character formatting.

	A	B
1		
2		This is the **final** notice.
3		
4		$x^2 + y^2$
5		
6		This is the ~~unapproved~~ final budget
7		
8		S ALES ARE INCREASING
9		
10		

Figure 48-1: Examples of individual character formatting.

Unfortunately, two of the most commonly used formatting attributes are not available on toolbar buttons: superscript and subscript formatting. If you would like to apply superscripts or subscripts, you need to access the Font tab in the Format Cells dialog box. Just press Ctrl+1 after you've selected the text to format.

NOTE

My Power Utility Pak add-in includes a handy tool that simplifies individual character formatting, including superscript and subscript formatting. You can use the coupon in the back of the book to order a discounted copy.

Part III

Displaying Times That Exceed 24 Hours

As you may know, Excel's time values are normal numbers that are formatted to display as a time. For example, 0 represents 12:00 AM, 0.50 represents noon (halfway through the day), and 0.75 represents 6:00 PM.

Because times are numbers, you can add them together. Figure 49-1 shows a worksheet that sums several time values. The formula in cell B8 is a simple SUM formula:

```
=SUM(B3:B7)
```

	A	B	C	D
1				
2	Date	Hours Worked		
3	Jan 4	8:30		
4	Jan 5	4:00		
5	Jan 6	8:00		
6	Jan 7	6:30		
7	Jan 8	4:00		
8	Total	7:00		
9				
10				

Figure 49-1: Summing time values may not display the correct result.

As you can see, the formula is returning an incorrect result. Because a day has only 24 hours, Excel normally ignores hours that exceed 24 hours. To force Excel to display times that exceed 24 hours, you need to modify the number formatting.

In this example, Excel uses the following number format:

```
h:mm
```

To display the correct value, place square brackets around the "h" part:

```
[h]:mm
```

Figure 49-2 shows the worksheet after making this number format change.

Part III

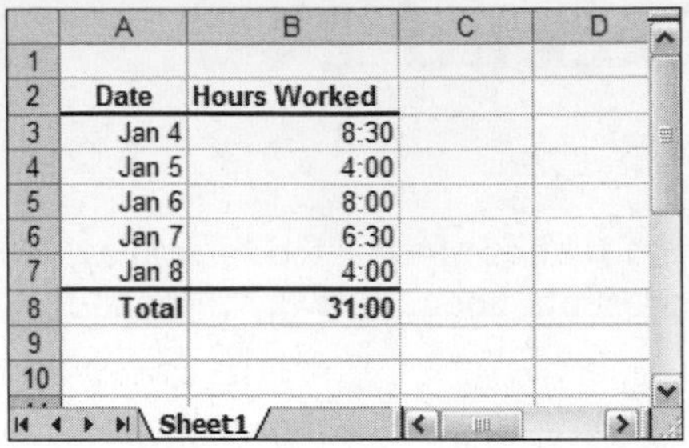

	A	B	C	D
1				
2	Date	Hours Worked		
3	Jan 4	8:30		
4	Jan 5	4:00		
5	Jan 6	8:00		
6	Jan 7	6:30		
7	Jan 8	4:00		
8	Total	31:00		
9				
10				

Sheet1

Figure 49-2: Adjusting the number format causes the cell to display the correct value.

Fixing Non-Numeric Numbers

If you import data from other sources, you may have discovered that Excel sometimes does not import values correctly. Specifically, you may find that Excel is treating your numbers as text. For example, you may sum a range of values, and find that the SUM formula returns 0 — even though the range apparently contains values.

To force Excel to change these "non-numeric" numbers to actual values, perform these steps:

1. Activate any empty cell on your worksheet.

2. Select Edit⇨Copy.

3. Select the range that contains the problematic values.

4. Select Edit⇨Paste Special to display the Paste Special dialog box.

5. In the Paste Special dialog box, select the Add operation.

6. Click OK.

Excel adds nothing to these values, but in the process, it coerces those cells to be actual values.

Using AutoFormats

One of Excel's best timesaving tools is AutoFormatting, accessed with the Format➪AutoFormat command. Figure 51-1 shows a typical table of data. The top table is unformatted, and the table at the bottom was formatted with a single click of the mouse.

	A	B	C	D	E	F	G	H	I
1									
2			Jan	Feb	Mar	Apr	May	Jun	TOTAL
3		Region 1	546	563	580	600	610	619	3518
4		Region 2	433	442	461	476	483	487	2782
5		Region 3	1032	1027	1034	1042	1054	1075	6264
6		Region 4	873	871	888	915	912	904	5363
7		TOTAL	2884	2903	2963	3033	3059	3085	17927
8									
9			Jan	Feb	Mar	Apr	May	Jun	TOTAL
10		Region 1	$ 546.00	$ 563.00	$ 580.00	$ 600.00	$ 610.00	$ 619.00	$ 3,518.00
11		Region 2	433.00	442.00	461.00	476.00	483.00	487.00	2,782.00
12		Region 3	1,032.00	1,027.00	1,034.00	1,042.00	1,054.00	1,075.00	6,264.00
13		Region 4	873.00	871.00	888.00	915.00	912.00	904.00	5,363.00
14		TOTAL	$2,884.00	$2,903.00	$2,963.00	$3,033.00	$3,059.00	$3,085.00	$17,927.00
15									

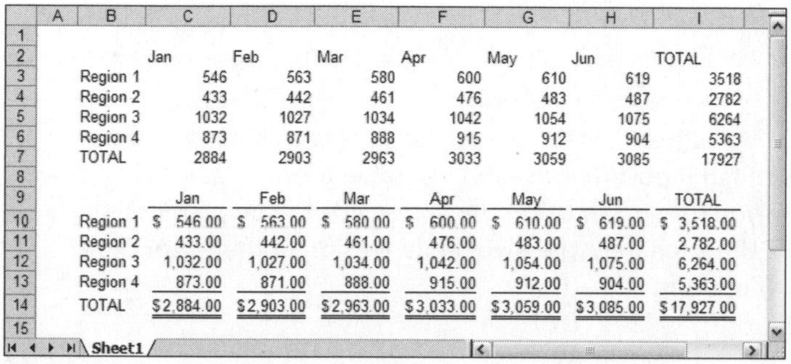

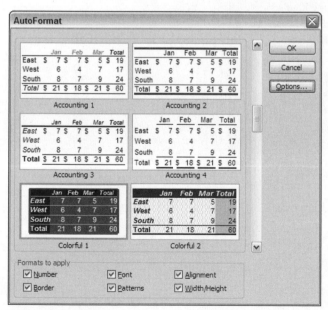

Figure 51-1: A table of data before and after using AutoFormatting.

Excel provides 15 different AutoFormats, and each of these can be customized a bit by clicking the Options button in the AutoFormat dialog box. When you click this button, the dialog box expands to show some options (see Figure 51-2).

Figure 51-2: The AutoFormat dialog box, with the options displayed.

Part III

When you apply an AutoFormat, up to six different formatting elements are applied: Number, Font, Alignment, Border, Patterns, and Width/Height. These correspond to the options in the AutoFormat dialog box. For example, you might like the Classic 3 AutoFormat, but you don't want Excel to automatically adjust the column width. Simply remove the check mark from the Width/Height option. When you turn these options on and off, the samples in the dialog box change to give you an idea of what you can expect when you apply the AutoFormat to your table.

NOTE

When you use AutoFormatting with a PivotTable, you can access an entirely different AutoFormat dialog box, with ten report formats and ten table formats (see Figure 51-3). Experiment with these, and you may be surprised how easy it is to completely change the look of your PivotTable. Unfortunately, the PivotTable version of the AutoFormat dialog box doesn't have any options.

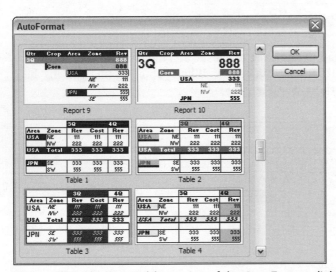

Figure 51-3: The PivotTable version of the AutoFormat dialog box.

A common question is "How can I add my own AutoFormats?" Unfortunately, that's not possible.

Dealing with Gridlines, Borders, and Underlines

If you need to draw attention to or delineate cells in a worksheet, one way to do it is with lines. Excel provides three options:

- Worksheet gridlines
- Cell borders
- Cell underlining

Worksheet gridlines is an all or none setting. Use the View tab of the Options dialog box (Tools⇨Options) to turn gridlines on or off for the active worksheet. You can also control whether cell gridlines are printed. Use the Sheet tab of the Page Setup dialog box (File⇨ Page Setup) to control this setting.

Cell borders can be applied to individual cells or to a range of cells. The Borders button on the Formatting toolbar provides some cell border options, but for complete control, you'll want to use the Border tab of the Format Cells dialog box (Format⇨Cells), which is shown in Figure 52-1. This dialog box gives you control over border color, line style, and location (for example, horizontal borders only). This dialog box works with the currently selected cell or range.

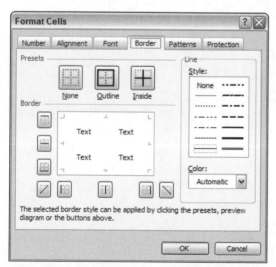

Figure 52-1: For optimal control over cell borders, use the Format Cells dialog box.

Cell underlining is completely independent of gridlines and cell borders. Excel provides four different types of underlining:

Part III

- Single

- Double

- Single Accounting

- Double Accounting

The Underline button on the Formatting toolbar toggles single underlining on and off for the selected cell or range. To apply the other three types of underlining, you must select the underline type from the Underline drop-down list in the Font tab of the Format Cells dialog box.

So how is the accounting underlining different from normal underlining? The difference is subtle. When accounting underlining is applied to a cell that contains text, the complete width of the cell is underlined. When using the Currency number format, the currency symbol is not underlined for the accounting underline formats. In addition, the underline appears slightly lower in the accounting underline formats, making the underlined data a bit more legible.

Figure 52-2 shows all four types of underlining for text (column A) and for values formatted as currency. Worksheet gridlines are turned off to make the underlining more visible.

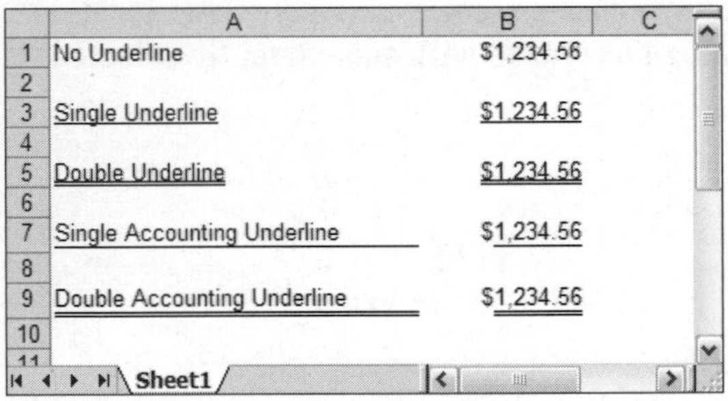

Figure 52-2: Examples of four types of underlining.

Creating 3D Formatting Effects

If you're the type who likes to apply lots of fancy formatting to your worksheet, you might like this. In this tip, I show you a way to produce a three-dimensional appearance in a cell or range. Figure 53-1 shows a few examples.

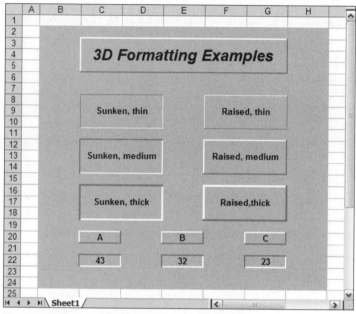

Figure 53-1: Examples of 3D formatting effects.

In order for this effect to work, the background range must use a colored pattern. For these examples, I used 25% Gray — but you can use any color you like.

Here's the step-by-step procedure for creating the sunken, thin effect, shown in range C8:D10 in Figure 53-1.

1. Select the background range (in this example, B2:H24), and make the background 25% Gray using the Fill Color tool on the Formatting toolbar.

2. Select C8:D10, and click the Merge and Center button on the Formatting toolbar. This is an optional step that merges the cells.

3. With the merged cells selected, select Format➪Cells.

4. In the Format Cells dialog box, click the Border tab.

5. Select 50% Gray from the Color drop-down list.

6. In the Style box, select the thinnest solid line.

7. In the Border section, click the left border and the top border.

Part III

8. Select White from the Color drop-down list.

9. In the Border section, click the right border and the bottom border. You won't notice any difference, because the background of the sample Text box is also white.

10. Click OK.

To create medium or thick line effects, select a thicker line type in Step 6.

To create a raised effect, make the top and right borders white, and the right and bottom borders 50% Gray.

Experiment with other colors and line styles. For example, using the double line option creates an even more convincing 3D effect.

Wrapping Text in a Cell

If you need to enter a lot of text into a cell, you have two choices:

- Allow the text to spill over into the adjacent cell on the right.
- Allow the text to wrap so that it displays on multiple lines within the cell.

If the cell to the right is not empty, the text will appear to be cut off if you don't wrap the text. Figure 54-1 illustrates how this works.

Figure 54-1: Examples of lengthy text in cells.

Cell B2 contains the default formatting. Because the cells to the right are empty, the entire text is visible.

Cell B4 contains the same text as B2, but it appears to be cut off because cell C4 is not empty.

Cell B6 uses the Wrap Text option, which is available in the Alignment tab of the Format Cells dialog box (accessible by choosing Format⇨Cells).

If you change the column width of a cell that uses Wrap Text, you will find that the row height does not change to compensate. For example, if you reduce the column width, then some of the text may not be displayed. If you increase the column width, you'll see extra white space in the cell. To fix the row height after changing the column width, choose Format⇨Row⇨Autofit.

To force a line break in a cell, press Alt+Enter. If the cell is not already formatted with Wrap Text, pressing Alt+Enter applies Wrap Text formatting automatically.

Part III

Seeing All Characters in a Font

You probably have dozens of fonts installed on your system. Here's a quick way to view the characters available in any font.

Start with a new worksheet, and then follow these steps:

1. Enter this formula into cell A1:

   ```
   =CHAR(ROW())
   ```

2. Copy cell A1 down the column to cell A255.

3. Click the Column A header to select the entire column.

4. Choose a font from the Font drop-down list on the Formatting toolbar.

5. Scroll down the worksheet to see the various characters in the selected font.

Repeat Step 4 as often as you like.

Figure 55-1 shows a partial view of the characters in the Bookshelf Symbol 7 font. The row number corresponds to the character number. You can enter these characters from the keyboard using the numeric keypad. For example, to enter the character shown in row 101, hold down the Alt key while you type **101** on the numeric keypad. For codes less than 100, enter a leading zero. Make sure that the cell (or character) is formatted using the correct font.

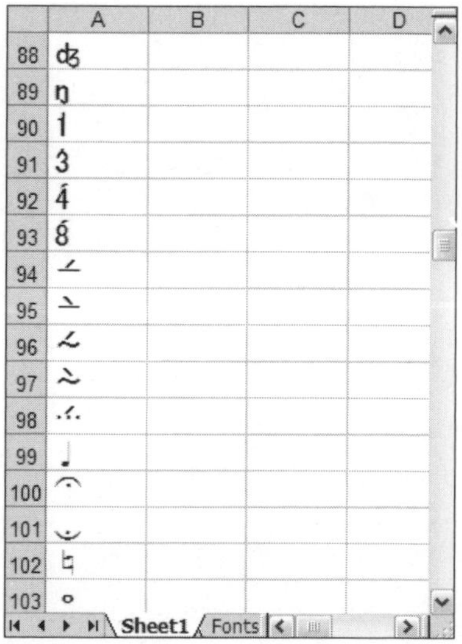

Figure 55-1: A few characters from the Bookshelf Symbol 7 font.

NOTE

This technique displays only the first 255 characters in the font. Unicode fonts contain many additional characters, which you can access using the Symbol dialog box. (See Tip 56 for more about using special characters.)

WARNING

If you plan to share your workbook with others, be careful about using nonstandard fonts (fonts that don't ship with Windows). If the font you specified is not available on your colleague's system, Excel will attempt to substitute the closest match. But it's not always successful.

Entering Special Characters

If you use a recent version of Excel, you can use the handy Symbol dialog box to locate and insert special characters into a cell (see Figure 56-1). You access this dialog box by choosing Insert⇨Symbol.

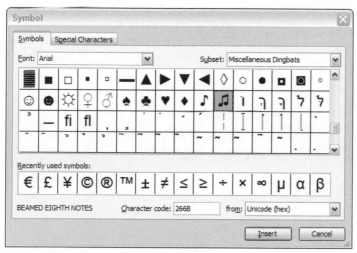

Figure 56-1: Characters in the Miscellaneous Dingbats subset of the Arial font.

In the Symbols tab, you select a font from the Font drop-down list. For most fonts, you'll also be able to select a subset of the font from the Subset drop-down list. Select the character you want and click the Insert button.

If you use a particular character frequently, you may prefer to make it more accessible. You can do this using Excel's AutoCorrect feature. Following are instructions for making the beamed eighth notes character (selected in Figure 56-1) easy to access:

1. Select an empty cell.

2. Choose Insert⇨Symbol, and use the Symbol dialog box to locate the character you want to use. In this case, the symbol is character code 266B, located in the Miscellaneous Dingbats subset.

3. Insert that symbol into the cell by clicking the Insert button.

4. Click Cancel to close the Symbol dialog box.

5. Press Ctrl+C to copy the character in the active cell.

6. Select Tools⇨AutoCorrect Options to display the AutoCorrect dialog box.

7. Click the AutoCorrect tab.

Part III

8. In the Replace field, enter a character sequence, such as **(m)**.

9. Activate the With field and press Ctrl+V to paste the special character.

10. Click OK to close the AutoCorrect dialog box.

After performing these steps, Excel will substitute the musical note symbol whenever you type **(m)**. When you select a replacement string, choose a character sequence that you don't normally type. Otherwise, you may find that Excel is making the substitution when you don't want it to happen. But remember, you can always press Ctrl+Z to override an AutoCorrect entry.

Using Named Styles

Perhaps one of the most under-utilized features in Excel is named styles. If you use Microsoft Word, you're probably familiar with the concept of styles. Excel's named styles feature is similar, but it's implemented much differently than it is in Word.

Named styles make it very easy to apply a set of predefined formatting options to a cell or range. In addition to saving time, using named styles also helps to ensure a consistent look across your worksheets.

A style can consist of settings for up to six different attributes:

- Number format
- Font (type, size, and color)
- Alignment (vertical and horizontal)
- Borders
- Pattern
- Protection (locked and hidden)

The real power of styles is apparent when you change a component of a style. All cells that use that named style automatically incorporate the change. Suppose that you apply a particular style to a dozen cells scattered throughout your worksheet. Later, you realize that these cells should have a font size of 14 points rather than 12 points. Rather than change each cell, simply edit the style. All cells with that particular style change automatically.

Using the Style Dialog Box

You work with styles in the Style dialog box, accessed by choosing Format⇨Style. Figure 57-1 shows the Style dialog box, and it displays the formatting attributes for the Normal style. (By default, all cells are assigned the Normal style.)

Figure 57-1: Use the Style dialog box to work with named styles.

Part III

Here's a quick example of how you can use styles to change the default font used throughout your workbook:

1. Choose Format⇨Style to display the Style dialog box.

2. Make sure that Normal appears in the Style Name drop-down list and click the Modify button. Excel displays the Format Cells dialog box.

3. Click the Font tab and choose the font and size that you want as the default.

4. Click OK to return to the Style dialog box.

5. Click OK again to close the Style dialog box.

The font for all cells that use the Normal style changes to the font that you specified. You can change the formatting attributes for the Normal style at any time.

Creating New Styles

You can, of course, define your own styles. For example, you might create a style called ColumnHeads, which is used for your column headings. To create a new style, follow these steps:

1. First select a cell and apply all the formatting that you want to include in the new style.

2. After you format the cell to your liking, choose Format⇨Style.

   Excel displays the Style dialog box. Excel displays the name of the current style of the cell (probably Normal) in the Style Name drop-down list box. This box is highlighted so that you can simply enter a new style name by typing it.

3. Enter a new style name in the Style Name drop-down list box (for example, **ColumnHeads**). Excel displays the words By Example to indicate that it's basing the style on the current cell.

   The check boxes display the current formats for the cell. By default, all check boxes are checked.

4. If you don't want the style to include one or more format categories, remove the check(s) from the appropriate box(es).

5. Click Add to create the style and click OK to close the dialog box.

You also can create a style from scratch in the Style dialog box. Just enter a style name and then click the Modify button to select the formatting.

NOTE

If you plan to work with named styles, you may want to add the Style button to one of your toolbars. Choose View⇨Toolbars⇨Customize, and click the Commands tab. The Style button is located in the Format category.

Understanding How Excel Handles Color

Excel has a dark secret that most users don't know: It can deal with only 56 different colors at a time. That's right. Your monitor can display millions of color, but Excel is stuck in the dark ages when it comes to colors.

Each workbook has its own 56-color palette. You can change any of the colors on this palette, but you can't add additional colors. To view the color palette for a workbook, select Tools⇨Options, and then click the Color tab in the Options dialog box (see Figure 58-1).

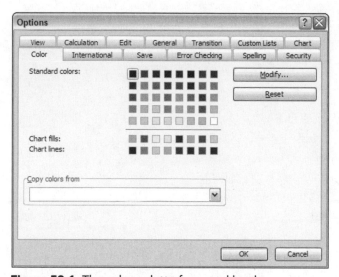

Figure 58-1: The color palette for a workbook.

Notice that the colors are arranged in seven rows of eight colors, and the rows are divided into three groups:

- **Standard colors (rows 1-5):** These 40 colors are the colors that appear when you use the Fill Color or Font Color buttons on the Formatting toolbar.

- **Chart fills (row 6):** These are the colors Excel uses when applying automatic formatting to chart series such as columns, bars, and areas. The colors are listed in the order in which they are used.

- **Chart lines (row 7):** These are the colors Excel uses when applying automatic formatting to line chart series. The colors are listed in the order in which they are used.

NOTE

Although the color palette consists of 56 colors, some of them are duplicated. In fact, the default color palette contains only 46 *different* colors.

Changing Colors

In some cases, you may want to modify the colors available. For example, if you're creating a chart, you may prefer to use different colors for the columns.

To modify any of the colors in the palette, click the color and then click the Modify button. This displays the Colors dialog box, shown in Figure 58-2. Use either the Standard tab or the Custom tab to select a new color, and then click OK. The Custom tab provides many more color choices — 16,777,216 colors, to be exact.

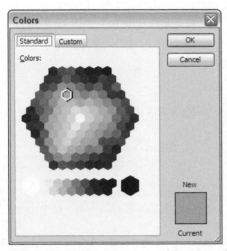

Figure 58-2: Changing one of Excel's colors.

When you change a color, elements in your workbook that used the old color will update to use the new color.

To return to the default color palette (and cancel any color changes you've made), click the Reset button on the Color tab of the Options dialog box.

You can also use the Color tab of the Options dialog box to copy the color palette from another workbook (which must be open) to the active workbook. Select a workbook from the drop-down list, and click OK. This might be useful if you've customized one or more of your colors and you would like to duplicate those colors in a different workbook.

Exceptions to the 56-Color Palette

As you work with Excel, you may notice that, in some situations, you see more than 56 colors. Specifically, the 56-color palette doesn't affect the following objects:

- AutoShapes
- Pictures

- Inserted or embedded objects, including WordArt, diagrams, and controls from the Control Toolbox toolbar

- Chart fills that use one of the preset gradients, a texture, or a picture (these options are available in the Fill Effects dialog box)

Setting Up Alternate Row Shading

Back in the old days, typical paper used by computer printers consisted of wide sheets, with holes on the side, and alternating green and white horizontal stripes. The green stripes were provided to make it easier to read the printed output.

This tip presents an easy way to set up a worksheet to display horizontal stripes, which I refer to as alternate row shading. It's done with Excel's Conditional Formatting feature. The best part is that it's completely dynamic. If you delete a row or add a row, the row shading adjusts itself automatically. Figure 59-1 shows an example of a range formatted with alternate row shading.

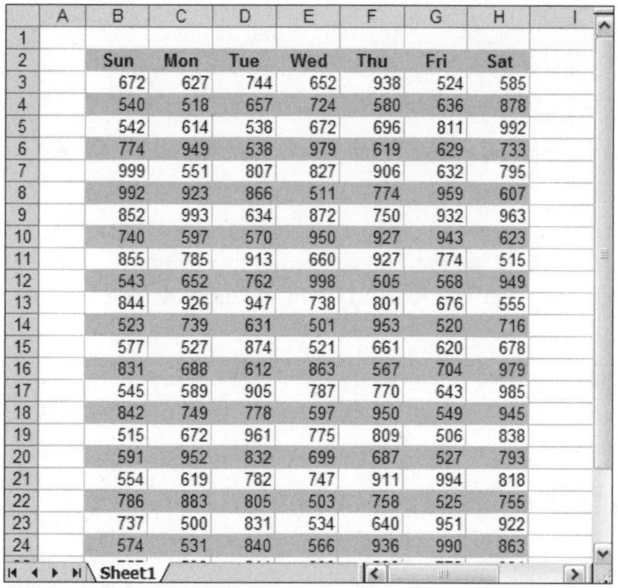

	A	B	C	D	E	F	G	H	I
1									
2		Sun	Mon	Tue	Wed	Thu	Fri	Sat	
3		672	627	744	652	938	524	585	
4		540	518	657	724	580	636	878	
5		542	614	538	672	696	811	992	
6		774	949	538	979	619	629	733	
7		999	551	807	827	906	632	795	
8		992	923	866	511	774	959	607	
9		852	993	634	872	750	932	963	
10		740	597	570	950	927	943	623	
11		855	785	913	660	927	774	515	
12		543	652	762	998	505	568	949	
13		844	926	947	738	801	676	555	
14		523	739	631	501	953	520	716	
15		577	527	874	521	661	620	678	
16		831	688	612	863	567	704	979	
17		545	589	905	787	770	643	985	
18		842	749	778	597	950	549	945	
19		515	672	961	775	809	506	838	
20		591	952	832	699	687	527	793	
21		554	619	782	747	911	994	818	
22		786	883	805	503	758	525	755	
23		737	500	831	534	640	951	922	
24		574	531	840	566	936	990	863	

Figure 59-1: Use Excel's Conditional Formatting feature to display alternate row shading.

Use the following steps to set up alternate row shading:

1. Select the range to be shaded.
2. Select Format⇨Conditional Formatting to display the Conditional Formatting dialog box.
3. In the Conditional Formatting dialog box, change the drop-down list to Formula Is, and then enter this formula in the field (see Figure 59-2):

   ```
   =MOD(ROW(),2)=0
   ```

4. Click the Format button to display the Format Cells dialog box.

5. Click the Patterns tab in the Format Cells dialog box.

6. Select a color for the shaded cells (a light color is a good choice).

7. Click OK to close the Format Cells dialog box, and then click OK again to close the Conditional Formatting dialog box.

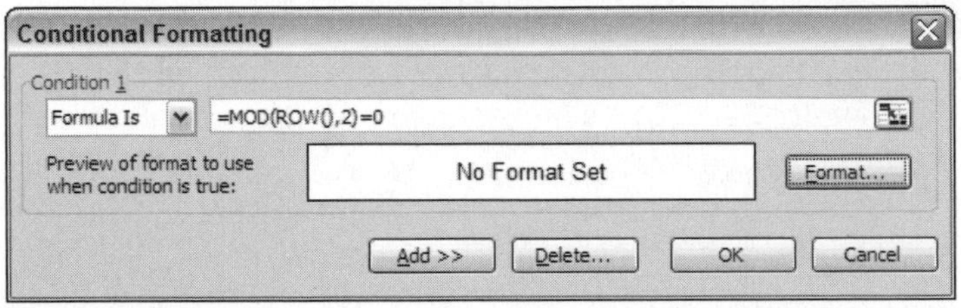

Figure 59-2: The Conditional Formatting formula that displays alternate row shading.

Try inserting or deleting rows within the formatted range. You'll see that the shading gets adjusted automatically.

This formula uses the ROW function (which returns the row number) and the MOD function (which returns the remainder of its first argument divided by its second argument). For cells in even-numbered rows, the MOD function returns 0, and cells in that row are formatted with shading.

For alternate shading of columns, use this modified formula:

```
=MOD(COLUMN(),2)=0
```

To apply shading to every *third* row, use this formula:

```
=MOD(ROW(),3)=0
```

Use the following formula to apply alternate shading in groups of four rows (that is, four rows shaded, followed by four rows not shaded):

```
=MOD(INT((ROW()-1)/4)+1,2)
```

Figure 59-3 shows yet another variation: checkerboard shading. This is accomplished with the following conditional formatting formula:

```
=MOD(ROW(),2)=MOD(COLUMN(),2)
```

	A	B	C	D	E	F	G	H	
1									
2		Sun	Mon	Tue	Wed	Thu	Fri	Sat	
3		672	627	744	652	938	524	585	
4		540	518	657	724	580	636	878	
5		542	614	538	672	696	811	992	
6		774	949	538	979	619	629	733	
7		999	551	807	827	906	632	795	
8		992	923	866	511	774	959	607	
9		852	993	634	872	750	932	963	
10		740	597	570	950	927	943	623	
11		855	785	913	660	927	774	515	
12		543	652	762	998	505	568	949	
13		844	926	947	738	801	676	555	
14		523	739	631	501	953	520	716	
15		577	527	874	521	661	620	678	
16		831	688	612	863	567	704	979	
17		545	589	905	787	770	643	985	
18		842	749	778	597	950	549	945	
19		515	672	961	775	809	506	838	
20		591	952	832	699	687	527	793	
21		554	619	782	747	911	994	818	

Sheet1

Figure 59-3: Using Conditional Formatting to apply checkerboard shading to a range.

Adding a Background Image to a Worksheet

Most of the time, simpler is better. But in some cases, you may want to spiff up a worksheet with something a bit fancy. One way to do that is to apply a background image. A background image in Excel is similar to the wallpaper that you may display on your Windows desktop or an image used as the background for a Web page.

Figure 60-1 shows an example of a worksheet that contains an appropriate background image — bricks for a masonry company.

Figure 60-1: You can add almost any image file as a worksheet background image.

NOTE

Before you get too excited about this feature, there is a caveat: The graphic background on a worksheet is for on-screen display only — it isn't printed when you print the worksheet.

To add a background image to a worksheet, choose Format⇨Sheet⇨Background. Excel displays a dialog box that enables you to choose a graphics file (all common graphic file formats are supported). When you locate a file, click OK.

Excel tiles the graphic across your worksheet. You'll probably want to turn off the gridline display, because the gridlines show through the graphic. Some backgrounds make reading text difficult, so you may want to use a solid background color for cells that contain text.

Part III

Part IV

Basic Formulas and Functions

The ability to create formulas is what makes a spreadsheet a spreadsheet. In this part, you'll find formula-related tips that can make your workbooks more powerful than ever.

Tips and Where to Find Them

Tip 61 When to Use Absolute References 159

Tip 62 When to Use Mixed References 161

Tip 63 Changing the Type of a Cell Reference 163

Tip 64 AutoSum Tricks 165

Tip 65 Using the Status Bar Selection Statistics Feature 167

Tip 66 Converting Formulas to Values 169

Tip 67 Transforming Data without Using Formulas 171

Tip 68 Transforming Data by Using Formulas 173

Tip 69 Deleting Values While Keeping Formulas 175

Tip 70 Dealing with Function Arguments 177

Tip 71 Annotating a Formula without Using a Comment 179

Tip 72 Making an Exact Copy of a Range of Formulas 181

Tip 73 Monitoring Formula Cells from Any Location 183

Tip 74 Displaying and Printing Formulas 185

Tip 75 Avoiding Error Displays in Formulas 187

Tip 76 Using Goal Seeking 189

Tip 77 Understanding the Secret about Names 191

Tip 78 Using Named Constants 193

Tip 79 Using Functions in Names 195

Tip 80 Editing Name References 197

Tip 81 Using Dynamic Names 199

Tip 82 Creating Worksheet-Level Names 201

Tip 83 Working with Pre-1900 Dates 203

Tip 84 Working with Negative Time Values 205

When to Use Absolute References

When you create a formula that refers to another cell or range, the cell or range reference can be relative or absolute. A *relative reference* is a cell reference that adjusts to its new location when the formula is copied and pasted. An *absolute reference* is a cell reference that does not change, even when the formula is copied and pasted elsewhere. An absolute reference is specified with two dollar signs. For example:

```
=$A$1
=SUM($A$1:$F$24)
```

A relative reference, on the other hand, does not use dollar signs:

```
=A1
=SUM(A1:F24)
```

The majority of cell and range references you will ever use are relative references. In fact, Excel creates relative cell references in formulas except when the formula includes cells in different worksheets or workbooks. So when do you use an absolute reference? The only time you even need to *think* about using an absolute reference is if you plan to copy the formula.

The easiest way to understand this is with an example. Figure 61-1 shows a simple worksheet. The formula in cell D2, which multiplies the quantity by the price, is

```
=B2*C2
```

This formula uses relative cell references. Therefore, when the formula is copied to the other cells, the references will adjust in a relative manner. For example, copy the formula to cell D3 and it becomes

```
=B3*C3
```

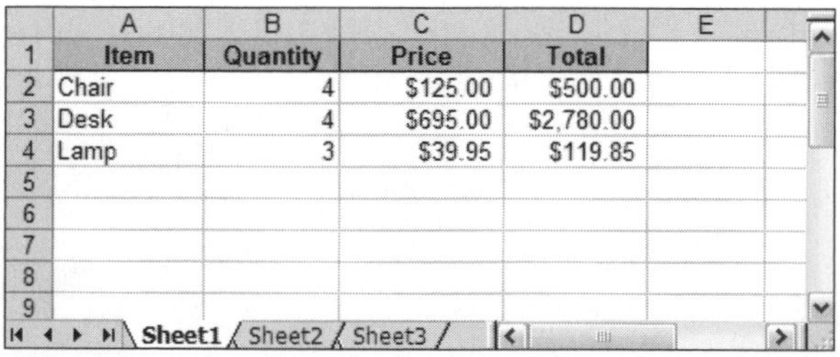

	A	B	C	D	E
1	Item	Quantity	Price	Total	
2	Chair	4	$125.00	$500.00	
3	Desk	4	$695.00	$2,780.00	
4	Lamp	3	$39.95	$119.85	
5					
6					
7					
8					
9					

Sheet1 / Sheet2 / Sheet3 /

Figure 61-1: Copying a formula that contains relative references.

Part IV

What if the cell references in D2 contained absolute references, like this?

```
=$B$2*$C$2
```

In this case, copying the formula to the cells below would produce incorrect results. The formula in cell D3 would be exactly the same as the formula in cell D2.

Now, I'll extend the example to calculate sales tax. The sales tax rate is stored in cell B7 (see Figure 61-2). In this situation, the formula in cell D2 is

```
=B2*C2*$B$7
```

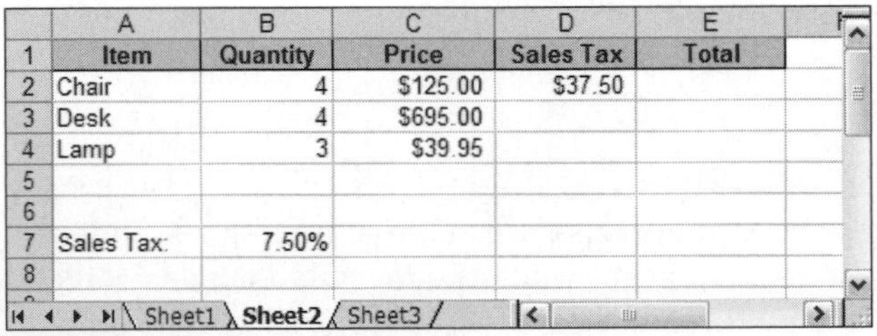

	A	B	C	D	E	F
1	Item	Quantity	Price	Sales Tax	Total	
2	Chair	4	$125.00	$37.50		
3	Desk	4	$695.00			
4	Lamp	3	$39.95			
5						
6						
7	Sales Tax:	7.50%				
8						

⏮ ◀ ▶ ⏭ \ Sheet1 \ **Sheet2** ⁄ Sheet3 ⁄

Figure 61-2: Formula references to the sales tax cell should be absolute.

The quantity is multiplied by the price, and the result is multiplied by the sales tax rate stored in cell B7. Notice that the reference to B7 is an absolute reference. When the formula in D2 is copied to the cells below, cell D3 will contain this formula:

```
=B3*C3*$B$7
```

The references to cells B2 and C2 were adjusted, but the reference to cell B7 was not — which is exactly what I want.

When to Use Mixed References

In the previous tip, I discuss absolute versus relative cell references. This tip covers an additional type of cell reference: A *mixed cell reference*, which is a cell reference where either the column or the row is absolute (and therefore doesn't change when the formula is copied and pasted). Mixed cell references aren't used too often, but as you see in this tip, there are some situations in which using mixed references will make your job much easier.

Where an absolute cell reference contains two dollar signs, a mixed cell reference, by comparison, contains only one dollar sign. Here are two examples of mixed references:

```
=$A1
=A$1
```

In the first example, the column part of the reference (A) is absolute, and the row part (1) is relative. In the second example, the column part of the reference is relative, and the row part is absolute.

Figure 62-1 shows a worksheet demonstrating a situation in which using mixed references is the best choice.

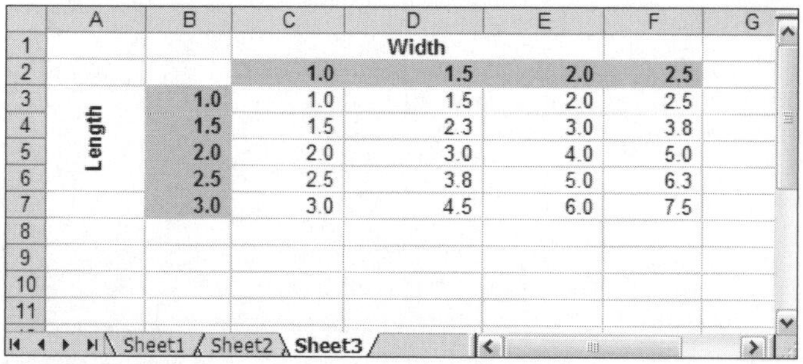

	A	B	C	D	E	F	G
1				Width			
2			1.0	1.5	2.0	2.5	
3		1.0	1.0	1.5	2.0	2.5	
4	Length	1.5	1.5	2.3	3.0	3.8	
5		2.0	2.0	3.0	4.0	5.0	
6		2.5	2.5	3.8	5.0	6.3	
7		3.0	3.0	4.5	6.0	7.5	
8							
9							
10							
11							

Sheet1 / Sheet2 \ **Sheet3** /

Figure 62-1: Using mixed cell references.

The formulas in the table calculate the area for various lengths and widths. Here's the formula in cell C3:

```
=$B3*C$2
```

Part IV

Notice that both cell references are mixed. The reference to cell B3 uses an absolute reference for the column ($B), and the reference to cell C2 uses an absolute reference for the row ($2). As a result, this formula can be copied down and across, and the calculations will be correct. For example, the formula in cell F7 is

```
=$B7*F$2
```

If C3 used either absolute or relative references, copying the formula would produce incorrect results.

Changing the Type of a Cell Reference

In Tips 61 and 62, I discuss absolute, relative, and mixed cell references. This tip describes an easy way to change the type of reference used when creating a formula.

You can enter nonrelative references (absolute or mixed) manually by simply typing dollar signs in the appropriate positions. Or you can use a handy shortcut: the F4 key. After you've entered a cell reference when creating a formula, you can press F4 repeatedly to have Excel cycle through all four reference types.

For example, if you enter **=A1** to start a formula, pressing F4 converts the cell reference to =$A$1. Pressing F4 again converts it to =A$1. Pressing it again displays =$A1. Pressing it one more time returns to the original =A1. Keep pressing F4 until Excel displays the type of reference that you want.

NOTE

When you name a cell or range, Excel (by default) uses an absolute reference for the name. For example, if you give the name SalesForecast to A1:A12, the Refers To field in the Define Name dialog box lists the reference as $A$1:$A$12. This is almost always what you want. If you copy a cell that has a named reference in its formula, the copied formula contains a reference to the original name.

AutoSum Tricks

Just about every Excel user knows about the AutoSum button, located on the Standard toolbar. Just click the button, and Excel analyzes the data surrounding the active cell and proposes a SUM formula. Click the AutoSum button again (or press Enter), and the formula is inserted. If you change your mind, press Esc.

If Excel incorrectly guesses the range to be summed, just select the correct range to be summed and press Enter. Easy and painless.

Following are some additional tricks related to AutoSum:

- If you use Excel 2002 or later, the AutoSum button can insert other types of formulas. Notice the little arrow on the right side of that button? Click it, and you'll see four other functions: AVERAGE, COUNT, MAX, and MIN. Click one of those items, and the appropriate formula is proposed. There's also a More Functions item, which simply displays the Insert Function dialog box — the same dialog box that appears when you select Insert⇨Function (or click the *fx* button to the left of the formula bar).

- If you need to enter a similar SUM formula into a range of cells, simply select the range before you click the AutoSum button. In this case, Excel inserts the functions for you without asking you — one formula in each of the selected cells.

- To sum both across and down a table of numbers, select the range of numbers — plus an additional column to the right and an additional row at the bottom. Click the AutoSum button, and Excel inserts the formulas that add the rows and the columns.

- A more efficient way to access AutoSum is to use your keyboard. Pressing Alt+= has exactly the same effect as clicking the AutoSum button.

- If you're working with a list that has AutoFiltering applied, using the AutoSum button inserts a SUBTOTAL formula rather than a SUM function. The SUBTOTAL function sums only the visible cells in the filtered list (see Figure 64-1). Most of the time, this is exactly what you want.

Figure 64-1: When working with a filtered list, the AutoSum button inserts a SUBTOTAL formula.

Part IV

- Unless you've applied a different number format to the cell that will hold the SUM formula, AutoSum will apply the same number format as the first cell in the range to be summed.

- To create a SUM formula that uses only *some* of the values in a column, select the cells to be summed, and then click the AutoSum button. Excel inserts the SUM formula in the first empty cell below the selected range.

Using the Status Bar Selection Statistics Feature

I'm always surprised when I encounter Excel users who have never noticed the handy selection statistics field in the status bar. When you select a range that contains values, Excel displays the sum of those selected values in the status bar, which is at the bottom of Excel's window. As you can see in Figure 65-1, the sum of the values in the selected cells is 7,583.

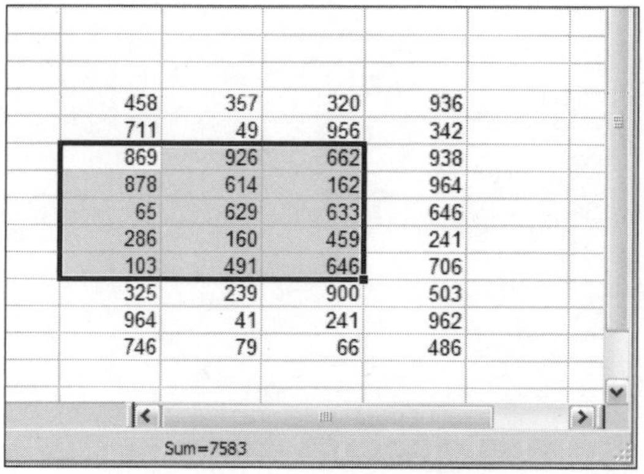

Figure 65-1: Excel displays the sum of the selected cells in the status bar.

If you'd prefer to see some other statistic relating to the selection, right-click the text in the status bar and make your selection from the shortcut menu (see Figure 65-2).

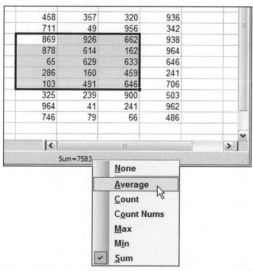

Figure 65-2: Excel offers a choice of six statistics about the selected range.

If you'd prefer to turn off this feature, select None.

When using this feature, remember that cells that contain text are ignored, except when the Count option is selected.

Converting Formulas to Values

If you have a range of cells that contain formulas, you can quickly convert these cells to values only. Here's how:

1. Select the range. It can include formula cells as well as nonformula cells.
2. Select Edit⇨Copy to copy the range.
3. Select Edit⇨Paste Special to display the Paste Special dialog box.
4. In the Paste Special dialog box, select the Value option.
5. Click OK.
6. Press Esc to cancel Copy mode.

Each of the formulas in the selected range will be replaced with its current value.

If you perform this operation on a regular basis, it pays to spend a few minutes and memorize the keystrokes:

1. Ctrl+C
2. Alt+ES
3. V
4. Enter
5. Esc

Repeat this keystroke sequence a few times, and it will become second nature.

Transforming Data without Using Formulas

Often, you'll have a range of cells containing data that must be transformed in some way. For example, you might want to increase all values by 5 percent. Or you may want to divide each value by 2. You can perform simple mathematical operations without using any formulas.

The following steps assume that you have values in a range, and you'd like to increase all values by 5 percent. For example, the range could contain a price list and you're raising all prices by 5 percent.

1. Activate any empty cell and enter **1.05**. You'll multiply the values by this number, which results in an increase of 5 percent.
2. Choose Edit⇨Copy to copy that cell.
3. Select the range to be transformed. It can include values, formulas, or text.
4. Choose Edit⇨Paste Special to display the Paste Special dialog box.
5. In the Paste Special dialog box, select the Multiply option.
6. Click OK.
7. Press Esc to cancel Copy mode.

The values in the range will be multiplied by the copied value (1.05). Formulas in the range will be modified accordingly. For example, assume the range originally contained this formula:

```
=SUM(B18:B22)
```

After performing the Paste Special operation, the formula would be converted to:

```
=(SUM(B18:B22))*1.05
```

This technique is limited to the four basic math operations: Add, Subtract, Multiply, and Divide.

Part IV

Transforming Data by Using Formulas

In Tip 67, I describe how to perform simple mathematical transformations on a range of numeric data. This tip describes the much more versatile method of transforming data by using temporary formulas.

Figure 68-1 shows a worksheet with names in column A. These names are in all caps, and the goal is to convert them to proper case (that is, only the first letter of each name will be uppercase).

	A	B	C	D
1	NAME	AMOUNT		
2	SERGEY DAVID	1,035		
3	ANTHONY MARKS	787		
4	DAVID KUNZ	958		
5	STEPHEN TON	361		
6	DEANA MOUGHAL	362		
7	ADRIAN FRANCINE	717		
8	RANDY ROZAK	373		
9	FRANCIS BRADY	100		
10	JON WILLIAMS	1,011		
11	JUSTIN KELLEY	673		
12	DAN LEMAN	495		
13	BRANDON SERIGANO	671		
14	RICHARD BECKMAN	403		
15	EDWARD KANE	559		
16	ARCEEB JACKMAN	421		
17	RACHEL NUTTER	824		
18	ALLEN PISSOURIOS	55		
19	VIEN COLLINS	754		
20	POWELL HESS	638		
21				

Sheet1

Figure 68-1: The goal is to transform the names in column A to proper case.

Follow these steps to transform the data in column A:

1. Create a temporary formula in an unused column. For this example, enter this formula in cell C2:

   ```
   =PROPER(A2)
   ```

2. Copy the formula down the column to accommodate all of the cells to be transformed.

3. Select the formula cells (in column C).

4. Choose Edit⇨Copy.

5. Select the original data cells (in column A).

6. Choose Edit⇨Paste Special to display the Paste Special dialog box.

7. In the Paste Special dialog box, select the Values option, and then click OK.

The original data is replaced with the transformed data (see Figure 68-2). When you are satisfied that the transformation was as you intended, you can delete the temporary formulas in column C.

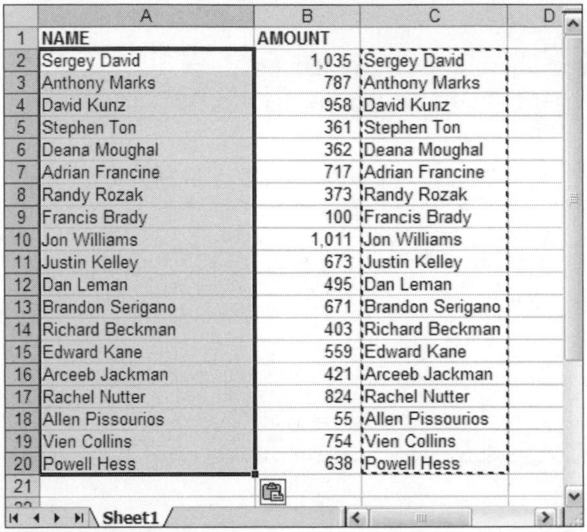

	A	B	C	D
1	NAME	AMOUNT		
2	Sergey David	1,035	Sergey David	
3	Anthony Marks	787	Anthony Marks	
4	David Kunz	958	David Kunz	
5	Stephen Ton	361	Stephen Ton	
6	Deana Moughal	362	Deana Moughal	
7	Adrian Francine	717	Adrian Francine	
8	Randy Rozak	373	Randy Rozak	
9	Francis Brady	100	Francis Brady	
10	Jon Williams	1,011	Jon Williams	
11	Justin Kelley	673	Justin Kelley	
12	Dan Leman	495	Dan Leman	
13	Brandon Serigano	671	Brandon Serigano	
14	Richard Beckman	403	Richard Beckman	
15	Edward Kane	559	Edward Kane	
16	Arceeb Jackman	421	Arceeb Jackman	
17	Rachel Nutter	824	Rachel Nutter	
18	Allen Pissourios	55	Allen Pissourios	
19	Vien Collins	754	Vien Collins	
20	Powell Hess	638	Powell Hess	
21				

Sheet1

Figure 68-2: The formula results from column C replace the original data.

You can adapt this technique for just about any type of data transformation you need. The key, of course, is constructing the proper transformation formula in Step 1.

Deleting Values While Keeping Formulas

A common type of spreadsheet model contains input cells and formulas that work with those input cells. If you would like to delete all of the values in the input cells, but keep the formulas intact, here's a simple way to do it:

1. Press F5 to display the Go To dialog box.

2. In the Go To dialog box, click the Special button to display the Go To Special dialog box.

3. In the Go To Special dialog box, select the Constants option and select Numbers.

4. Click OK, and the nonformula numeric cells will be selected.

5. Press Delete to delete the values.

To make things even easier, you can specify a name for the input cells. After Step 4, select Insert⇨Name⇨Define to display the Define Name dialog box. Enter a name for the selected cells — something like InputCells.

After naming the input cells, you can select the name directly from the Go To dialog box, saving a few mouse clicks.

Part IV

Dealing with Function Arguments

Excel has dozens of useful functions, and each of them has its own unique set of arguments. You've probably memorized the arguments for functions that you use frequently, but what about the other functions?

The best way to insert a function is to use the Insert Function dialog box. Display this dialog box by choosing Insert➪Function, by pressing Shift+F3, or by clicking the *fx* button to the left of the formula bar. If you don't know the name of the function you need, you can search for it by entering some text in the Search for a Function field and clicking the Go button (see Figure 70-1). When you've identified the function, click OK, and you'll see the Function Arguments dialog box, which guides you through the function's arguments.

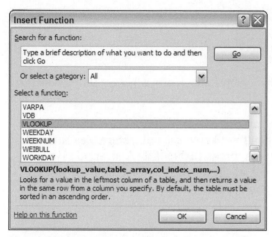

Figure 70-1: Use the Insert Function dialog box to help find the function you need.

If you already know the function you need, you can save a bit of time and enter the function manually. In Excel 2002 or later, you'll get a small pop-up display of the argument name, as shown in Figure 70-2. Notice that the argument names are shown in hyperlinks. You can click an argument name and go directly to Excel's Help system.

Figure 70-2: When you enter a function manually, Excel provides you with the names of the arguments.

For more help with the arguments for a manually entered function, press Ctrl+A to display the Function Arguments dialog box (see Figure 70-3).

Part IV

NOTE
This key combination works only if you haven't yet entered any arguments for the function.

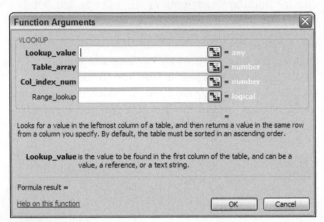

Figure 70-3: Press Ctrl+A to display the Function Arguments dialog box while entering a function.

In some cases, you may want to insert "dummy" arguments for a function — placeholders that will be filled in later. This is useful if you don't yet know the cell references that will be used. To insert argument names as placeholders, press Ctrl+Shift+A after you type the function's name. Excel uses the argument's names as arguments. For example, if you press Ctrl+Shift+A while entering the VLOOKUP function, Excel inserts the following:

```
=VLOOKUP(lookup_value,table_array,col_index_num,range_lookup)
```

The formula will, of course, return an error, so you'll need to replace the dummy arguments with actual values or cell references.

Annotating a Formula without Using a Comment

Excel's comment feature is a great way to annotate your formulas. Just select Insert⇨ Comment to add a comment to a cell, and you can then describe the formula any way you like inside the comment.

This tip describes another, less obtrusive, way to annotate a formula. The trick involves Excel's rarely used N function (this function is included in Excel primarily for compatibility with Lotus 1-2-3 files). The N function takes one argument, and this argument is converted to a value. When the argument is a text string, the N function returns 0. So you can take advantage of this and modify the formula so it uses the N function.

Consider this simple formula:

```
=A4*.075
```

You can modify the formula to contain a comment. Because the N function returns 0, the comment has no effect on how the formula works:

```
=A4*.075+N("7.5% represents the home office cut")
```

Making an Exact Copy of a Range of Formulas

When you copy a cell that contains a formula, Excel adjusts all of the relative cell references. For example, assume cell D1 contains this formula:

```
=A1*B1
```

When you copy this cell, the two cell references are changed relative to the destination. If you copy D1 to D12, for example, the copied formula is

```
=A12*B12
```

Sometimes, you may prefer to make an exact copy of a formula. One way is to convert all of the cell references to absolute references (for example, change =A1*B1 to =$A$1*$B$1). Another way is to (temporarily) remove the equal sign from the formula, which converts the formula to text. Then you can copy the cell and manually insert the equal sign into the original formula and the copied formula.

But what if you have a large range of formulas, and you'd like to make an exact copy of those formulas? Editing each formula is tedious and error-prone. Here's a trick that does the job. For the following steps, assume that you want to copy the formulas in A1:D10 on Sheet1, and make an exact copy in A13:D22, also on Sheet1:

1. Insert a new (temporary) worksheet before the sheet that contains the formulas to be copied. I assume this sheet is named Sheet2.

2. Select the source range (A1:D10 in this example).

3. Group the source sheet with the empty sheet. To do this, press Ctrl while you click the sheet tab for the temporary sheet.

4. Select Edit⇨Fill⇨Across Worksheets, and then choose the All option in the Fill Across Worksheets dialog box.

5. Ungroup the sheets by clicking the sheet tab for Sheet2.

6. In Sheet2, the copied range will be selected. Choose Edit⇨Cut.

7. Activate cell A13 (in Sheet2) and press Enter to paste the cut cells. A13:D22 will be selected.

8. Regroup the sheets by Ctrl+clicking the sheet tab for Sheet1.

9. Once again, choose Edit⇨Fill⇨Across Worksheets.

10. Activate Sheet1, and you'll find that A13:D22 contains an exact replica of the formulas in A1:D10.

Monitoring Formula Cells from Any Location

If you have a spreadsheet model, you may find it helpful to monitor the values in a few key cells as you change various input cells. Excel 2002 introduced a handy feature, called the Watch Window, which makes this sort of thing very simple. Using the Watch Window, you can keep an eye on any number of cells, regardless of which worksheet or workbook is active.

To watch a cell, activate the cell, right-click, and choose Add Watch from the shortcut menu. Excel displays a floating Watch Window that shows the current value of that cell. Figure 73-1 shows the Watch Window, with several cells being monitored.

Book	Sheet	Name	Cell	Value	Formula
Loan Amortiz...	Calculator	pmt	C9	$1,461.31	=-PMT(C3/1200,C4*12,C7,0)
Loan Amortiz...	Payment Amo...		F15	128,011.72	=IF(B15="","",F14-D15)
Loan Amortiz...	Payment Amo...		E148	75,428.78	=IF(A148=(1+(A2)),SUM(E$...

Figure 73-1: Using the Watch Window to monitor the value of formula cells.

You can customize the display in the Watch Window as follows:

- Click and drag a border to change the size of the window.

- Drag it to the edge of Excel's window, and it will become docked rather than free-floating.

- Click and drag the borders in the header to change the width of the columns displayed. By dragging a column border all the way to the left, you can hide the column.

- Click on one of the headers to sort the contents by that column.

Part IV

Displaying and Printing Formulas

When you enter a formula into a cell, Excel displays the calculated value of the formula. To view a formula, activate the cell, and Excel shows the formula in the formula bar.

If you would like to view all of your formulas, switch to formula view mode. You can do this in the Options dialog box, accessible by choosing Tools⇨Options. Click the View tab, and place a check mark next to the Formulas check box. Excel then displays the formulas, rather than their results. In addition, you can also see which cells are referenced by the selected formula because Excel displays those cells with a colored border. In Figure 74-1, C10 is the selected cell, and it references cells A2 and A10, which are displayed with a colored border.

NOTE

A more efficient way to toggle formula view mode is to press Ctrl+` (that's the accent character found on the key above Tab that also includes the tilde, ~).

	A	B	C	D
1				
2		**Payment Number**	**Total Payment**	**Principle Payment**
3		0		
4		=IF(A4<=(A2),A4,"")	=IF(A4<=(A2),Calculator!C	=IF(A4<=(A2),-PPMT(Calcula =IF
5		=IF(A5<=(A2),A5,"")	=IF(A5<=(A2),Calculator!C	=IF(A5<=(A2),-PPMT(Calcula =IF
6		=IF(A6<=(A2),A6,"")	=IF(A6<=(A2),Calculator!C	=IF(A6<=(A2),-PPMT(Calcula =IF
7		=IF(A7<=(A2),A7,"")	=IF(A7<=(A2),Calculator!C	=IF(A7<=(A2),-PPMT(Calcula =IF
8		=IF(A8<=(A2),A8,"")	=IF(A8<=(A2),Calculator!C	=IF(A8<=(A2),-PPMT(Calcula =IF
9		=IF(A9<=(A2),A9,"")	=IF(A9<=(A2),Calculator!C	=IF(A9<=(A2),-PPMT(Calcula =IF
10		=IF(A10<=(A2),A10,"")	=IF(A10<=(A2),Calculator!$C	=IF(A10<=(A2),-PPMT(Calcu =IF
11		=IF(A11<=(A2),A11,"")	=IF(A11<=(A2),Calculator!$C	=IF(A11<=(A2),-PPMT(Calcu =IF
12		=IF(A12<=(A2),A12,"")	=IF(A12<=(A2),Calculator!$C	=IF(A12<=(A2),-PPMT(Calcu =IF
13		=IF(A13<=(A2),A13,"")	=IF(A13<=(A2),Calculator!$C	=IF(A13<=(A2),-PPMT(Calcu =IF
14		=IF(A14<=(A2),A14,"")	=IF(A14<=(A2),Calculator!$C	=IF(A14<=(A2),-PPMT(Calcu =IF
15		=IF(A15<=(A2),A15,"")	=IF(A15<=(A2),Calculator!$C	=IF(A15<=(A2),-PPMT(Calcu =IF
16		=IF(A16<=(A2),A16,IF(A16=(	=IF(A16=(1+(A2)),SUM(C$4:(	=IF(A16=(1+(A2)),SUM(D$4:[=IF
17		=IF(A17<=(A2),A17,"")	=IF(A17<=(A2),Calculator!$C	=IF(A17<=(A2),-PPMT(Calcu =IF
18		=IF(A18<=(A2),A18,"")	=IF(A18<=(A2),Calculator!$C	=IF(A18<=(A2),-PPMT(Calcu =IF
19		=IF(A19<=(A2),A19,"")	=IF(A19<=(A2),Calculator!$C	=IF(A19<=(A2),-PPMT(Calcu =IF
20		=IF(A20<=(A2),A20,"")	=IF(A20<=(A2),Calculator!$C	=IF(A20<=(A2),-PPMT(Calcu =IF

Calculator \ **Payment Amortization** /

Figure 74-1: Excel's formula view mode displays the actual formulas rather than their results.

In practice, you may find that formula view mode is virtually worthless. Although Excel widens the columns, it's rare that you can actually see the entire formula in a cell. And if you print the sheet in formula view, you usually end up with a meaningless mess.

If you would like to document a worksheet by printing its formulas, your best bet is to locate a VBA macro to do the job. Do a Web search for *Excel print formulas* and you'll find lots of examples.

Avoiding Error Displays in Formulas

Sometimes a formula may return an error, such as #REF! or $DIV/0!. Usually, you'll want to know when a formula error occurs, but in some cases, you may prefer to simply avoid displaying the error messages. Figure 75-1 shows an example.

	A	B	C	D	E	F
1	Month	Total Sales	No. Reps	Average		
2	Jan	1,934,333	10	193,433		
3	Feb	2,098,344	12	174,862		
4	Mar	2,756,920	14	196,923		
5	Apr	2,840,983	14	202,927		
6	May			#DIV/0!		
7	Jun			#DIV/0!		
8	Jul			#DIV/0!		
9	Aug			#DIV/0!		
10	Sep			#DIV/0!		
11	Oct			#DIV/0!		
12	Nov			#DIV/0!		
13	Dec			#DIV/0!		
14						

Figure 75-1: The formulas in column D display an error if the data is missing.

Column D contains formulas that calculate the average sales volume. For example, cell D2 contains this formula:

```
=B2/C2
```

As you can see, the formula displays an error if the cells used in the calculation are empty. If you'd prefer to hide those error values, you can do so by using an IF function to check for an error.

For this example, change the formula in cell D1 to

```
=IF(ISERROR(B2/C2),"",B2/C2)
```

The ISERROR function returns TRUE if its argument evaluates to an error. In such a case, the IF function returns an empty string. Otherwise, the IF function returns the calculated value. As you can see in Figure 75-2, when this formula is copied down the column, the result is a bit more visually pleasing.

Part IV

You can adapt this technique to any formula. The original formula serves as the argument for the ISERROR function, and it repeats as the last argument of the IF function as follows:

```
=IF(ISERROR(OriginalFormula),"",OriginalFormula)
```

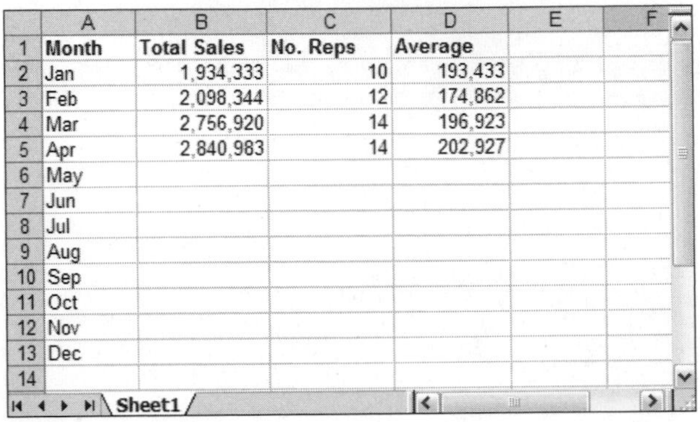

	A	B	C	D	E	F
1	Month	Total Sales	No. Reps	Average		
2	Jan	1,934,333	10	193,433		
3	Feb	2,098,344	12	174,862		
4	Mar	2,756,920	14	196,923		
5	Apr	2,840,983	14	202,927		
6	May					
7	Jun					
8	Jul					
9	Aug					
10	Sep					
11	Oct					
12	Nov					
13	Dec					
14						

Sheet1

Figure 75-2: Using an IF function to hide error values.

Using Goal Seeking

Many Excel worksheets are set up to do what-if analysis. For example, you might have a sales projection worksheet that allows you to answer questions such as, "What is the total profit if sales increase by 20 percent?" If you set up your worksheet properly, you can change the value in one cell to see what happens to the profit cell.

Excel offers a useful tool that can best be described as what-if analysis in reverse. If you know what a formula result *should* be, Excel can tell you the value that you need to enter in an input cell to produce that result. In other words, you can ask a question such as, "How much do sales need to increase to produce a profit of $1.2 million?"

Figure 76-1 shows a simple worksheet that calculates mortgage loan information. This worksheet has four input cells (C4:C7) and four formula cells (C10:C13).

Figure 76-1: Figuring a monthly mortgage payment is usually a series of time-consuming trial and error calculations entered in a worksheet as shown here. Excel, however, provides a tool to save you a lot of time and trouble.

Assume that you're in the market for a new home and you know that you can afford $1,800 per month in mortgage payments. You also know that a lender can issue a fixed-rate mortgage loan for 6.50 percent, based on an 80 percent loan-to-value (that is, a 20 percent down payment). The question is, "What is the maximum purchase price I can handle?" In other words, what value in cell C4 causes the formula in cell C11 to result in $1,800? One approach is to simply plug a bunch of values into cell C4 until C11 displays $1,800; however, Excel can determine the answer much more efficiently.

To answer this question, follow these steps:

1. Select Tools⇨Goal Seek. Excel displays the Goal Seek dialog box, as shown in Figure 76-2.

2. Complete the three fields in the dialog box (to the right of the worksheet in Figure 76-2) similar to forming a sentence: You want to set cell C11 to 1800 by changing cell C4.

Enter this information in the dialog box either by typing the cell references or by pointing with the mouse.

3. Click OK to begin the goal-seeking process.

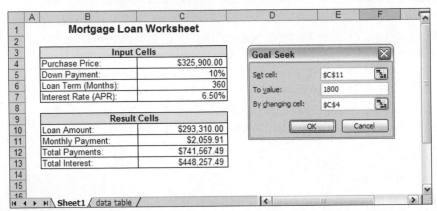

Figure 76-2: Enter the information in the Goal Seek dialog box to the right of the mortgage loan worksheet.

In less than a second, Excel displays the Goal Seek Status dialog box, which shows the target value and the value that Excel calculated. In this case, Excel finds an exact value. The worksheet now displays the found value in cell C4 ($284,779). As a result of this value, the monthly payment amount is $1,800. At this point, you have two options:

- Click OK to replace the original value with the found value.

- Click Cancel to restore your worksheet to the way it was before you chose Tools⇨ Goal Seek.

This is a simple example. The power of goal seeking is more apparent when you're dealing with a complex model with many interrelated formulas.

Understanding the Secret about Names

Most Excel users have at least a rudimentary understanding of named cells and named ranges. You can use the Insert⇨Name⇨Define command to provide a meaningful name to a cell or range. Then, you can use those defined names in your formulas.

For example, if you give the name Sales to range A2:A13, then you can write a formula such as =SUM(Sales). Just about every Excel user I've known refers to this concept as *named ranges* or *named cells* (even I did, in the first paragraph). Actually, this terminology is not quite accurate.

Here's the secret to understanding names: *When you create a name, you're actually creating a named formula. Unlike a normal formula, a named formula doesn't exist in a cell. Rather, it exists in Excel's memory.*

While this is not exactly an earth-shaking revelation, keeping this secret in mind will help you understand some advanced naming techniques.

When you work with the Define Name dialog box, the Refers To field contains the formula, and the Names in Workbook field contains the formula's name. You'll find that the contents of the Refers To field always begin with an equal sign, which makes it a formula.

As you can see in Figure 77-1, the workbook contains a name (InterestRate) for cell B1 on Sheet1. The Refers To field lists the following formula:

```
=Sheet1!$B$1
```

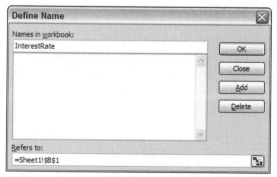

Figure 77-1: Technically, the name InterestRate is a named formula, not a named cell.

Whenever you use the name InterestRate, Excel actually evaluates the formula named InterestRate and returns the result. For example, you might type this formula into a cell:

```
=InterestRate*1.05
```

Part IV

When Excel evaluates this formula, it first evaluates the formula named InterestRate (which exists only in memory, not in a cell). It then multiplies the result of this named formula by 1.05 and displays the result. This cell formula, of course, is equivalent to the following formula, which uses the actual cell reference instead of the name:

```
=Sheet1!$B$1*1.05
```

Using Named Constants

This tip describes a useful technique that can remove some clutter from your worksheets: Named constants.

Consider a worksheet that generates an invoice and calculates sales tax for a sales amount. The common approach is to insert the sales tax rate value into a cell, and then use this cell reference in your formulas. To make things easier, you probably would name this cell something like SalesTax.

You can store your sales tax rate using a name (and avoid using a cell). Figure 78-1 demonstrates the following steps:

1. Choose Insert⇨Name⇨Define (or press Ctrl+F3) to bring up the Define Name dialog box.

2. Enter the name (in this case, **SalesTax**) into the Names in Workbook field.

3. Click the Refers To field, delete its contents, and replace it with a simple formula, such as **=.075**

4. Click OK to close the dialog box.

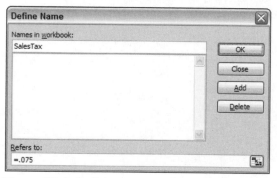

Figure 78-1: Defining a name that refers to a constant.

The preceding steps create a named formula that doesn't use any cell references. To try it out, enter the following formula into any cell:

```
=SalesTax
```

This simple formula returns .075, the result of the formula named SalesTax. Because this named formula always returns the same result, you can think of it as a *named constant*. And you can use this constant in a more complex formula, such as the following:

```
=A1*SalesTax
```

SalesTax is a workbook-level name, so you can use it in any worksheet in the workbook.

A named constant can also consist of text. For example, you can define a constant for a company's name. You can use the Define Name dialog box to create the following formula named MS:

```
="Microsoft Corporation"
```

Then you can use a cell formula such as:

```
="Annual Report: "&MS
```

This formula returns the text *Annual Report: Microsoft Corporation*.

NOTE

Names that do not refer to ranges do not appear in the Name box or in the Go To dialog box (which appears when you press F5). This makes sense, because these constants don't reside anywhere tangible. They *do* appear in the Paste Names dialog box, however, which *does* make sense, because you'll use these names in formulas.

As you might expect, you can change the value of the constant at any time by accessing the Define Name dialog box and simply changing the value in the Refers To field. When you close the dialog box, Excel uses the new value to recalculate the formulas that use this name.

Using Functions in Names

Tip 78 described how to create a named constant. This tip takes the concept one step further and describes how to use worksheet functions in your names.

Figure 79-1 shows an example of a named formula. In this case, the formula is named ThisMonth, and the actual formula is:

```
=MONTH(TODAY())
```

Figure 79-1: Defining a named formula that uses worksheet functions.

The named formula uses two worksheet functions. The TODAY function returns the current date and the MONTH function returns the month number of its date argument. Therefore, you can enter a formula such as the following into a cell and it will return the number of the current month. For example, if the current month is April, the following formula returns 4:

```
=ThisMonth
```

A more useful named formula would return the actual month name as text. To do so, create a formula named MonthName, defined as follows:

```
=TEXT(TODAY(),"mmmm")
```

Now enter the following formula into a cell, and it returns the current month name as text. In the month of April, the formula returns the text *April*.

```
=MonthName
```

Here's another example of a named formula that uses a function. Create a formula with the name SumColAr, defined as follows:

```
=SUM(Sheet1!$A:A$)
```

Part IV

As you might expect, this named formula returns the sum of all values in column A.

NOTE

Note that the name is defined using absolute references. This is critical. If you use relative references, the formula would evaluate differently depending on the location of the active cell.

Editing Name References

This is a simple tip, but I didn't learn it until I had been using Excel for about 10 years!

When you're working in the Define Name dialog box, you may need to change the contents of the Refers To field. Figure 80-1 shows an example. The name CalcArea refers to this range:

```
=Sheet1!$E$1:$K$490
```

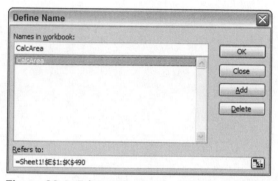

Figure 80-1: Editing the contents of the Refers To field can be tricky.

Let's say you want to edit this formula so that it extends only to row 480 instead of row 490. Your first inclination would probably be to activate the Refers To field, and then use the left arrow key to move the insertion point to the left. But, as you'll notice, that field is in point mode, so the arrow keys are used to specify a range selection.

This was a continual source of frustration for me, until someone pointed out that pressing F2 switches between point mode and edit mode. The Define Name dialog box is still frustrating, but knowing the F2 trick certainly helps.

Using Dynamic Names

This tip describes a very useful concept that can save you lots of time: The *dynamic named formula,* which is a named formula that refers to a range that is not fixed in size. This idea can be difficult to grasp, so I provide a quick example.

Examine the worksheet shown in Figure 81-1. This sheet contains a listing of sales by month, through the month of May.

Figure 81-1: You can use a dynamic named formula to represent the sales data in column B.

Suppose you want to create a name (SalesData) for the data in column B, and you don't want this name to refer to empty cells. In other words, the reference for the SalesData range would change each month as you add a new sales figure. You could, of course, use the Define Name dialog box to change the range name definition each month. Or you could create a dynamic named formula that changes automatically as you enter new data (or delete existing data).

To create a dynamic named formula, start by re-creating the worksheet shown in Figure 81-1. Then follow these steps:

1. Select Insert⇨Name⇨Define to display the Define Name dialog box.

2. Enter **SalesData** in the Names in Workbook field.

3. Enter the following formula in the Refers To field (see Figure 81-2):

   ```
   =OFFSET(Sheet1!$B$1,0,0,COUNTA(Sheet1!$B:$B),1)
   ```

4. Click OK to close the Define Name dialog box.

The preceding steps created a named formula that uses Excel's OFFSET and COUNTA functions to return a range that changes, based on the number of nonempty cells in column B. To try out this formula, enter the following formula into any cell not in column B:

```
=SUM(SalesData)
```

Part IV

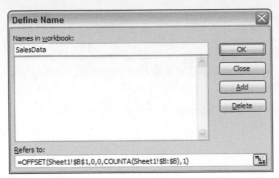

Figure 81-2: Creating a dynamic named formula.

This formula returns the sum of the values in column B. Note that SalesData does not display in the Name box and does not appear in the Go To dialog box. You can, however, bring up the Go To dialog box and type **SalesData** to select the range.

NOTE

This formula works only for data that does not contain gaps. In this example, if cell B3 is empty, the SalesData name will not include the last value in the column.

At this point, you may be wondering about the value of this exercise. After all, a simple formula such as the following does the same job, without the need to define a formula:

```
=SUM(B:B)
```

One of the most common uses for a dynamic named formula is setting up data to be used in a chart. You can use this technique to create a chart with a data series that adjusts automatically as you enter new data:

```
=Sheet1!$E$1:$K$490
```

CROSS-REFERENCE

For more on charts, turn to Part VI.

Creating Worksheet-Level Names

Normally, when you name a cell or range, you can use that name in all worksheets in the workbook. For example, if you create a name called RegionTotal that refers to the cell M32 on Sheet1, you can use this name in any formula in any worksheet. This is referred to as a workbook-level name (or a global name). By default, all cell and range names are workbook-level names.

What if you have several worksheets in a workbook and you want to use the same name (such as RegionTotal) on each sheet? In this case, you need to create worksheet-level names (sometimes referred to as local names).

To define a worksheet-level name RegionTotal, activate the worksheet in which you want to define the name and choose Insert⇨Name⇨Define. The Define Name dialog box then appears. In the Names in Workbook field, precede the worksheet-level name with the worksheet name, followed by an exclamation point. For example, to define the name RegionTotal on Sheet2, activate Sheet2 and enter the following in the Names in Workbook field of the Define Name dialog box:

```
Sheet2!RegionTotal
```

If the worksheet name contains at least one space, enclose the worksheet name in apostrophes, like this:

```
'Marketing Dept'!RegionTotal
```

You can also create a worksheet-level name by using the Name box. Select the cell or range you want named, click in the Name box, and type the name. Make sure you precede the name with the sheet's name and an exclamation point (as shown in the preceding examples). Press Enter to create the name.

When you write a formula that uses a worksheet-level name on the sheet in which you defined it, you don't need to include the worksheet name in the range name. (The Name box won't display the worksheet name either.) If you use the name in a formula on a *different* worksheet, however, you must use the entire name (sheet name, exclamation point, and name).

NOTE

Only the worksheet-level names on the current sheet appear in the Name box. Similarly, only worksheet-level names in the current sheet appear in the list when you open the Paste Name dialog box (by pressing F3) or the Define Name dialog box.

Working with Pre-1900 Dates

According to Excel, the world began on January 1, 1900. If you work with historical information, you may have noticed that Excel does not recognize pre-1900 dates. For example, if you enter **July 4, 1776** into a cell, Excel interprets it as text, not a date.

Unfortunately, the only way to work with pre-1900 dates is to enter the date into a cell as text. You can't, however, perform any manipulation on dates recognized as text. For example, you can't change its numeric formatting, you can't determine which day of the week this date occurred on, and you can't calculate the date that occurs seven days later.

If you need to be able to sort by dates that precede 1900, you can do so by entering the year, month, and day into separate cells. Figure 83-1 shows a simple example.

	A	B	C	D	E
1	President Birthdays				
2					
3	President	Year	Month	Day	
4	Abraham Lincoln	1809	2	12	
5	Franklin D. Roosevelt	1882	1	30	
6	James A. Garfield	1831	11	19	
7	Warren G. Harding	1865	11	2	
8	William Henry Harrison	1773	2	9	
9	William McKinley	1843	1	29	
10	Zachary Taylor	1784	11	24	
11					
12					

Figure 83-1: To allow sorting by pre-1900 dates, enter the year, month, and day into separate cells.

To sort the presidents by birthday, first do an ascending sort on column D, then an ascending sort on column C, and finally an ascending sort on column B. The result is shown in Figure 83-2.

	A	B	C	D	E
1	President Birthdays				
2					
3	President	Year	Month	Day	
4	William Henry Harrison	1773	2	9	
5	Zachary Taylor	1784	11	24	
6	Abraham Lincoln	1809	2	12	
7	James A. Garfield	1831	11	19	
8	William McKinley	1843	1	29	
9	Warren G. Harding	1865	11	2	
10	Franklin D. Roosevelt	1882	1	30	
11					
12					

Figure 83-2: The presidents sorted by birthday, after performing three sorts.

Part IV

NOTE

I've created an Excel add-in, XDATE, which contains a number of functions that make it possible to work with pre-1900 dates. You can download a free copy from my Web site at www.j-walk.com/ss.

Working with Negative Time Values

Because Excel stores dates and times as numeric values, it's possible to add or subtract one from the other. Figure 84-1 shows a simple example that keeps track of hours worked. The total is calculated in cell B8 using this formula (and formatted using the [h]:mm number format):

```
=SUM(B2:B6)
```

Cell B9 calculates the amount of time required to make up a 40-hour work week using this formula:

```
=(40/24)-B8
```

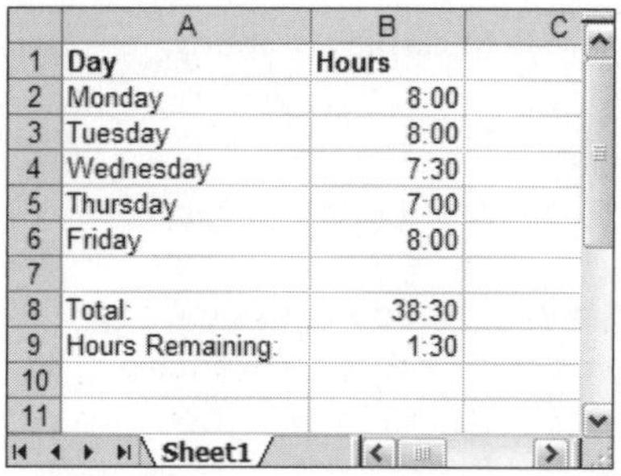

	A	B	C
1	Day	Hours	
2	Monday	8:00	
3	Tuesday	8:00	
4	Wednesday	7:30	
5	Thursday	7:00	
6	Friday	8:00	
7			
8	Total:	38:30	
9	Hours Remaining:	1:30	
10			
11			

Figure 84-1: Cell B8 displays the time left in a 40-hour work week.

But what if the number of hours worked exceeds 40 hours? In such a case, the formula in cell B9 returns a negative number. But, as you can see in Figure 84-2, Excel can't deal with a negative time value.

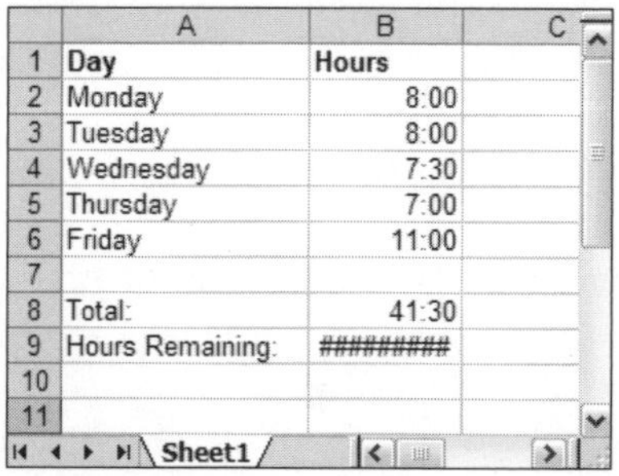

	A	B	C
1	Day	Hours	
2	Monday	8:00	
3	Tuesday	8:00	
4	Wednesday	7:30	
5	Thursday	7:00	
6	Friday	11:00	
7			
8	Total:	41:30	
9	Hours Remaining:	########	
10			
11			

Figure 84-2: Excel displays a series of hash marks for negative time values.

By default, Excel uses a date system that begins with January 1, 1900. A negative time value generates a date/time combination that falls before this date, which is invalid.

One solution is to use the optional 1904 date system, which assigns the date serial number 1 to January 2, 1904. Select Tools⇨Options to display the Options dialog box. Click the Calculation tab, and check the 1904 Date System check box to change the starting date to January 2, 1904. Your negative times will now be displayed correctly, as shown in Figure 84-3.

	A	B	C
1	Day	Hours	
2	Monday	8:00	
3	Tuesday	8:00	
4	Wednesday	7:30	
5	Thursday	7:00	
6	Friday	11:00	
7			
8	Total:	41:30	
9	Hours Remaining:	-1:30	
10			
11			

Figure 84-3: Switching to the 1904 date system causes negative times to display properly.

WARNING

Be careful if your workbook contains links to other workbooks that don't use the 1904 date system. In such a case, the mismatch of date systems could cause erroneous results.

Part V

Useful Formula Examples

In this part, you'll find many formula examples. Some are useful as is. Others can be adapted to your own needs.

Tips and Where to Find Them

Tip 85 Calculating Holidays 209

Tip 86 Calculating a Weighted Average 213

Tip 87 Calculating a Person's Age 215

Tip 88 Ranking Values with an Array Formula 217

Tip 89 Counting Characters in a Cell 219

Tip 90 Expressing a Number as an Ordinal 221

Tip 91 Extracting Words from a String 223

Tip 92 Parsing Names 225

Tip 93 Removing Titles from Names 227

Tip 94 Generating a Series of Dates 229

Tip 95 Determining Specific Dates 231

Tip 96 Displaying a Calendar in a Range 235

Tip 97 Various Methods of Rounding Numbers 237

Tip 98 Rounding Time Values 241

Tip 99 Returning the Last Nonblank Cell in a Column or Row 243

Tip 100 Using the COUNTIF Function 245

Tip 101 Counting Cells That Meet Multiple Criteria 247

Tip 102 Counting Distinct Entries in a Range 251

Tip 103 Calculating Single-Criterion Conditional Sums 253

Tip 104 Calculating Multiple-Criterion Conditional Sums 255

Tip 105 Looking Up an Exact Value 257

Tip 106 Performing a Two-Way Lookup 259

Tip 107 Performing a Two-Column Lookup 261

Tip 108 Performing a Lookup Using an Array 263

Tip 109 Using the INDIRECT Function 265

Tip 110 Creating Megaformulas 267

Calculating Holidays

Determining the date for a particular holiday can be tricky. Some holidays, such as New Year's Day and Independence Day (U.S.), are no-brainers because they always occur on the same date. For these kinds of holidays, you can simply use the DATE function. For example, to calculate New Year's Day (which always falls on January 1) for a specific year in cell A1, you can enter this function:

```
=DATE(A1,1,1)
```

Other holidays are defined in terms of a particular occurrence of a particular weekday in a particular month. For example, Labor Day in the U.S. falls on the first Monday in September.

The formulas that follow all assume that the year is in cell A1. Notice that because New Year's Day, Independence Day, Veterans Day, and Christmas Day all fall on the same days of the year, their dates can be calculated using the simple DATE function.

New Year's Day

This holiday always falls on January 1:

```
=DATE(A1,1,1)
```

Martin Luther King Jr. Day

This holiday occurs on the third Monday in January. The following formula calculates Martin Luther King Jr. Day for the year in cell A1:

```
=DATE(A1,1,1)+IF(2<WEEKDAY(DATE(A1,1,1)),7-WEEKDAY(DATE(A1,1,1))
+2,2-WEEKDAY(DATE(A1,1,1)))+((3-1)*7)
```

Presidents' Day

Presidents' Day occurs on the third Monday in February. This formula calculates Presidents' Day for the year in cell A1:

```
=DATE(A1,2,1)+IF(2<WEEKDAY(DATE(A1,2,1)),7-WEEKDAY(DATE(A1,2,1))
+2,2-WEEKDAY(DATE(A1,2,1)))+((3-1)*7)
```

Easter

Calculating the date for Easter is difficult because of the way Easter is determined. Easter Day is the first Sunday after the next full moon occurs after the vernal equinox. I found these formulas to calculate Easter on the Web. I have no idea how they work:

```
=DOLLAR(("4/"&A1)/7+MOD(19*MOD(A1,19)-7,30)*14%,)*7-6
```

This one is slightly shorter, but equally obtuse:

```
=FLOOR("5/"&DAY(MINUTE(A1/38)/2+56)&"/"&A1,7)-34
```

Memorial Day

The last Monday in May is Memorial Day. This formula calculates Memorial Day for the year in cell A1:

```
=DATE(A1,6,1)+IF(2<WEEKDAY(DATE(A1,6,1)),7-WEEKDAY(DATE(A1,6,1))
+2,2-WEEKDAY(DATE(A1,6,1)))+((1-1)*7)-7
```

Notice that this formula actually calculates the first Monday in June, and then subtracts 7 from the result to return the last Monday in May.

Independence Day

This holiday always falls on July 4:

```
=DATE(A1,7,4)
```

Labor Day

Labor Day occurs on the first Monday in September. This formula calculates Labor Day for the year in cell A1:

```
=DATE(A1,9,1)+IF(2<WEEKDAY(DATE(A1,9,1)),7-WEEKDAY(DATE(A1,9,1))
+2,2-WEEKDAY(DATE(A1,9,1)))+((1-1)*7)
```

Columbus Day

This holiday occurs on the second Monday in October. The following formula calculates Columbus Day for the year in cell A1:

```
=DATE(A1,10,1)+IF(2<WEEKDAY(DATE(A1,10,1)),7-WEEKDAY(DATE(A1,10,1))
+2,2-WEEKDAY(DATE(A1,10,1)))+((2-1)*7)
```

Veterans Day

This holiday always falls on November 11:

```
=DATE(A1,11,11)
```

Thanksgiving Day

Thanksgiving Day is celebrated on the fourth Thursday in November. This formula calculates Thanksgiving Day for the year in cell A1:

```
=DATE(A1,11,1)+IF(5<WEEKDAY(DATE(A1,11,1)),7-WEEKDAY(DATE(A1,11,1))
+5,5-WEEKDAY(DATE(A1,11,1)))+((4-1)*7)
```

Christmas Day

This holiday always falls on December 25:

```
=DATE(A1,12,25)
```

Calculating a Weighted Average

Excel's AVERAGE function returns the average (or mean) of a range of data. Often, users need to calculate a weighted average. You can search all day, and you won't find a function to do the calculation. You can, however, calculate a weighted average by creating a formula that uses the SUMPRODUCT and the SUM function.

Figure 86-1 shows a simple spreadsheet that contains 30 days of gasoline prices. For example, the price was $2.48 for the first four days. Then it decreased to $2.41 for two days. The price then dipped to $2.39 for three days, and so on.

	A	B	C	D
1	Gas Prices For January			
2				
3		Price	No. Days	
4		2.48	4	
5		2.41	2	
6		2.39	3	
7		2.35	1	
8		2.34	1	
9		2.41	2	
10		2.37	2	
11		2.42	4	
12		2.41	3	
13		2.47	8	
14				
15	Average:	2.405		
16	Wt. Avg:	2.428		
17				

Sheet1

Figure 86-1: The formula in cell B16 calculates the weighted average of the gas prices.

Cell B15 contains a formula that uses the AVERAGE function:

```
=AVERAGE(B4:B13)
```

But, if you think about it, this formula does not return an accurate result. Rather, the prices must be weighted by factoring in the number of days each price was in effect. In other words, a weighted average is the appropriate type of calculation.

The following formula, in cell B16, does the job:

```
=SUMPRODUCT(B4:B13,C4:C13)/SUM(C4:C13)
```

Calculating a Person's Age

Calculating a person's age in Excel is a bit tricky, because the calculation depends not only on the current year, but also the current day. And then there's the complications resulting from leap years.

In this tip, I present three methods to calculate a person's age. These formulas assume that cell B1 contains the date of birth, and that cell B2 contains the current day (see Figure 87-1).

	A	B	C
1	Date of Birth:	5/19/73	
2	Today:	3/15/05	
3	Age:	31	
4			
5			
6			

Figure 87-1: Calculating a person's age.

Method 1

The following formula subtracts the date of birth from the current date, and divides by 365.25. The INT function then eliminates the decimal part of the result.

```
=INT((B2-B1)/365.25)
```

This formula is not 100 percent accurate because it divides by the average number of days in a year. For example, consider a child who is exactly one year old. This formula returns 0, not 1.

Method 2

A more accurate way to calculate age uses the YEARFRAC function, which is available only when the Analysis Toolpak add-in is installed:

```
=INT(YEARFRAC(B2, B1))
```

Method 3

The third method for calculating age uses the DATEDIF function. Depending on which version of Excel you have, this function may or may not be documented in Excel's Help.

```
=DATEDIF(B1,B2,"Y")
```

Part V

And if you're a real stickler for accuracy, here's another version:

```
=DATEDIF(B1,B2,"y") & " years, "&DATEDIF(B1,B2,"ym") &
" months, "&DATEDIF(B1,B2,"md") & " days"
```

This function returns a text string like this:

```
31 years, 9 months, 24 days
```

Ranking Values with an Array Formula

Often, computing the rank orders for the values in a range of data is helpful. For example, if you have a worksheet containing the annual sales figures for 20 salespeople, you may want to know how each person ranks, from highest to lowest.

If you've used Excel's RANK function, you may have noticed that the ranks produced by this function don't handle ties the way that you may like. For example, if two values are tied for third place, the RANK function gives both of them a rank of 3. You may prefer to assign each an average (or midpoint) of the ranks — in other words, a rank of 3.5 for both values tied for third place.

Figure 88-1 shows a worksheet that uses two methods to rank a column of values. The first method (column C) uses Excel's RANK function. Column D uses array formulas to compute the ranks. The range B2:B9 is named Sales.

	A	B	C	D	E
1	Salesperson	Sales	Excel's Rank Function	Ranks With Array Formula	
2	Adams	45,000	7	7	
3	Bigelow	90,000	3	3.5	
4	Fredericks	90,000	3	3.5	
5	Georgio	54,000	6	6	
6	Jensen	25,000	8	8	
7	Juarez	101,000	1	1	
8	Martin	85,000	5	5	
9	Swenson	92,000	2	2	
10					
11					

Figure 88-1: Ranking data with Excel's RANK function and with array formulas.

The following is the array formula in cell D5, which is copied to the cells below it:

```
=SUM(1*(B5<=Sales))-(SUM(1*(B5=Sales))-1)/2
```

NOTE

An array formula is a special type of formula that works with internal arrays of data. When you enter an array formula, you must press Ctrl+Shift+Enter (not just Enter) to indicate that it's an array formula. Excel will display curly braces around the formula to remind you that it's an array formula.

Counting Characters in a Cell

This tip contains formula examples that count characters in a cell.

Counting Specific Characters in a Cell

The following formula counts the number of Bs (uppercase only) in the string in cell A1:

```
=LEN(A1)-LEN(SUBSTITUTE(A1,"B",""))
```

This formula works by using the SUBSTITUTE function to create a new string (in memory) that has all Bs removed. Then the length of this string is subtracted from the length of the original string. The result reveals the number of Bs in the original string.

For example, if cell A1 contains the text *Bubble Chart*, the formula would return 1.

The following formula is a bit more versatile. It counts the number of Bs (both upper- and lowercase) in the string in cell A1.

```
=LEN(A1)-LEN(SUBSTITUTE(UPPER(A1),"B",""))
```

If cell A1 contains the text *Bubble Chart*, the formula would return 3.

Counting the Occurrences of a Substring in a Cell

The following formula works with more than one character. It returns the number of occurrences of a particular substring (contained in cell B1) within a string (contained in cell A1). The substring can consist of any number of characters.

```
=(LEN(A1)-LEN(SUBSTITUTE(A1,B1,"")))/LEN(B1)
```

For example, if cell A1 contains the text *Blonde On Blonde* and B1 contains the text *Blonde*, the formula returns 2.

The comparison is case sensitive, so if B1 contains the text *blonde*, the formula returns 0. The following formula is a modified version that performs a case-insensitive comparison:

```
=(LEN(A1)-LEN(SUBSTITUTE(UPPER(A1),UPPER(B1),"")))/LEN(B1)
```

Expressing a Number as an Ordinal

You may need to express a value as an ordinal number. For example, *Today is the 21st day of the month*. In this case, the number 21 converts to an ordinal number by appending the characters *st* to the number. Excel doesn't have a number format to do this, but it can be accomplished by using a formula.

The specific characters appended to a number (*st*, *nd*, *rd*, or *th*) depend on the number. The pattern is a little convoluted, making the construction of a formula tricky. Most numbers will use the *th* suffix. Exceptions occur for numbers that end with 1, 2, or 3 — except if the preceding number is a 1 (numbers that end with 11, 12, or 13). These may seem like fairly complex rules, but you can translate them into an Excel formula.

The formula that follows converts the number in cell A1 (assumed to be an integer) to an ordinal number:

```
=A1&IF(OR(VALUE(RIGHT(A1,2))={11,12,13}),"th",IF(OR(VALUE(RIGHT(A1))={1,2,3}),
CHOOSE(RIGHT(A1),"st","nd","rd"),"th"))
```

This is a rather complicated formula, so it may help to examine its components. Basically, the formula works as follows:

1. If the last two digits of the number consist of 11, 12, or 13, then use *th*.

2. If Rule #1 does not apply, then check the last digit. If the last digit is 1, use *st*. If the last digit is 2, use *nd*. If the last digit is 3, use *rd*.

3. If neither Rule #1 nor Rule #2 apply, use *th*.

Figure 90-1 shows the formula in use.

	A	B	C	D
1	Number	Ordinal		
2	1	1st		
3	4	4th		
4	7	7th		
5	10	10th		
6	13	13th		
7	16	16th		
8	19	19th		
9	22	22nd		
10	25	25th		
11	28	28th		
12	31	31st		
13	34	34th		
14	37	37th		
15	40	40th		
16	43	43rd		
17	46	46th		
18	49	49th		
19	52	52nd		
20				
21				

Figure 90-1: Using a formula to express a number as an ordinal.

Part V

Extracting Words from a String

The formulas in this tip are useful for extracting words from text contained in a cell. For example, you can use a formula to extract the first word in a sentence.

Extracting the First Word of a String

To extract the first word of a string, a formula must locate the position of the first space character, and then use this information as an argument for the LEFT function. The following formula does just that:

```
=LEFT(A1,FIND(" ",A1)-1)
```

This formula returns all of the text prior to the first space in cell A1. However, the formula has a slight problem: It returns an error if the text in cell A1 contains no space characters because it consists of a single word. A slightly more complex formula solves the problem by using an IF function and an ISERR function to check for the error:

```
=IF(ISERR(FIND(" ",A1)),A1,LEFT(A1,FIND(" ",A1)-1))
```

Extracting the Last Word of a String

Extracting the last word of a string is more complicated, because the FIND function only works from left to right. Therefore, the problem rests with locating the *last* space character. The formula that follows, however, solves this problem. It returns the last word of a string (all the text following the last space character):

```
=RIGHT(A1,LEN(A1)-FIND("*",SUBSTITUTE(A1," ","*",LEN(A1)-LEN
(SUBSTITUTE(A1," ","")))))
```

This formula, however, has the same problem as the first formula in the preceding section: It fails if the string does not contain at least one space character. The following modified formula uses an IF function to count the number of spaces in cell A1. If it contains no spaces, the entire contents of cell A1 are returned. Otherwise, the previous formula kicks in.

```
=IF(ISERR(FIND(" ",A1)),A1,RIGHT(A1,LEN(A1)-FIND("*",SUBSTITUTE
(A1," ","*",LEN(A1)-LEN(SUBSTITUTE(A1," ","")))))))
```

Extracting All but the First Word of a String

The following formula returns the contents of cell A1, except for the first word:

```
=RIGHT(A1,LEN(A1)-FIND(" ",A1,1))
```

If cell A1 contains *2006 Operating Budget*, the formula returns *Operating Budget*.

This formula returns an error if the cell contains only one word. The following formula solves this problem, and returns an empty string if the cell does not contain multiple words:

```
=IF(ISERR(FIND(" ",A1)),"",RIGHT(A1,LEN(A1)-FIND(" ",A1,1)))
```

Parsing Names

Suppose you have a list consisting of people's names in a single column. You have to separate these names into three columns: one for the first name, one for the middle name or initial, and one for the last name. This task is more complicated than you may initially think, because not every name in the column has a middle name or middle initial. However, you can still do it.

NOTE

The task becomes a *lot* more complicated if the list contains names with titles (such as Mrs. or Dr.) or names followed by additional details (such as Jr. or III). In fact, the following formulas will *not* handle these complex cases. However, they still give you a significant head start if you're willing to do a bit of manual editing to handle the special cases.

The formulas that follow all assume that the name appears in cell A1.

You can easily construct a formula to return the first name:

```
=LEFT(A1,FIND(" ",A1)-1)
```

This formula returns the last name:

```
=RIGHT(A1,LEN(A1)-FIND("*",SUBSTITUTE(A1," ","*",LEN(A1)-
LEN(SUBSTITUTE(A1," ","")))))
```

The formula that follows extracts the middle name. It assumes that the first name is in B1 and the last name is in D1.

```
=IF(LEN(B1&D1)+2>=LEN(A1),"",MID(A1,LEN(B1)+2,LEN(A1)-LEN(B1&D1)-2))
```

As you can see in Figure 92-1, the formulas work fairly well. There are a few problems, however — notably names that contain four words. But, as I mention earlier, you can clean these cases up manually.

	A	B	C	D
1	Full Name	First	Middle	Last
2	John Q. Public	John	Q.	Public
3	Lisa Smith	Lisa		Smith
4	J.R. Robins	J.R.		Robins
5	A. Baxter	A.		Baxter
6	Roger R. Burns	Roger	R.	Burns
7	John P. Van Williams	John	P. Van	Williams
8	Mr. Ted G. Smith	Mr.	Ted G.	Smith
9				
10				

Figure 92-1: This worksheet uses formulas to extract the first name, middle name (or initial), and last name from a list of names in column A.

Part V

NOTE

In many cases, you can eliminate the use of formulas and use Excel's Data➪Text to Columns command to parse strings into their component parts. Selecting this command displays Excel's Convert Text to Columns Wizard, which consists of a series of dialog boxes that walk you through the steps to convert a single column of data into multiple columns. Generally, you'll want to select the Delimited option (in Step 1) and use Space as the delimiter (in Step 2).

Removing Titles from Names

If you have a list of names, you may need to remove titles (such as Mr., Ms., or Mrs.) from the names. You may wish to perform this operation before you parse the name, as described in Tip 92.

You can use the formula that follows to remove three common titles (Mr., Ms., and Mrs.) from a name. For example, if cell A1 contains *Mr. Fred Mertz*, the formula would return *Fred Mertz*.

```
=IF(OR(LEFT(A1,2)="Mr",LEFT(A1,3)="Mrs",LEFT(A1,2)="Ms"),
RIGHT(A1,LEN(A1) -FIND(" ",A1)),A1)
```

This formula tests for three conditions. If you need to test for more, just add additional arguments to the OR function.

Generating a Series of Dates

Often, you'll want to insert a series of dates into a worksheet. For example, in tracking weekly sales, you may want to enter a series of dates, each separated by seven days. These dates will serve to identify the sales figures.

Using the AutoFill Feature

The most efficient way to enter a series of dates doesn't require any formulas — just use Excel's AutoFill feature to insert a series of dates. Enter the first date, and then drag the cell's fill handle while pressing the right mouse button (right-drag the cell's fill handle). Release the mouse button and select an option from the shortcut menu (see Figure 94-1).

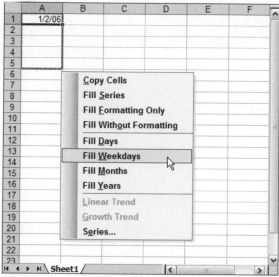

Figure 94-1: Using Excel's AutoFill feature to create a series of dates.

Using Formulas

The advantage of using formulas (rather than the AutoFill feature) to create a series of dates is that you can change the first date and the others will update automatically. You need to enter the starting date into a cell, and then use formulas (copied down the column) to generate the additional dates.

The following examples assume that you entered the first date of the series into cell A1 and the formula into cell A2. You can then copy this formula down the column as many times as needed.

To generate a series of dates separated by seven days, use this formula:

```
=A1+7
```

To generate a series of dates separated by one month, use this formula:

```
=DATE(YEAR(A1),MONTH(A1)+1,DAY(A1))
```

To generate a series of dates separated by one year, use this formula:

```
=DATE(YEAR(A1)+1,MONTH(A1),DAY(A1))
```

To generate a series of weekdays only (no Saturdays or Sundays), use the formula that follows. This formula assumes that the date in cell A1 is not a weekend day.

```
=IF(WEEKDAY(A1)=6,A1+3,A1+1)
```

Determining Specific Dates

This tip contains a number of useful formulas that return a specific date.

Determining the Day of the Year

January 1 is the first day of the year, and December 31 is the last day. But what about all of those days in between? The following formula returns the day of the year for a date stored in cell A1:

```
=A1-DATE(YEAR(A1),1,0)
```

The day of the year is sometimes referred to as a *Julian date*.

The following formula returns the number of days remaining in the year from a particular date (assumed to be in cell A1):

```
=DATE(YEAR(A1),12,31)-A1
```

 NOTE
When you enter either of these formulas, Excel automatically applies date formatting to the cell. You need to apply a nondate number format to view the result as a number.

Determining the Day of the Week

If you need to determine the day of the week for a date, the WEEKDAY function will do the job. The WEEKDAY function accepts a date argument and returns an integer between 1 and 7 that corresponds to the day of the week. The following formula, for example, returns 1 because the first day of the year 2006 falls on a Sunday:

```
=WEEKDAY(DATE(2006,1,1))
```

The WEEKDAY function uses an optional second argument that specifies the day numbering system for the result. If you specify 2 as the second argument, the function returns 1 for Monday, 2 for Tuesday, and so on. If you specify 3 as the second argument, the function returns 0 for Monday, 1 for Tuesday, and so on.

 NOTE
You can also determine the day of the week for a cell that contains a date by applying a custom number format. A cell that uses the following custom number format displays the day of the week, spelled out:

    dddd

Keep in mind that the cell really contains the full date, not just the day number.

Part V

Determining the Date of the Most Recent Sunday

The formula in this section returns the most recent specified day. You can use the following formula to return the date for the previous Sunday. If the current day is a Sunday, the formula returns the current date (you will need to format the cell to display as a date):

```
=TODAY()-MOD(TODAY()-1,7)
```

To modify this formula to find the date of a day other than Sunday, change the 1 to a different number between 2 (for Monday) and 7 (for Saturday).

Determining the First Day of the Week after a Date

The following formula returns the specified day of the week that occurs after a particular date. For example, you can use this formula to determine the date of the first Monday after June 1, 2006.

The formula assumes that cell A1 contains a date, and cell A2 contains a number between 1 and 7 (1 for Sunday, 2 for Monday, and so on).

```
=A1+A2-WEEKDAY(A1)+(A2<WEEKDAY(A1))*7
```

If cell A1 contains June 1, 2006, and cell A2 contains 2 (for Monday), the formula returns June 5, 2006. This is the first Monday after June 1, 2006 (which is a Thursday).

Determining the nth Occurrence of a Day of the Week in a Month

You may need a formula to determine the date for a particular occurrence of a weekday. For example, suppose your company payday falls on the second Friday of each month, and you need to determine the paydays for each month of the year. The following formula will make this type of calculation:

```
=DATE(A1,A2,1)+A3-WEEKDAY(DATE(A1,A2,1))+(A4-(A3>=WEEKDAY
(DATE(A1,A2,1))))*7
```

This formula assumes that

- Cell A1 contains a year.
- Cell A2 contains a month.
- Cell A3 contains a day number (1 for Sunday, 2 for Monday, and so on).
- Cell A4 contains the occurrence number (for example, 2 to select the second occurrence of the weekday specified in cell A3).

If you use this formula to determine the date of the first Friday in June 2006, it returns June 2, 2006.

Determining the Last Day of a Month

To determine the date that corresponds to the last day of a month, you can use the DATE function. However, you need to increment the month by 1, and use a day value of 0. In other words, the "0th" day of the next month is the last day of the current month.

The following formula assumes that a date is stored in cell A1. The formula returns the date that corresponds to the last day of the month.

```
=DATE(YEAR(A1),MONTH(A1)+1,0)
```

You can use a variation of this formula to determine how many days comprise a specified month. The formula that follows returns an integer that corresponds to the number of days in the month for the date in cell A1 (make sure that you format the cell as a number, not a date):

```
=DAY(DATE(YEAR(A1),MONTH(A1)+1,0))
```

Determining a Date's Quarter

For financial reports, you might find it useful to present information in terms of quarters. The following formula returns an integer between 1 and 4 that corresponds to the calendar quarter for the date in cell A1:

```
=ROUNDUP(MONTH(A1)/3,0)
```

This formula divides the month number by 3, and then rounds up the result.

Displaying a Calendar in a Range

This tip describes how to create a "live" calendar in a range of cells. Figure 96-1 shows an example. If you change the date that's displayed at the top of the calendar, the calendar recalculates to display the dates for the month and year.

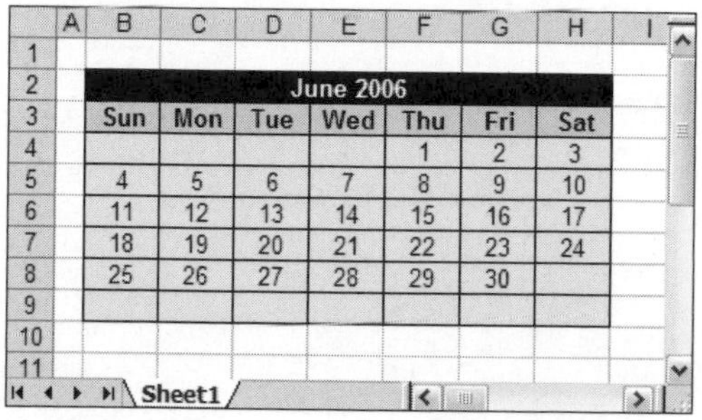

Figure 96-1: This calendar was created with a complex array formula.

To create this calendar in the range B2:H9, follow these steps:

1. Select B2:H2, and then merge the cells by clicking the Merge and Center button on the Formatting toolbar.

2. Enter a date into the merged range. The day of the month isn't important.

3. Enter the abbreviated day names in the range B3:H3.

4. Select B4:H9, and then enter this array formula. Remember, to enter an array formula, press Ctrl+Shift+Enter (not just Enter).

```
=IF(MONTH(DATE(YEAR(B2),MONTH(B2),1))<>
MONTH(DATE(YEAR(B2),MONTH(B2),1)-
(WEEKDAY(DATE(YEAR(B2),MONTH(B2),1))-1)
+{0;1;2;3;4;5}*7+{1,2,3,4,5,6,7}-1),"",
DATE(YEAR(B2),MONTH(B2),1)-
WEEKDAY(DATE(YEAR(B2),MONTH(B2),1))-1)+
{0;1;2;3;4;5}*7+{1,2,3,4,5,6,7}-1)
```

5. Format the range B4:H9 to use this custom number format, which displays only the day: d.

6. Adjust the column widths, and format the cells as you like.

Change the date and year, and the calendar will update automatically. After creating this calendar, you can copy the range to any other worksheet or workbook.

Various Methods of Rounding Numbers

Rounding numbers is a common task in Excel, and you'll find quite a few functions that round values in various ways.

It's important to understand the difference between rounding a value and formatting a value. When you *format* a number to display a specific number of decimal places, formulas that refer to that number use the actual value, which may differ from the displayed value. When you *round* a number, formulas that refer to that value use the rounded number.

Table 97-1 summarizes Excel's rounding functions.

TABLE 97-1   EXCEL'S ROUNDING FUNCTIONS

Function	Description
CEILING	Rounds a number up (away from zero) to the nearest specified multiple
DOLLARDE*	Converts a dollar price expressed as a fraction into a decimal number
DOLLARFR*	Converts a dollar price expressed as a decimal into a fractional number
EVEN	Rounds positive numbers up (away from zero) to the nearest even integer; rounds negative numbers down (away from zero) to the nearest even integer
FLOOR	Rounds a number down (toward zero) to the nearest specified multiple
INT	Rounds a number down to make it an integer
MROUND*	Rounds a number to a specified multiple
ODD	Rounds numbers up (away from zero) to the nearest odd integer; rounds negative numbers down (away from zero) to the nearest odd integer
ROUND	Rounds a number to a specified number of digits
ROUNDDOWN	Rounds a number down (toward zero) to a specified number of digits
ROUNDUP	Rounds a number up (away from zero) to a specified number of digits
TRUNC	Truncates a number to a specified number of significant digits

* This function is available only when the Analysis ToolPak add-in is installed.

The following sections provide examples of formulas that use various types of rounding.

Part V

Rounding to the Nearest Multiple

The MROUND function (part of the Analysis ToolPak add-in) is useful for rounding values to the nearest multiple. For example, you can use this function to round a number to the nearest 5. The following formula returns 135:

```
=MROUND(133,5)
```

Rounding Currency Values

Often, you need to round currency values. For example, a calculated price may be something like $45.78923. In such a case, you'll want to round the calculated price to the nearest penny. This may sound simple, but there are actually three ways to round such a value:

- Round it up to the nearest penny.
- Round it down to the nearest penny.
- Round it to the nearest penny (the rounding may be up or down).

The following formula assumes a dollar and cents value is in cell A1. The formula rounds the value to the nearest penny. For example, if cell A1 contains $12.421, the formula returns $12.42.

```
=ROUND(A1,2)
```

If you need to round the value up to the nearest penny, use the CEILING function. The following formula rounds the value in cell A1 up to the nearest penny. If, for example, cell A1 contains $12.421, the formula returns $12.43.

```
=CEILING(A1,0.01)
```

To round a dollar value down, use the FLOOR function. The following formula, for example, rounds the dollar value in cell A1 down to the nearest penny. If cell A1 contains $12.421, the formula returns $12.42.

```
=FLOOR(A1,0.01)
```

To round a dollar value up to the nearest nickel, use this formula:

```
=CEILING(A1,0.05)
```

Using the INT and TRUNC Functions

On the surface, the INT and TRUNC functions seem similar. Both convert a value to an integer. The TRUNC function simply removes the fractional part of a number. The INT function rounds a number down to the nearest integer, based on the value of the fractional part of the number.

In practice, INT and TRUNC return different results only when using negative numbers. For example, the following formula returns –14.0:

```
=TRUNC(-14.2)
```

The next formula returns –15.0 because –14.3 is rounded down to the next lower integer:

```
=INT(-14.2)
```

The TRUNC function takes an additional (optional) argument that's useful for truncating decimal values. For example, the formula that follows returns 54.33 (the value truncated to two decimal places):

```
=TRUNC(54.3333333,2)
```

Rounding to *n* Significant Digits

In some cases, you may need to round a value to a particular number of significant digits. For example, you might want to express the value 1,432,187 in terms of two significant digits (that is, as 1,400,000). The value 9,187,877 expressed in terms of three significant digits is 9,180,000.

If the value is a positive number with no decimal places, the following formula does the job. This formula rounds the number in cell A1 to two significant digits. To round to a different number of significant digits, replace the 2 in this formula with a different number.

```
=ROUNDDOWN(A1,2-LEN(A1))
```

For nonintegers and negative numbers, the solution gets a bit trickier. The formula that follows provides a more general solution that rounds the value in cell A1 to the number of significant digits specified in cell A2. This formula works for positive and negative integers and nonintegers.

```
=ROUND(A1,A2-1-INT(LOG10(ABS(A1))))
```

For example, if cell A1 contains 1.27845 and cell A2 contains 3, the formula returns 1.28000 (the value, rounded to three significant digits).

Rounding Time Values

You may need to create a formula that rounds a time to a particular number of minutes. For example, you may need to enter your company's time records rounded to the nearest 15 minutes. This tip presents examples of various ways to round a time value.

The following formula rounds the time in cell A1 to the nearest minute:

```
=ROUND(A1*1440,0)/1440
```

The formula works by multiplying the time by 1440 (to get total minutes). This value is passed to the ROUND function, and the result is divided by 1440. For example, if cell A1 contains 11:52:34, the formula returns 11:53:00.

The following formula resembles this example, except that it rounds the time in cell A1 to the nearest hour:

```
=ROUND(A1*24,0)/24
```

If cell A1 contains 5:21:31, the formula returns 5:00:00.

The following formula rounds the time in cell A1 to the nearest 15 minutes (quarter of an hour):

```
=ROUND(A1*24/0.25,0)*(0.25/24)
```

In this formula, 0.25 represents the fractional hour. To round a time to the nearest 30 minutes, change 0.25 to 0.5, as in the following formula:

```
=ROUND(A1*24/0.5,0)*(0.5/24)
```

Part V

Returning the Last Nonblank Cell in a Column or Row

Suppose you have a worksheet that you update frequently by adding new data to columns. You might need a way to reference the last value in a particular column (the value most recently entered).

Figure 99-1 shows an example. New data is entered daily, and the goal is to create a formula that returns the last value in column C.

	A	B	C	D
1	Date	Amount	Running Total	
2	6/1/05	604	604	
3	6/2/05	532	1136	
4	6/3/05	314	1450	
5	6/4/05	873	2323	
6	6/5/05	704	3027	
7	6/6/05	532	3559	
8	6/7/05	763	4322	
9	6/8/05	983	5305	
10	6/9/05			
11	6/10/05			
12	6/11/05			
13	6/12/05			
14	6/13/05			
15	6/14/05			
16	6/15/05			
17				
18				

Figure 99-1: Use a formula to return the last nonempty cell in column C.

If column C contains no empty cells, the solution is relatively simple:

```
=OFFSET(C1,COUNTA(C:C)-1,0)
```

This formula uses the COUNTA function to count the number of nonempty cells in column C. This value (minus 1) is used as the second argument for the OFFSET function. For example, if the last value is in row 100, COUNTA returns 100. The OFFSET function returns the value in the cell 99 rows down from cell D1, in the same column.

If column D has one or more empty cells interspersed, which is frequently the case, the preceding formula won't work because the COUNTA function doesn't count the empty cells. The following array formula returns the contents of the last nonempty cell in the first 500 rows of column D:

```
=INDEX(D1:D500,MAX(ROW(D1:D500)*(D1:D500<>"")))
```

 NOTE
Press Ctrl+Shift+Enter (not just Enter) to enter an array formula.

Part V

You can, of course, modify the formula to work with a column other than column D. To use a different column, change the four column references from D to whatever column you need. If the last nonempty cell occurs in a row beyond row 500, you need to change the two instances of 500 to a larger number. The fewer rows referenced in the formula, the faster the calculation speed.

The following array formula is similar to the previous formula, but it returns the last nonempty cell in a row (in this case, row 1):

```
=INDEX(1:1,MAX(COLUMN(1:1)*(1:1<>"")))
```

To use this formula for a different row, change the 1:1 reference to correspond to the correct row number.

Using the COUNTIF Function

Excel's COUNT and COUNTA functions are useful for basic counting, but sometimes you need more flexibility. This tip contains many examples of Excel's powerful COUNTIF function, useful for counting cells based on various types of criteria.

These formulas all work with a range named Data. As you can see in Table 100-1, the criteria argument proves quite flexible. You can use constants, expressions, functions, cell references, and even wildcard characters (* and ?).

TABLE 100-1   COUNTIF FORMULAS

Formula	What It Does
=COUNTIF(Data,12)	Returns the number of cells containing the value 12
=COUNTIF(Data,"<0")	Returns the number of cells containing a negative value
=COUNTIF(Data,"<>0")	Returns the number of cells not equal to 0
=COUNTIF(Data,">5")	Returns the number of cells greater than 5
=COUNTIF(Data,A1)	Returns the number of cells equal to the contents of cell A1
=COUNTIF(Data,">"&A1)	Returns the number of cells greater than the value in cell A1
=COUNTIF(Data,"*")	Returns the number of cells containing text
=COUNTIF(Data,"???")	Returns the number of text cells containing exactly three characters
=COUNTIF(Data,"budget")	Returns the number of cells containing the single word budget and nothing else (not case sensitive)
=COUNTIF(Data,"*budget*")	Returns the number of cells containing the text budget anywhere within the text
=COUNTIF(Data,"A*")	Returns the number of cells containing text that begins with the letter A (not case sensitive)

continued

Part V

TABLE 100-1   COUNTIF FORMULAS *(continued)*

Formula	What It Does
`=COUNTIF(Data,TODAY())`	Returns the number of cells containing the current date
`=COUNTIF(Data,">"&AVERAGE(Data))`	Returns the number of cells with a value greater than the average
`=COUNTIF(Data,">"&AVERAGE(Data)+STDEV(Data)*3)`	Returns the number of values exceeding three standard deviations above the mean
`=COUNTIF(Data,3)+COUNTIF(Data,-3)`	Returns the number of cells containing the value 3 or –3
`=COUNTIF(Data,TRUE)`	Returns the number of cells containing logical TRUE
`=COUNTIF(Data,TRUE)+COUNTIF(Data,FALSE)`	Returns the number of cells containing a logical value (TRUE or FALSE)
`=COUNTIF(Data,"#N/A")`	Returns the number of cells containing the #N/A error value

Counting Cells That Meet Multiple Criteria

Tip 100 presents examples of formulas that use the COUNTIF function. Those formulas are useful for counting cells that match a single criterion. The formula examples in this tip are useful when you need to count cells only if two or more criteria are met. These criteria can be based on the cells that are being counted or based on a range of corresponding cells.

Using "And" Criteria

The And criterion counts cells if all specified conditions are met. A common example is a formula that counts the number of values that fall within a numerical range. For example, you may want to count cells that contain a value greater than 0 *and* less than or equal to 12. Any cell that has a positive value less than or equal to 12 will be included in the count. For this example, the COUNTIF function will do the job:

```
=COUNTIF(Data,">0")-COUNTIF(Data,">12")
```

This formula counts the number of values that are greater than 0 and then subtracts the number of values that are greater than 12. The result is the number of cells that contain a value greater than 0 and less than or equal to 12.

Creating this type of formula can be confusing, because the formula refers to a condition ">12" even though the goal is to count values that are less than or equal to 12. An alternate technique is to use an array formula, such as the one that follows. You may find creating this type of formula easier.

```
=SUM((Data>0)*(Data<=12))
```

 NOTE

Remember, when you enter an array formula, press Ctrl+Shift+Enter, not just Enter.

Figure 101-1 shows a simple worksheet that I use for some of the examples that follow. This sheet shows sales data categorized by Month, SalesRep, and Type. The worksheet contains named ranges that correspond to the labels in Row 1.

Sometimes, the counting criteria will be based on cells other than the cells being counted. You may, for example, want to count the number of sales that meet the following criteria:

- Month is January, *and*
- SalesRep is Brooks, *and*
- Amount is greater than 1000

	A	B	C	D	E
1	**Month**	**SalesRep**	**Type**	**Amount**	
2	January	Albert	New	85	
3	January	Albert	New	675	
4	January	Brooks	New	130	
5	January	Cook	New	1350	
6	January	Cook	Existing	685	
7	January	Brooks	New	1350	
8	January	Cook	New	475	
9	January	Brooks	New	1205	
10	February	Brooks	Existing	450	
11	February	Albert	New	495	
12	February	Cook	New	210	
13	February	Cook	Existing	1050	
14	February	Albert	New	140	
15	February	Brooks	New	900	
16	February	Brooks	New	900	
17	February	Cook	New	95	
18	February	Cook	New	780	
19	March	Brooks	New	900	
20	March	Albert	Existing	875	
21	March	Brooks	New	50	
22	March	Brooks	New	875	
23	March	Cook	Existing	225	
24	March	Cook	New	175	
25	March	Brooks	Existing	400	
26	March	Albert	New	840	
27	March	Cook	New	132	
28					
29					

Figure 101-1: This worksheet demonstrates various counting techniques that use multiple criteria.

The following array formula returns the number of items that meet all three criteria:

```
=SUM((Month="January")*(SalesRep="Brooks")*(Amount>1000))
```

Using "Or" Criteria

To count cells using an Or criterion, you can sometimes use multiple COUNTIF functions. The following formula, for example, counts the number of 1s, 3s, and 5s in the range named *Data*:

```
=COUNTIF(Data,1)+COUNTIF(Data,3)+COUNTIF(Data,5)
```

You can also use the COUNTIF function in an array formula. The following array formula, for example, returns the same result as the previous formula:

```
=SUM(COUNTIF(Data,{1,3,5}))
```

But if you base your Or criteria on cells other than the cells being counted, the COUNTIF function won't work. Refer to Figure 101-1. Suppose you want to count the number of sales that meet the following criteria:

- Month is January, *or*
- SalesRep is Brooks, *or*
- Amount is greater than 1000

The following array formula returns the correct count:

```
=SUM(IF((Month="January")+(SalesRep="Brooks")+(Amount>1000),1))
```

Combining "And" and "Or" Criteria

You can combine And and Or criteria when counting. For example, perhaps you want to count sales that meet the following criteria:

- Month is January, *and*
- SalesRep is Brooks, *or*
- SalesRep is Cook

This array formula returns the number of sales that meet the criteria:

```
=SUM((Month="January")*IF((SalesRep="Brooks")+(SalesRep="Cook"),1))
```

Counting Distinct Entries in a Range

A common Excel question is "How can I count the number of distinct entries in a range?"

The simplest approach is to use an array formula. The following array formula returns the number of different entries in a range named Data:

```
=SUM(1/COUNTIF(Data,Data))
```

 NOTE
Enter an array formula by pressing Ctrl+Shift+Enter, not just Enter.

Figure 102-1 demonstrates using an array formula to count the number of different entries in the range A1:C12. The formula in cell D3 (an array formula) is

```
=SUM(1/COUNTIF(A1:C12,A1:C12))
```

This formula returns 3, because range A1:C12 contains three different entries.

	A	B	C	D	E	F
1	cat	dog	dog			
2	dog	dog	dog			
3	rabbit	dog	rabbit	3	animals	
4	dog	cat	dog			
5	dog	dog	dog			
6	cat	dog	rabbit			
7	dog	cat	dog			
8	dog	dog	rabbit			
9	dog	dog	dog			
10	cat	cat	rabbit			
11	dog	dog	rabbit			
12	dog	dog	rabbit			
13						

Sheet1

Figure 102-1: The array formula in cell D3 counts the number of distinct entries in a range.

Calculating Single-Criterion Conditional Sums

Excel's SUM function is easily the most commonly used function. But sometimes, you'll need more flexibility than the SUM function provides. The SUMIF function is useful when you need to compute conditional sums. For example, you might need to calculate the sum of just the negative values in a range of cells.

The examples in this tip demonstrate how to use the SUMIF function for conditional sums using a single criterion.

These formulas are based on the worksheet shown in Figure 103-1, which is set up to track invoices. Column F contains a formula that subtracts the date in column E from the date in column D. A negative number in column F indicates that the payment is past due. The worksheet uses named ranges that correspond to the labels in row 1.

	A	B	C	D	E	F
1	InvoiceNum	Office	Amount	DateDue	Today	Difference
2	AG-0145	Oregon	$5,000.00	3-Apr	6-May	-33
3	AG-0189	California	$450.00	21-Apr	6-May	-15
4	AG-0220	Washington	$3,211.56	30-Apr	6-May	-6
5	AG-0310	Oregon	$250.00	2-May	6-May	-4
6	AG-0355	Washington	$125.50	6-May	6-May	0
7	AG-0409	Washington	$3,000.00	12-May	6-May	6
8	AG-0581	Oregon	$2,100.00	25-May	6-May	19
9	AG-0600	Oregon	$335.39	25-May	6-May	19
10	AG-0602	Washington	$65.00	30-May	6-May	24
11	AG-0633	California	$250.00	1-Jun	6-May	26
12	TOTAL		$14,787.45			36
13						
14						

Sheet1

Figure 103-1: A negative value in column F indicates a past-due payment.

Summing Only Negative Values

The following formula returns the sum of the negative values in column F. In other words, it returns the total number of past-due days for all invoices. For this worksheet, the formula returns –58.

```
=SUMIF(Difference,"<0")
```

The SUMIF function can use three arguments. Because you omit the third argument, the second argument ("<0") applies to the values in the Difference range.

Summing Values Based on a Different Range

The following formula returns the sum of the past-due invoice amounts (in column C):

```
=SUMIF(Difference,"<0",Amount)
```

Part V

This formula uses the values in the Difference range to determine whether the corresponding values in the Amount range contribute to the sum.

Summing Values Based on a Text Comparison

The following formula returns the total invoice amounts for the Oregon office:

```
=SUMIF(Office,"=Oregon",Amount)
```

Using the equal sign is optional. The following formula has the same result:

```
=SUMIF(Office,"Oregon",Amount)
```

To sum the invoice amounts for all offices *except* Oregon, use this formula:

```
=SUMIF(Office,"<>Oregon",Amount)
```

Summing Values Based on a Date Comparison

The following formula returns the total invoice amounts that have a due date after June 1, 2005:

```
=SUMIF(DateDue,">="&DATE(2005,6,1),Amount)
```

Notice that the second argument for the SUMIF function is an expression. The expression uses the DATE function, which returns a date. Also, the comparison operator, enclosed in quotation marks, is concatenated (using the & operator) with the result of the DATE function.

The formula that follows returns the total invoice amounts that have a future due date (including today):

```
=SUMIF(DateDue,">="&TODAY(),Amount)
```

Calculating Multiple-Criterion Conditional Sums

Tip 103 contains summing examples that use a single comparison criterion. The examples in this tip involve summing cells based on multiple criteria. Because the SUMIF function does not work with multiple criteria, you need to use an array formula.

Figure 104-1 shows the sample worksheet again, for your reference. The formulas in this tip, of course, can be adapted to your own worksheets.

	A	B	C	D	E	F
1	InvoiceNum	Office	Amount	DateDue	Today	Difference
2	AG-0145	Oregon	$5,000.00	3-Apr	6-May	-33
3	AG-0189	California	$450.00	21-Apr	6-May	-15
4	AG-0220	Washington	$3,211.56	30-Apr	6-May	-6
5	AG-0310	Oregon	$250.00	2-May	6-May	-4
6	AG-0355	Washington	$125.50	6-May	6-May	0
7	AG-0409	Washington	$3,000.00	12-May	6-May	6
8	AG-0581	Oregon	$2,100.00	25-May	6-May	19
9	AG-0600	Oregon	$335.39	25-May	6-May	19
10	AG-0602	Washington	$65.00	30-May	6-May	24
11	AG-0633	California	$250.00	1-Jun	6-May	26
12	TOTAL		$14,787.45			36
13						
14						

Sheet1

Figure 104-1: This worksheet demonstrates summing based on multiple criteria.

Using "And" Criteria

Suppose you want to get a sum of the invoice amounts that are past due, *and* associated with the Oregon office. In other words, the value in the Amount range will be summed only if both of the following criteria are met:

- The corresponding value in the Difference range is negative.

- The corresponding text in the Office range is "Oregon."

The following array formula does the job:

```
=SUM((Difference<0)*(Office="Oregon")*Amount)
```

NOTE

You enter array formulas by pressing Ctrl+Shift+Enter.

An alternative nonarray formula is

```
=SUMPRODUCT(1*(Difference<0),1*(Office="Oregon"),Amount)
```

Part V

Using "Or" Criteria

Suppose you want to get a sum of past-due invoice amounts, *or* ones associated with the Oregon office. In other words, the value in the Amount range will be summed if either of the following criteria is met:

- The corresponding value in the Difference range is negative.
- The corresponding text in the Office range is "Oregon."

The following array formula does the job:

```
=SUM(IF((Office="Oregon")+(Difference<0),1,0)*Amount)
```

A plus sign (+) joins the conditions, and you can include more than two conditions.

Using "And" and "Or" Criteria

Things get a bit tricky when your criteria consists of both And and Or operations. For example, you may want to sum the values in the Amount range when both of the following conditions are met:

- The corresponding value in the Difference range is negative.
- The corresponding text in the Office range is "Oregon" or "California."

Notice that the second condition actually consists of two conditions, joined with Or. The following array formula does the trick:

```
=SUM((Difference<0)*IF((Office="Oregon")+(Office="California"),1)*Amount)
```

Looking Up an Exact Value

Excel's VLOOKUP and HLOOKUP formulas are useful if you need to return a value from a table (in a range) by looking up another value.

The classic example of a lookup formula involves an income tax rate schedule (see Figure 105-1). The tax rate schedule shows the income tax rates for various income levels. The following formula (in cell B3) returns the tax rate for the income in cell B2:

```
=VLOOKUP(B2,D2:F7,3)
```

	A	B	C	D	E	F
1				Income is Greater Than or Equal To...	But Less Than or Equal To...	Tax Rate
2	Enter Income:	$64,500		$0	$2,650	15.00%
3	The Tax Rate is:	36.00%		$2,651	$27,300	28.00%
4				$27,301	$58,500	31.00%
5				$58,501	$131,800	36.00%
6				$131,801	$284,700	39.60%
7				$284,701		45.25%
8						
9						
10						
11						

Figure 105-1: Using VLOOKUP to look up a tax rate.

The tax table example demonstrates that VLOOKUP and HLOOKUP don't require an exact match between the value to be looked up and the values in the lookup table. But in some cases, you may *require* a perfect match. For example, when looking up an employee number, you would require a perfect match for the number.

To look up an exact value only, use the VLOOKUP (or HLOOKUP) function with the optional fourth argument set to FALSE.

Figure 105-2 shows a worksheet with a lookup table that contains employee numbers (column C) and employee names (column D). The lookup table is named EmpList. The formula in cell B2, which follows, looks up the employee number entered in cell B1 and returns the corresponding employee name:

```
=VLOOKUP(B1,EmpList,2,FALSE)
```

Because the last argument for the VLOOKUP function is FALSE, the function returns a value only if an exact match is found. If the value is not found, the formula returns #N/A. This, of course, is exactly what you want to happen because returning an approximate match for an employee number makes no sense. Also, notice that the employee numbers in column C are not in ascending order. If the last argument for VLOOKUP is FALSE, the values need not be in ascending order.

Part V

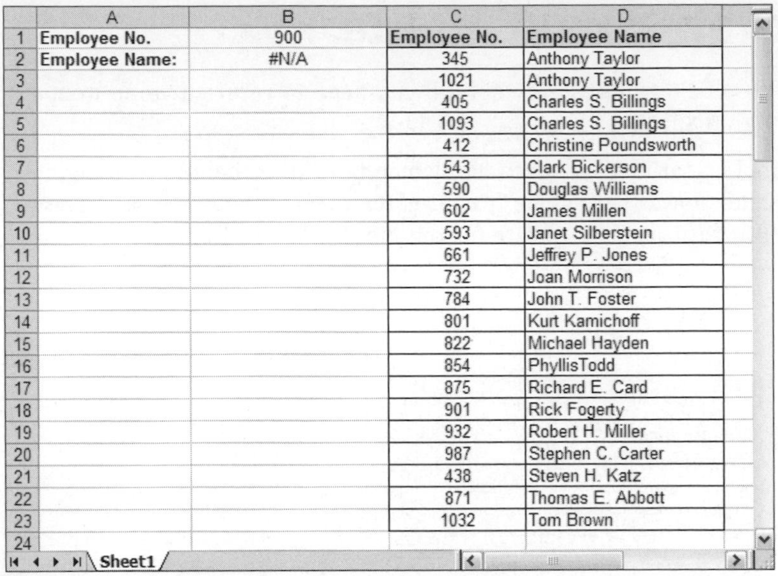

	A	B	C	D
1	Employee No.	900	Employee No.	Employee Name
2	Employee Name:	#N/A	345	Anthony Taylor
3			1021	Anthony Taylor
4			405	Charles S. Billings
5			1093	Charles S. Billings
6			412	Christine Poundsworth
7			543	Clark Bickerson
8			590	Douglas Williams
9			602	James Millen
10			593	Janet Silberstein
11			661	Jeffrey P. Jones
12			732	Joan Morrison
13			784	John T. Foster
14			801	Kurt Kamichoff
15			822	Michael Hayden
16			854	PhyllisTodd
17			875	Richard E. Card
18			901	Rick Fogerty
19			932	Robert H. Miller
20			987	Stephen C. Carter
21			438	Steven H. Katz
22			871	Thomas E. Abbott
23			1032	Tom Brown
24				

Sheet1

Figure 105-2: This lookup table requires an exact match.

If you prefer to see something other than #N/A when the employee number is not found, you can use an IF function to test for the #N/A result (using the ISNA function) and substitute a different string. The following formula displays the text "Not Found" rather than #N/A:

```
=IF(ISNA(VLOOKUP(B1,EmpList,2,FALSE)),"Not Found",VLOOKUP(B1,EmpList,2,FALSE))
```

Performing a Two-Way Lookup

A *two-way lookup* identifies the value at the intersection of a column and a row. This tip describes two methods to perform a two-way lookup.

Using a Formula

Figure 106-1 shows a worksheet with a table that displays product sales by month. To retrieve sales for a particular month and product, the user enters a month in cell B1 and a product name in cell B2.

	A	B	C	D	E	F	G	H
1	Month:	July			Widgets	Sprockets	Snapholytes	Combined
2	Product:	Sprockets		January	2,892	1,771	4,718	9,381
3				February	3,380	4,711	2,615	10,706
4	Month Offset:	8		March	3,744	3,223	5,312	12,279
5	Product Offset:	3		April	3,221	2,438	1,108	6,767
6	Sales:	3,337		May	4,839	1,999	1,994	8,832
7				June	3,767	5,140	3,830	12,737
8				July	5,467	3,337	3,232	12,036
9				August	3,154	4,895	1,607	9,656
10				September	1,718	2,040	1,563	5,321
11				October	1,548	1,061	2,590	5,199
12				November	5,083	3,558	3,960	12,601
13				December	5,753	2,839	3,013	11,605
14				Total	44,566	37,012	35,542	117,120
15								

Figure 106-1: This table demonstrates a two-way lookup.

To simplify things, the worksheet uses the following named ranges:

Name	Refers To
Month	B1
Product	B2
Table	D1:H14
MonthList	D1:D14
ProductList	D1:H1

The following formula (in cell B4) uses the MATCH function to return the position of the Month within the MonthList range. For example, if the month is January, the formula returns 2 because January is the second item in the MonthList range (the first item is a blank cell, D1).

```
=MATCH(Month,MonthList,0)
```

The formula in cell B5 works similarly, but it uses the ProductList range.

```
=MATCH(Product,ProductList,0)
```

The final formula, in cell B6, returns the corresponding sales amount. It uses the INDEX function with the results from cells B4 and B5.

```
=INDEX(Table,B4,B5)
```

You can, of course, combine these formulas into a single formula, as shown here:

```
=INDEX(Table,MATCH(Month,MonthList,0),MATCH(Product,ProductList,0))
```

 NOTE
You can use the Lookup Wizard add-in to create this type of formula (see Figure 106-2). The Lookup Wizard add-in is distributed with Excel. Choose Tools⇨Add-Ins to install the add-in. After you install the Lookup Wizard add-in, you access it by choosing Tools⇨ Lookup.

Lookup Wizard - Step 1 of 4

The Lookup Wizard helps you write a formula that finds the value at the intersection of a column and a row.

	2/15/94	10/10/94	7/25/95
8:45	5.31	30	51.55
10:15	10.84	13	84.87
15:30	12.83	66	83.87
18:45	15.98	16.89	95.02

Where is the range to search, including the row and column labels?

```
Sheet1!$D$1:$H$14
```

Cancel   < Back   Next >   Finish

Figure 106-2: The Lookup Wizard add-in can create a formula that performs a two-way lookup.

Using Implicit Intersection

The second method to accomplish a two-way lookup is quite a bit simpler, but it requires that you create a name for each row and column in the table.

A quick way to name each row and column is to select the table and choose Insert⇨ Name⇨Create. After creating the names, you can use a simple formula to perform the two-way lookup, such as the following:

```
=Sprockets July
```

This formula, which uses the range intersection operator (a space), returns July sales for Sprockets.

Performing a Two-Column Lookup

Some situations may require a lookup based on the values in two columns. Figure 107-1 shows an example.

	A	B	C	D	E	F
1	Make:	Jeep		**Make**	**Model**	**Code**
2	Model:	Grand Cherokee		Chevy	Blazer	C-094
3	Code:	J-701		Chevy	Tahoe	C-823
4				Ford	Explorer	F-772
5				Ford	Expedition	F-229
6				Isuzu	Rodeo	I-897
7				Isuzu	Trooper	I-900
8				Jeep	Cherokee	J-983
9				Jeep	Grand Cherokee	J-701
10				Nissan	Pathfinder	N-231
11				Toyota	4Runner	T-871
12				Toyota	Land Cruiser	T-981
13						

Sheet1

Figure 107-1: This workbook performs a lookup by using information in two columns (D and E).

The lookup table contains automobile makes and models, and a corresponding code for each. The technique described here allows you to look up the value based on the car's make and model.

The worksheet uses named ranges, as shown here:

Range	Name
F2:F12	Code
B1	Make
B2	Model
D2:D12	Range1
E2:E12	Range2

The following array formula displays the corresponding code for an automobile make and model:

```
=INDEX(Code,MATCH(Make&Model,Range1&Range2,0))
```

NOTE

When you enter an array formula, press Ctrl+Shift+Enter (not just Enter).

Part V

This formula works by concatenating the contents of Make and Model, and then searching for this text in an array consisting of the corresponding concatenated text in Range1 and Range2.

Performing a Lookup Using an Array

If your lookup table is small, you may be able to avoid using a table altogether and store the lookup information in an array. This tip describes a typical lookup problem that uses a standard lookup table — and an alternative method that uses an array.

Using a Lookup Table

Figure 108-1 shows a worksheet with student test scores. The range E2:F6 (named GradeList) displays a lookup table used to assign a letter grade to a test score.

	A	B	C	D	E	F	
1	Student	Score	Grade		Score	Grade	
2	Adams	36	F		0	F	
3	Baker	68	D		40	D	
4	Camden	50	D		70	C	
5	Dailey	77	C		80	B	
6	Gomez	92	A		90	A	
7	Hernandez	100	A				
8	Jackson	74	C				
9	Maplethorpe	45	D				
10	Paulson	60	D				
11	Ramirez	89	B				
12	Sosa	99	A				
13	Thompson	91	A				
14	Wilson	59	D				
15							

Figure 108-1: Looking up letter grades for test scores.

Column C contains formulas that use the VLOOKUP function and the lookup table to assign a grade based on the score in column B. The formula in C2, for example, is

```
=VLOOKUP(B2,GradeList,2)
```

Using an Array

When the lookup table is small (as in this example), you can use a literal array in place of the lookup table. This can remove a bit of clutter on your worksheet. The formula that follows, for example, returns a letter grade without using a lookup table. Rather, the information in the lookup table is hard-coded into an array constant. Note the use of curly braces to indicate the array, and note the use of semicolons to separate "rows."

```
=VLOOKUP(B2,{0,"F";40,"D";70,"C";80,"B";90,"A"},2)
```

Another approach, which uses a more legible formula, is to use the LOOKUP function with two array arguments:

```
=LOOKUP(B2,{0,40,70,80,90},{"F","D","C","B","A"})
```

Part V

Using the INDIRECT Function

To make a formula more flexible, you can use Excel's INDIRECT function to create a range reference. This rarely used function accepts a text argument that resembles a range reference, and then converts it to an actual range reference. When you understand how this function works, you can use it to create more powerful interactive spreadsheets.

Figure 109-1 shows a simple example. The formula in cell E5 is

```
=SUM(INDIRECT("B"&E2&":B"&E3))
```

	A	B	C	D	E	F
1	**Month**	**Sales**				
2	Jan	45,322		First Row	2	
3	Feb	38,900		Last Row	4	
4	Mar	59,832				
5	Apr	65,985		**SUM:**	144,054	
6	May	45,001				
7	Jun	78,323				
8	Jul	69,212				
9	Aug	72,090				
10	Sep	69,832				
11	Oct	65,874				
12	Nov	71,293				
13	Dec	43,505				

Sheet1

Figure 109-1: Using the INDIRECT function to sum user-supplied rows.

Notice that the argument for the INDIRECT function uses the concatenation operator to build a range reference using the values in cells E2 and E3. So, if E2 contains 2 and E3 contains 4, the range reference evaluates to this string:

```
"B2:B4"
```

The indirect function converts that string to an actual range reference, which is then passed to the SUM function. In effect, the formula returns:

```
=SUM(B2:B4)
```

When you change the values in E2 or E3, the formula updates to display the sum of the specified rows.

Figure 109-2 shows another example, this time using a worksheet reference.

Column A, on the Summary worksheet, contains text that corresponds to other worksheets in the workbook. Column B contains formulas that reference these text items. For example, the formula in cell B2 is

```
=SUM(INDIRECT(A2&"!F1:F10"))
```

Part V

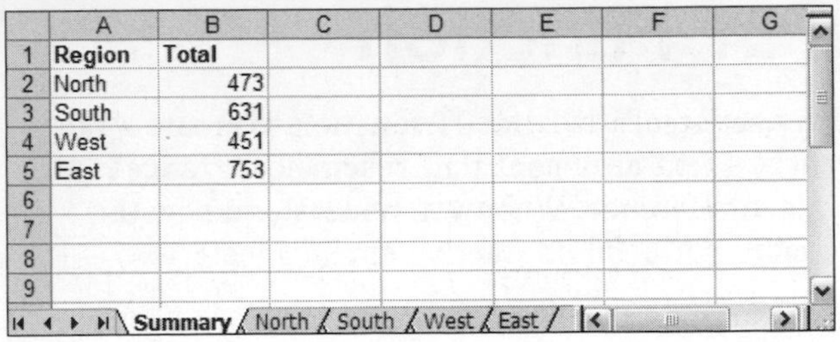

	A	B	C	D	E	F	G
1	Region	Total					
2	North	473					
3	South	631					
4	West	451					
5	East	753					
6							
7							
8							
9							

Summary / North / South / West / East

Figure 109-2: Using the INDIRECT function to create references.

This formula concatenates the text in A2 with a range reference. The INDIRECT function evaluates the result and converts it to an actual range reference. The result is equivalent to this formula:

```
=SUM(North!F1:F10)
```

That formula is copied down the column. Each formula returns the sum of range F1:F10 on the corresponding worksheet.

Creating Megaformulas

This tip describes a method of combining several intermediate formulas to create a single long formula (a *megaformula*). In the past, you may have seen some lengthy formulas that were virtually incomprehensible. Here, you'll learn how they were created.

The goal is to create a single formula that removes the middle name (for example, "Billy Joe Shaver" becomes "Billy Shaver." Figure 110-1 shows a worksheet with some names, plus six columns of intermediate formulas that accomplish the goal. Notice that the formulas aren't perfect; they can't handle a single-word name.

	A	B	C	D	E	F	G	H	I	J
1	Robert E. Lee	Robert E. Lee	7	10	10	Robert	Lee	Robert Lee		Robert Lee
2	Jim Jones	Jim Jones	4	#VALUE!	4	Jim	Jones	Jim Jones		Jim Jones
3	R. L Burnside	R. L Burnside	3	5	5	R.	Burnside	R. Burnside		R. Burnside
4	Michael J. Hammer	Michael J. Hammer	8	11	11	Michael	Hammer	Michael Hammer		Michael Hammer
5	T. Henry Jackson	T. Henry Jackson	3	9	9	T.	Jackson	T. Jackson		T. Jackson
6	Frank J Thomas	Frank J Thomas	6	8	8	Frank	Thomas	Frank Thomas		Frank Thomas
7	Enya	Enya	#####	#VALUE!	#####	#VALUE!	#VALUE!	#VALUE!		#VALUE!
8	Mary Richards Helton	Mary Richards Helton	5	14	14	Mary	Helton	Mary Helton		Mary Helton
9	Tom A. Smith	Tom A. Smith	4	7	7	Tom	Smith	Tom Smith		Tom Smith
10										
11										
12										
13										

multiple formulas / megaformula / VBA function

Figure 110-1: Removing the middle names and initials requires six intermediate formulas.

The formulas are listed in Table 110-1.

TABLE 110-1 INTERMEDIATE FORMULAS

Cell	Intermediate Formula	What It Does
B1	=TRIM(A1)	Removes excess spaces
C1	=FIND(" ",B1,1)	Locates the first space
D1	=FIND(" ",B1,C1+1)	Locates the second space, if any
E1	=IF(ISERROR(D1),C1,D1)	Uses the first space if no second space exists
F1	=LEFT(B1,C1-1)	Extracts the first name
G1	=RIGHT(B1,LEN(B1)-E1)	Extracts the last name
H1	=F1&" "&G1	Concatenates the two names

With a bit of work, you can eliminate all the intermediate formulas and replace them with a single megaformula. You do so by creating all the intermediate formulas and then editing the final result formula (in this case, the formula in column H) by replacing each cell reference with a copy of the formula in the cell referred to. Fortunately, you can use the

Clipboard to copy and paste the formulas instead of typing them over again. Keep repeating this process until cell H1 contains nothing but references to cell A1. You end up with the following megaformula in one cell:

```
=LEFT(TRIM(A1),FIND(" ",TRIM(A1),1)-1)&" "&RIGHT
(TRIM(A1),LEN(TRIM(A1))-IF(ISERROR(FIND(" ",
TRIM(A1),FIND(" ",TRIM(A1),1)+1)),FIND(" ",TRIM(A1),1),
FIND(" ",TRIM(A1),FIND(" ",TRIM(A1),1)+1)))
```

When you're satisfied that the megaformula works, you can delete the columns that hold the intermediate formulas because they are no longer used. If you're still not clear about this process, take a look at the step-by-step procedure:

1. Examine the formula in H1. This formula contains two cell references (F1 and G1):

   ```
   =F1&" "&G1
   ```

2. Activate cell G1 and copy the contents of the formula (without the equal sign) to the Clipboard.

3. Activate cell H1 and replace the reference to cell G1 with the Clipboard contents. Now cell H1 contains the following formula:

   ```
   =F1&" "&RIGHT(B1,LEN(B1)-E1)
   ```

4. Activate cell F1 and copy the contents of the formula (without the equal sign) to the Clipboard.

5. Activate cell H1 and replace the reference to cell F1 with the Clipboard contents. Now the formula in cell H1 is as follows:

   ```
   =LEFT(B1,C1-1)&" "&RIGHT(B1,LEN(B1)-E1)
   ```

6. Now cell H1 contains references to three cells (B1, C1, and E1). The formulas in those cells will replace each of the references to those cells.

7. Replace the reference to cell E1 with the formula in E1. The result is

   ```
   =LEFT(B1,C1-1)&" "&RIGHT(B1,LEN(B1)-IF(ISERROR(D1),C1,D1))
   ```

8. Notice that the formula in cell H1 now contains two references to cell D1. Copy the formula from D1 and replace both of the references to cell D1. The formula now looks like this:

   ```
   =LEFT(B1,C1-1)&" "&RIGHT(B1,LEN(B1)-IF(ISERROR(FIND
   (" ",B1,C1+1)),C1,FIND(" ",B1,C1+1)))
   ```

9. Replace the four references to cell C1 with the formula contained in cell C1. The formula in cell H1 is as follows:

   ```
   =LEFT(B1,FIND(" ",B1,1)-1)&" "&RIGHT(B1,LEN(B1)-IF
   (ISERROR(FIND(" ",B1,FIND(" ",B1,1)+1)),FIND(" ",B1,1),
   FIND(" ",B1,FIND(" ",B1,1)+1)))
   ```

10. Finally, replace the nine references to cell B1 with the formula in cell B1. The result is

```
=LEFT(TRIM(A1),FIND(" ",TRIM(A1),1)-1)&" "&RIGHT(TRIM(A1),
LEN(TRIM(A1))-IF(ISERROR(FIND(" ",TRIM(A1),FIND(" ",
TRIM(A1),1)+1)),FIND(" ",TRIM(A1),1),FIND(" ",TRIM(A1),
FIND(" ",TRIM(A1),1)+1)))
```

Notice that the formula in cell H1 now contains references only to cell A1. The mega-formula is complete, and it performs exactly the same tasks as all the intermediate formulas (which you can now delete).

You can, of course, adapt this technique to your own needs. A nice by-product is that a single megaformula usually calculates faster than a series of formulas.

Part VI

Charts and Graphics

A well-conceived chart can make a range of incomprehensible numbers make sense. The tips in this part deal with various aspects of chart making.

Tips and Where to Find Them

Tip 111   Creating a Text Chart Directly in a Range   273

Tip 112   Annotating a Chart   275

Tip 113   Creating a Self-Expanding Chart   277

Tip 114   Creating Combination Charts   281

Tip 115   Dealing with Missing Data in a Line Chart   283

Tip 116   Creating a Gantt Chart   285

Tip 117   Creating a Thermometer-Style Chart   287

Tip 118   Creating a Picture Chart   291

Tip 119   Plotting Single-Variable Mathematical Functions   293

Tip 120   Plotting Two-Variable Mathematical Functions   295

Tip 121   Creating a Semi-Transparent Chart Series   297

Tip 122   Saving a Chart as a Graphics File   299

Tip 123   Making Charts the Same Size   301

Tip 124   Displaying Multiple Charts on a Chart Sheet   303

Tip 125   Freezing a Chart   305

Tip 126   Adding a Watermark to a Worksheet   307

Tip 127   Changing the Shape of a Cell Comment   309

Tip 128   Inserting a Graphic into a Cell Comment   311

Creating a Text Chart Directly in a Range

Excel's charts offer great ways to present data, but sometimes a standard chart may be too unwieldy, especially if you have to visually summarize many values. In this case, you might want to forego a standard chart. But how do you create a chart without creating a chart? Simple. Use a range of cells to depict your data. An example is shown in Figure 111-1.

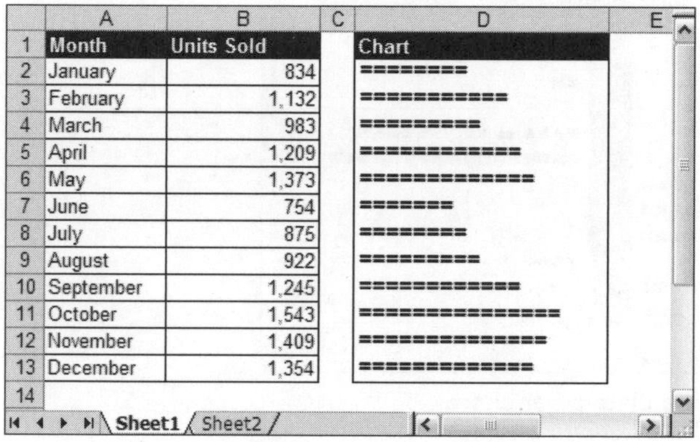

	A	B	C	D	E
1	Month	Units Sold		Chart	
2	January	834		========	
3	February	1,132		===========	
4	March	983		==========	
5	April	1,209		============	
6	May	1,373		=============	
7	June	754		=======	
8	July	875		========	
9	August	922		=========	
10	September	1,245		============	
11	October	1,543		===============	
12	November	1,409		==============	
13	December	1,354		=============	
14					

Sheet1 / Sheet2 /

Figure 111-1: A crude histogram created directly in a range of cells.

Column D contains formulas that feature the rarely used REPT function. This function repeats a text string a specified number of times. For example, the formula below prints five asterisks:

```
=REPT("*",5)
```

In the example shown in Figure 111-1, cell D2 contains this formula, which was copied down the column:

```
=REPT("=",B2/100)
```

Notice that the formula divides the value in column B by 100. This is a way to scale the chart. After all, you don't really want to see 834 characters in a cell, do you? For improved accuracy, you can include the ROUND function:

```
=REPT("=",ROUND(B2/100,0))
```

Without the ROUND function, the formula simply truncates the result of the division; that is, it disregards the decimal part of the argument. For example, the value 1,373 in column B displays 13 characters (13.73 without the decimal portion) in column D. Using ROUND rounds the result up to 14 characters.

You can use this type of graphical display in place of a column chart. As long as you don't require strict accuracy (due to rounding errors), this type of nonchart might fit the bill nicely.

Figure 111-2 shows another example. The formulas in columns E and G graphically depict monthly budget variances by displaying a series of characters. This display makes it very easy to see which budget items are under and which exceed the budget. This bar chart example uses the character *n*, which appears as a small square in the Wingdings font.

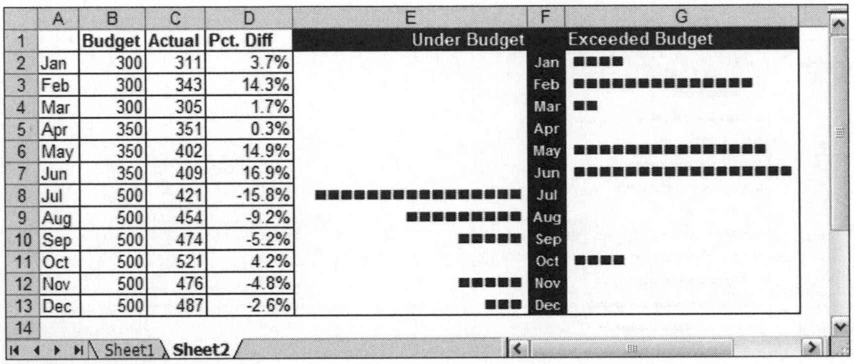

	A	B	C	D	E	F	G
1		Budget	Actual	Pct. Diff	Under Budget		Exceeded Budget
2	Jan	300	311	3.7%		Jan	■■■■
3	Feb	300	343	14.3%		Feb	■■■■■■■■■■■■■■
4	Mar	300	305	1.7%		Mar	■■
5	Apr	350	351	0.3%		Apr	
6	May	350	402	14.9%		May	■■■■■■■■■■■■■■■
7	Jun	350	409	16.9%		Jun	■■■■■■■■■■■■■■■■■
8	Jul	500	421	-15.8%	■■■■■■■■■■■■■■■■	Jul	
9	Aug	500	454	-9.2%	■■■■■■■■■	Aug	
10	Sep	500	474	-5.2%	■■■■■	Sep	
11	Oct	500	521	4.2%		Oct	■■■■
12	Nov	500	476	-4.8%	■■■■■	Nov	
13	Dec	500	487	-2.6%	■■■	Dec	
14							

Figure 111-2: Using the Wingdings font to simulate a bar chart.

The key formulas are:

```
E2: =IF(D2<0,REPT("n",ROUND(D2*-100,0)),"")
F2: =A2
G2: =IF(D2>0,REPT("n",ROUND(D2*100,0)),"")
```

For this example, follow these steps to set up the bar chart after entering the preceding formulas:

1. Assign the Wingdings font to cells E2 and G2.
2. Copy the formulas down columns E, F, and G to accommodate all the data.
3. Right-align the text in column E and adjust any other formatting.

Depending on the numerical range of your data, you may need to change the scaling. Experiment by replacing the 100 value in the formulas. You can substitute any character you like for the *n* in the formulas to produce a different character in the chart.

Annotating a Chart

When you create a chart, you might want to provide some text annotation. The question is, how do you add free-floating text to a chart? It's a common question, and the answer is amazingly simple: Select the chart and just start typing. When you're finished, press Enter.

The result is a free-floating text box in the center of the chart. You can move and resize the text box and apply any formatting you like (right-click the text box and choose Format Text Box from the shortcut menu). Figure 112-1 shows a chart with a text box.

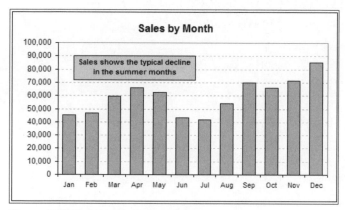

Figure 112-1: A text box in a chart.

You can also create a text box in which the text is linked to a cell. The procedure is just as easy: Select the chart, type an equal sign (=), click the cell that has the text, and press Enter. The text box is then linked to the specified cell. Change the contents of the cell, and the text box is updated.

Creating a Self-Expanding Chart

This tip describes how to create a chart that expands automatically when you add new data to a worksheet. Figure 113-1 illustrates the problem. The chart displays all of the data in the sheet. But when new data is entered, the chart series must be manually expanded to include the new data. Wouldn't it be nice if Excel could do this automatically?

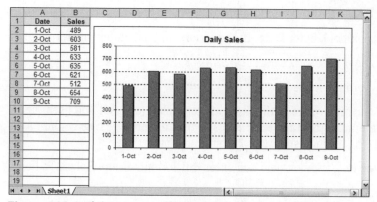

Figure 113-1: If this was a self-expanding chart, it would update automatically when additional data was entered.

First, the good news. If you use Excel 2003 or later, Excel can update the chart for you. If you're using a previous version, a self-expanding chart is possible, but it requires a bit of setup work.

For Excel 2003

To create a self-expanding chart in Excel, follow these simple steps:

1. Create your chart as usual.

2. Select the range that contains the data used by the chart.

3. Choose Data➪List➪Create List.

That's all there is to it. Excel recognizes the data as an official list, and data added to the list will be shown in the chart.

For Versions Prior to Excel 2003

To make the chart self-expanding, you need to create named formulas and then substitute the names in the chart's Source Data dialog box. The instructions here refer to the chart shown in Figure 113-1.

First, create the named formulas:

1. Select Insert⇨Name⇨Define to display the Define Name dialog box.

2. In the Names In Workbook field, enter **Date**. In the Refers To field, enter this formula:

   `=OFFSET(Sheet1!$A$2,0,0,COUNTA(Sheet1!$A:$A)-1,1)`

3. Click Add to create the formula named Date.

   Note that the OFFSET function refers to the first category label (cell A2) and uses the COUNTA function to determine the number of labels in the column. Because column A has a heading in row 1, the formula subtracts 1 from the number.

4. Type **Sales** in the Names In Workbook field and enter this formula in the Refers To field:

   `=OFFSET(Sheet1!$B$2,0,0,COUNTA(Sheet1!$B:$B)-1,1)`

5. Click Add to create the formula named Sales.

6. Click Close to close the Define Name dialog box.

After you perform these steps, the workbook contains two new names: Date and Sales. Next, modify the chart so it uses these two names by following these steps:

1. Activate the chart and select Chart⇨Source Data to display the Source Data dialog box.

2. In the Values field, enter **Sheet1!Sales**.

3. In the Category (x) Axis Labels field, enter **Sheet1!Date**.

4. Verify that the dialog box looks like Figure 113-2 and click OK.

After performing these steps, you'll find that the chart expands when you add new data to the bottom of the list.

If your chart has more than one data series, you need to create an additional named formula for each series and then make sure that you update the series via the Source Data dialog box.

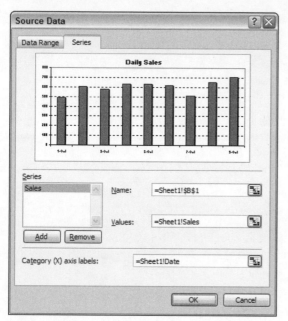

Figure 113-2: Specifying the named formulas in the Source Data dialog box.

Creating Combination Charts

Typically, a chart uses a single style: a column chart, a line chart, a pie chart, and so on. If your chart has more than one data series, you may want to display multiple styles within the same chart — a combination chart is just what you need.

One way to create a combination chart is to use the Chart Wizard (Insert⇨Chart). In Step 1 of 4 in the Chart Wizard dialog box, click the Custom Types tab. There, you have access to several combination charts (see Figure 114-1).

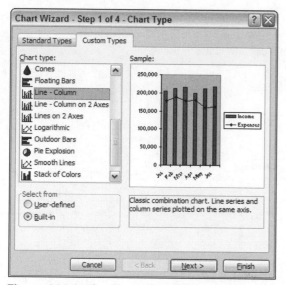

Figure 114-1: The Chart Wizard lets you choose from several combination chart types.

If you've already created your chart, it's easy to convert it to a combination chart. Follow these steps:

1. Click the series that you want to change.
2. Select Chart⇨Chart Type.
3. On the Standard Types tab, select the chart type for the selected series.

Figure 114-2 shows a chart that started out as a column chart. A few mouse clicks later, one of the series (Expenses in this case) is converted from columns to a line.

If your chart plots data with drastically different scales, you may want to use a second value axis for one of the chart series. Double-click the series you want to change to display the Format Data Series dialog box. Click the Axis tab, and select the Secondary Axis option.

Figure 114-3 shows a combination chart that uses a second axis.

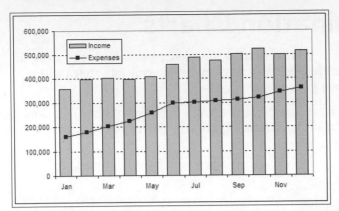

Figure 114-2: Creating a combination chart from a column chart.

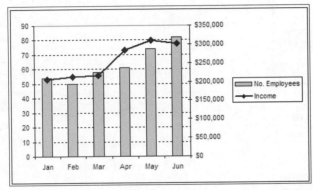

Figure 114-3: A combination chart that uses a second value axis.

Dealing with Missing Data in a Line Chart

When you create a line chart in Excel, missing data points (blank cells) are not plotted, which leaves gaps in the chart. Excel provides two other ways of handling missing data:

- Treat the missing data as zero.

- Interpolate the data by connecting the line between the nonmissing data points.

Figure 115-1 shows the default behavior for missing data. The two missing data values are not plotted. In some cases, you may want to use a different approach.

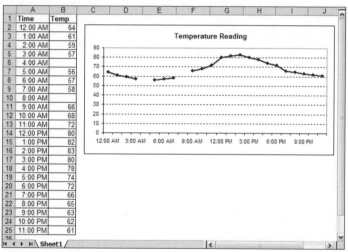

Figure 115-1: By default, Excel does not plot missing data in a line chart.

You don't use the Chart Options dialog box to specify how Excel deals with missing data. Rather, you use the Options dialog box as follows: Select your chart and choose Tools⇨ Options. In the Options dialog box, click the Chart tab and then select the appropriate option. Your choice will apply to all data series in the selected chart (this is not a global setting for all charts).

Figure 115-2 shows how these options look. The top chart uses the Zero option (which plots missing data as zero values), and the bottom chart uses the Interpolated setting. In this example, interpolating the missing data seems the better choice, given the data's time-based nature.

NOTE

You can also represent missing data with the formula =NA() instead of leaving a cell blank. The chart will use interpolation for data cells that contain this formula, regardless of the setting in the Options dialog box.

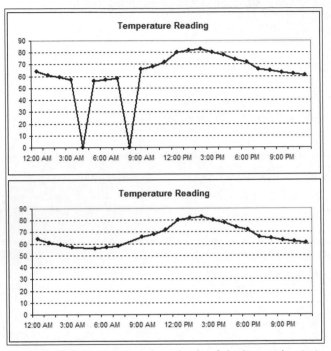

Figure 115-2: Two optional methods of dealing with missing data in a line chart.

Creating a Gantt Chart

A Gantt chart is a horizontal bar chart that's often used in project management applications. Although Excel doesn't support Gantt charts per se, you can fake it — as long as your project isn't too complicated.

Figure 116-1 shows a Gantt chart set up to depict the schedule for a project. The task names, start dates, and durations are in columns A:C. The chart depicts this schedule of events. The horizontal axis represents the total timespan of the project, and each bar represents a task. This makes it easy to see the duration for each task and spot overlapping tasks.

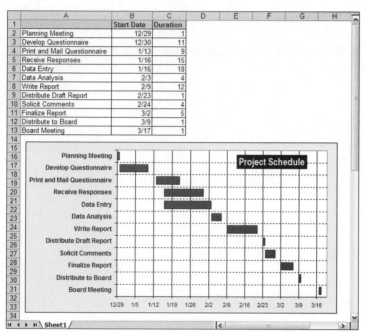

Figure 116-1: A simple Gantt chart.

Following are the steps required to create a Gantt chart from the data shown in Figure 116-1.

1. Use the Chart Wizard to create a stacked-bar chart: Select the range A1:C13, click the Chart Wizard button, and choose Bar as the Chart Type and Stack Bar as the Chart Sub-Type.

2. In Step 3 of the Chart Wizard, remove the legend and then click Finish to create an embedded chart.

3. Adjust the height of the chart so that all the axis labels are visible. You can also accomplish this by using a smaller font size for the category axis labels.

4. Display the Format Axis dialog box for the value (horizontal) axis by double-clicking the horizontal axis. Adjust the horizontal Axis Minimum and Maximum values to correspond to the earliest and latest dates in the data (note that you can enter a date into the Minimum or Maximum box). You also may want to set the Major Axis Unit to 7 to indicate weeks.

5. Display the Format Axis dialog box for the category (vertical) axis. In the Scale tab, select the option labeled Categories in Reverse Order, and select the option labeled Value (Y) Axis Crosses at Maximum Category.

6. Select the first data series and access the Format Data Series dialog box by selecting Format Data Series. On the Patterns tab, set Border to None and Area to None. This makes the first data series invisible.

7. Apply other formatting and tweaks as desired.

Although this is no substitute for Gantt charts that are generated by project management software, it's an easy way to depict a simple project.

Creating a Thermometer-Style Chart

You're probably familiar with a thermometer-style display that shows the percentage of a task that's completed. It's very easy to create such a display in Excel. The trick involves creating a chart that uses a single cell (which holds a percentage value) as a data series.

Setting Up the Percentage Formula

Figure 117-1 shows a worksheet set up to track daily progress toward a goal: 1,000 new customers in a 15-day period. Cell B18 contains the goal value, and cell B19 contains this simple SUM formula:

```
=SUM(B2:B16)
```

Cell B21 contains the following formula that calculates the percent of goal:

```
=B19/B18
```

As you enter new data in column B, the formulas display the current results.

	A	B	C
1	Day	New Customers	
2	Day 1	90	
3	Day 2	83	
4	Day 3	132	
5	Day 4	87	
6	Day 5	102	
7	Day 6	132	
8	Day 7		
9	Day 8		
10	Day 9		
11	Day 10		
12	Day 11		
13	Day 12		
14	Day 13		
15	Day 14		
16	Day 15		
17			
18	Goal:	1,000	
19	Total:	626	
20			
21		63%	
22			

Figure 117-1: This information will be plotted as a thermometer chat.

Creating the Chart

To create the chart, select cell B21, and click the Chart Wizard button. In Step 1 of the Chart Wizard, select Column as the Chart Type. Notice the blank row before cell B21. Without this blank row, Excel uses the entire data block for the chart, not just the single cell. Because B21 is isolated from the other data, the Chart Wizard uses only the single cell.

Figure 117-2 shows the basic chart.

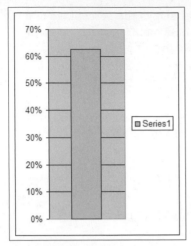

Figure 117-2: This chart will be transformed into a thermometer chart.

Fixing Up the Thermometer

Now make some other changes to make the chart more presentable:

1. Choose Chart⇨Chart Options to display the Chart Options dialog box.

2. In the Title tab of the Chart Options dialog box, add a Chart Title (for this example, New Customer Promotion).

3. In the Axes tab of the Chart Options dialog box, remove the check mark from Category (x) Axis to remove the horizontal axis.

4. In the Gridlines tab of the Chart Options dialog box, remove the check mark from Major Gridlines.

5. In the Legend tab of the Chart Options dialog box, remove the check mark from Show Legend.

6. In the Data Labels tab of the Chart Options dialog box, select the Value check box.

7. Click OK to close the Chart Options dialog box.

8. Double-click the column in the chart to display the Format Data Series dialog box.

9. On the Options tab of the Format Data Series dialog box, change the Gap Width setting to 0.

10. Click OK to close the Format Data Series dialog box.

11. Double-click the vertical axis to access the Format Axis dialog box.

12. In the Format Axis dialog box, select the Scale tab and set the Minimum to 0 and the Maximum to 1.

You can then make any other adjustments to get the look you desire. Figure 117-3 shows the thermometer chart after making these adjustments, and applying some additional formatting.

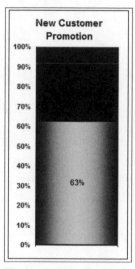

Figure 117-3: The drab column chart has been converted into an attractive thermometer chart.

Creating a Picture Chart

Excel offers a wide variety of chart types, but sometimes you may want something else for added impact. One of the easiest ways to make a chart more interesting is to replace the series elements (bars, columns, area, pie slices, or line markers) with a graphic image.

Figure 118-1 shows a column chart composed of a graphic image.

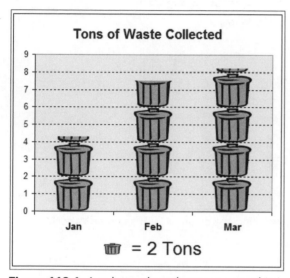

Figure 118-1: A column chart that uses a graphic image.

To convert a chart data series to pictures, follow these steps:

1. Start with a column or bar chart (either standard or 3D).

2. Select the chart series and choose Format⇨Selected Data Series to access the chart's Format Data Series dialog box.

3. Select the Patterns tab and click the Fill Effects button to get the Fill Effects dialog box.

4. In the Fill Effects dialog box, click the Picture tab and then click the Select Picture button to locate the graphics file that you want to use.

You'll probably need to play around with the settings to make your graphics work out the way you'd like.

An even easier method involves the Windows Clipboard. Here are the steps:

1. Copy any graphic image to the Clipboard. This can even include Autoshapes that you create using Excel's Drawing toolbar.

2. Select the chart column or bar series.

3. Choose Edit⇔Paste.

Figure 118-2 shows a before-and-after view of a column chart. In the second chart, the columns were replaced with an Autoshape (with shadow). The Autoshape was placed on a worksheet and then copied to the Clipboard.

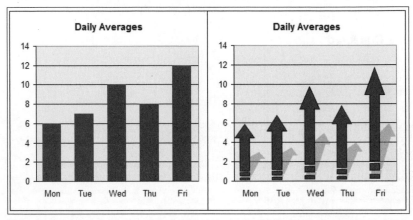

Figure 118-2: A column chart, before and after replacing the columns with a copied Autoshape.

Plotting Single-Variable Mathematical Functions

An X-Y chart (otherwise known as a Cartesian plane) is useful for plotting various mathematical and trigonometric functions. For example, Figure 119-1 shows a plot of the SIN function. The chart plots y for values of x (expressed in radians) from -5 to $+5$ in increments of 0.5. Each pair of x and y values appears as a data point in the chart, and the points connect with a line.

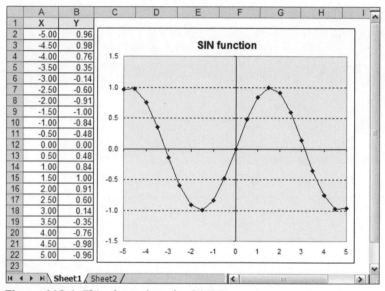

Figure 119-1: This chart plots the SIN(x).

The function is expressed as

```
y = SIN(x)
```

The corresponding formula in cell B2 (which is copied to the cells below) is

```
=SIN(A2)
```

To create this chart, follow these steps:

1. Select A1:B22.

2. Click the Chart Wizard button.

3. In Step 1 of the Chart Wizard, select X-Y (Scatter) and one of the subtypes that use connected lines.

4. Click Finish to create the chart.

5. You can then fine-tune the chart in terms of appearance.

Change the values in column A for different values of x. And, of course, you can use any single-variable formula you like in column B. For more accurate charts, increase the number of values plotted and make the increments in column A smaller.

Plotting Two-Variable Mathematical Functions

The preceding tip describes how to plot functions that use a single variable (x). You also can plot functions that use two variables. For example, the following function calculates a value of z for various values of two variables $(x$ and $y)$:

z = SIN(x)*COS(y)

Figure 120-1 shows a surface chart that plots the value of z for 21 x values ranging from −3 to 0 and for 21 y values ranging from 2 to 5. Both x and y use an increment of 0.15.

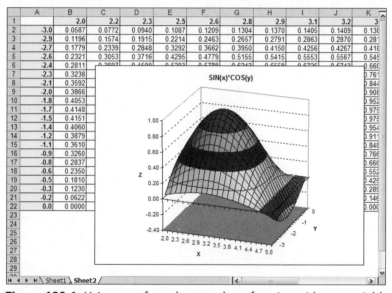

Figure 120-1: Using a surface chart to plot a function with two variables.

The x values are in A2:A22, and the y values are in B1:V1. The formula in cell B2, which is copied to the other cells in the table, is:

= SIN($A2)*COS(B$1)

To create this chart, follow these steps:

1. Select A1:V22.
2. Click the Chart Wizard button.

Part VI

3. In Step 1 of the Chart Wizard, select Surface and the first subtype.

4. Click Finish to create the chart.

You can then fine-tune the chart in terms of appearance.

As long as the x and y values have equal increments, you can specify any two-variable formula you like. You may need to adjust the starting values and increment values for the x and y variables. For a smoother plot, use more x and y values with a smaller increment.

Creating a Semi-Transparent Chart Series

If you've used a recent version of Excel for Macintosh, you may have noticed that the program supports semi-transparent chart series. In other words, it's possible to create a see-through chart series, as shown in the bottom chart in Figure 121-1 (notice that the gridlines are visible behind the columns).

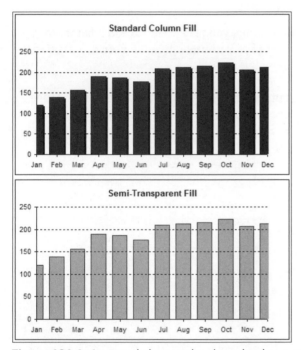

Figure 121-1: A normal chart and a chart that has a semi-transparent chart series.

Unfortunately, Excel for Windows is a bit behind in the chart department, so in order to create a semi-transparent chart series, you need to perform a few tricks. This technique makes it possible to create an Excel chart that's just a little bit different than the norm.

Here are the steps required:

1. Create your chart as usual. It must be a bar chart, a column chart, or an area chart.
2. Display the Drawing toolbar, and add a Rectangle AutoShape to your worksheet.
3. Double-click the Rectangle to display the Format AutoShape dialog box.
4. In the AutoShape dialog box, select the Colors and Lines tab.
5. Use the Color control to select a color.

6. Use the Transparency scroll bar to specify a transparency setting. Start with 80%. You can always adjust it if necessary.

7. For best results, use the Line Color control and specify No Line.

8. Close the Format AutoShape dialog box.

9. Select the AutoShape. Press Shift, and select Copy⇨Picture (this command is available only when the Shift key is pressed). Accept the default settings.

10. Activate your chart and click the bar or column series.

11. Choose Edit⇨Paste to paste the copied AutoShape.

12. If you formatted the AutoShape without a border, you may prefer to add a border to your chart series. Double-click the series and use the Patterns tab in the Format Data Series dialog box.

If the level of transparency is not what you had in mind, you'll find that you can't change the transparency directly in the chart. You need to modify the Transparency setting in the Format AutoShape dialog box and then repeat Steps 9–11.

Saving a Chart as a Graphics File

Oddly, Excel doesn't provide a direct way to convert a chart into a standalone graphics file, such as a GIF or a JPG file. It can, however, be done. Here I present three methods (one uses a VBA macro).

Method 1: Paste the Chart into a Graphics Program

This method requires other software — namely, a graphics program. Select your chart and choose Edit⇨Copy. Then access your graphics program and choose Edit⇨Paste. Then you can save the file by using whatever graphics file format you like.

You may need to experiment a bit to get optimal results. For example, you may need to copy the chart as a picture. To do so, select the chart, press Shift, and then choose Edit⇨ Copy Picture. (The Copy Picture command is available only when you press Shift.)

Method 2: Save as an HTML File

To convert all of the charts in a workbook to GIF files, save your workbook in HTML format and then locate the GIF files that are created.

1. Make sure your workbook is saved.

2. Choose File⇨Save As.

3. In the Save As dialog box, choose Web Page (*.htm, *.html) from the Save As Type drop-down list.

4. Choose the Entire Workbook option.

5. Select a directory if you like (and make a note of the directory). Your desktop is a good choice because it's easy to find.

6. Give the file a name and click Save.

7. Close the workbook.

8. Activate an Explorer window and locate the directory where you saved the file. You'll find a subdirectory with a name that corresponds to the filename with "_files" appended. Open that directory and you'll find a GIF file that corresponds to each chart in your workbook.

Method 3: Use a VBA Macro

This method uses a simple VBA macro that saves each chart on the active sheet as a GIF file.

To create the macro, press Alt+F11 to activate the Visual Basic editor. Select your workbook in the Projects window and choose Insert⇨Module to insert a new VBA module. Then type the following procedure into the module:

```
Sub SaveChartsAsGIF()
    Dim ChtObj As ChartObject
    Dim Fname As String
    For Each ChtObj In ActiveSheet.ChartObjects
        Fname = ThisWorkbook.Path & "\" & ChtObj.Name & ".gif"
        ChtObj.Chart.Export Filename:=Fname, FilterName:="gif"
  Next ChtObj
End Sub
```

After the macro is entered, press Alt+F11 to reactivate Excel. Then activate the worksheet that contains your charts. Press Alt+F8 to display the Macro dialog box. Select the SaveChartsAsGIF macro and click Run.

The procedure uses the chart's name as the GIF filename, and the file is stored in the same directory as the workbook. If you prefer to use the JPG format, change the two instances of "gif" to "jpg."

Making Charts the Same Size

If you have several embedded charts on a worksheet, you might want to make them all exactly the same size. Figure 123-1 shows a worksheet with four charts. Wouldn't they look better if they were all the same size and nicely aligned?

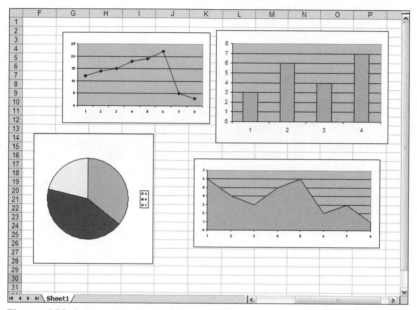

Figure 123-1: You can precisely control the size of the charts by selecting them as objects.

To make all of the charts the same size, first identify the chart that is already the size you want. In this case, you want to make all the charts the same size as the column chart in the upper right.

1. Ctrl+click the chart to select it as an object.

2. Right-click and choose Format Object to display the Format Object dialog box.

3. Click the Size tab and make a note of the Height and Width displayed in the dialog box.

4. Click Cancel to close the Format Object dialog box.

5. Ctrl+click the other three charts (so all four are selected as objects).

6. Right-click any of the selected charts and choose Format Object.

7. Enter the Height and Width you noted from Step 3 and click OK.

The charts are now exactly the same size.

You can align the charts manually, or you can use the Draw⇨Align commands on the Drawing toolbar. Figure 123-2 shows the end result.

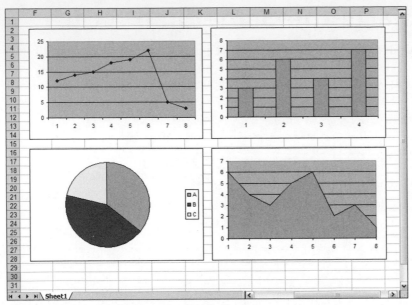

Figure 123-2: Four charts, resized and aligned.

Displaying Multiple Charts on a Chart Sheet

An Excel chart can appear embedded in a worksheet, or it can reside in a separate Chart sheet. Most Excel users think that a Chart sheet can hold only one chart. If you know the trick, you can store multiple charts on a single Chart sheet.

Here's how to do it:

1. Create your charts as usual, embedding them in a worksheet.

2. Select any blank cell in the worksheet and press F11. This creates an empty Chart sheet to hold the embedded charts.

3. Reactivate your worksheet, click an embedded chart, and select Chart⇨Location to display the Chart Location dialog box.

4. In the Chart Location dialog box, choose the As Object In option and specify the empty Chart sheet. Excel transfers the embedded chart to your Chart sheet.

5. Select your remaining charts and choose Chart⇨Location to move them to the Chart sheet. Note that you must move each chart separately. (You can't select multiple charts.)

Now you can arrange and size the charts any way you like. Putting multiple charts on a single Chart sheet lets you use the View⇨Sized with Window command (available when the Chart sheet is active) to scale the charts to the current window size and dimensions.

Figure 124-1 shows an example of a Chart sheet that contains four charts.

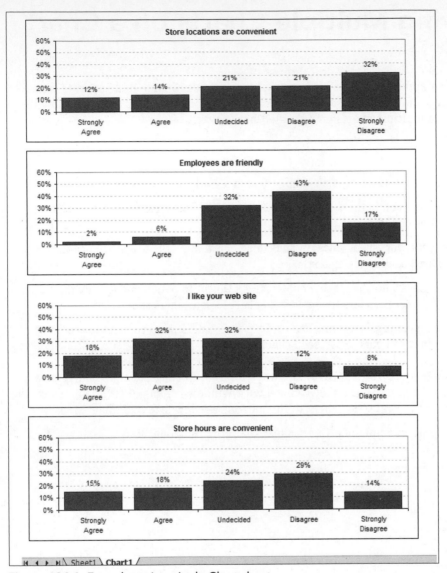

Figure 124-1: Four charts in a single Chart sheet.

Freezing a Chart

Normally, an Excel chart uses data stored in a range. Change the data, and the chart updates automatically. Usually, that's a good thing. But sometimes you want to "unlink" the chart from its data range and produce a static chart — a snapshot of a chart that never changes. For example, if you plot data generated by various what-if scenarios, you may want to save a chart that represents some baseline so that you can compare it with other scenarios. There are two ways to "freeze" a chart:

- Convert the chart to a picture
- Convert the range references to arrays

Converting a Chart into a Picture

To convert a chart to a static picture, follow these steps:

1. Create the chart as usual and make any modifications.

2. Click the chart to activate it.

3. Press the Shift key and choose Edit⇨Copy Picture to display the Copy Picture dialog box. (The Copy Picture menu item is available only when you press the Shift key.)

4. In the Copy Picture dialog box, choose As Shown When Printed for the Appearance option, and As Shown On Screen for the Size option.

5. Click any cell to deselect the chart.

6. Choose Edit⇨Paste.

The result is a picture of the original chart. This chart can be edited as a picture, but not as a chart. In other words, you can no longer modify properties such as chart type, data labels, and so on. It's a dead chart — just what you wanted.

Converting Range References into Arrays

The other way to unlink a chart from its data is to convert the SERIES formula range references to arrays. Follow these steps:

1. Activate your chart.

2. Click the chart series. The chart SERIES will appear in the formula bar.

3. Click the formula bar.

4. Press F9, and then press Enter.

Repeat this procedure for each series in the chart.

Figure 125-1 shows a pie chart that has been unlinked from its data range. Notice that the formula bar displays arrays, not range references. The original data is in I3:J6. The converted SERIES formula is:

```
=SERIES(,{"Work","Sleep","Drive","Eat","Other"},{9,7,2,1,5},1)
```

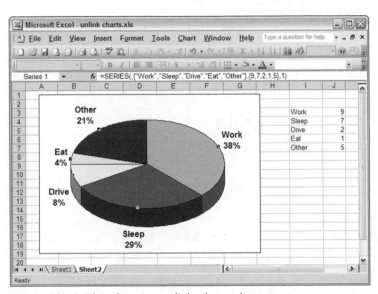

Figure 125-1: This chart is not linked to a data range.

Adding a Watermark to a Worksheet

Sometimes you need to print a watermark on an Excel sheet. For example, you might want to print the word DRAFT in large letters, just to make it perfectly clear that the document is not a final version.

As you may know, Excel has the ability to display a graphic on a worksheet. Just choose Format⇨Sheet⇨Background and select a graphic file. Although it might seem like a perfect candidate for displaying a watermark, it has one big problem: The graphic is for on-screen viewing only; it's not printed!

One solution is to use Word Art. Choose Insert⇨Picture⇨Word Art, and you have lots of options for your watermark display. Figure 126-1 shows some Word Art formatted to be transparent (shown in Print Preview mode).

If you're generating a multipage printout, you want to copy the Word Art to each printed page. The easiest way to do that is to select View⇨Page Break Preview, which displays your worksheet zoomed out, with page breaks clearly delineated.

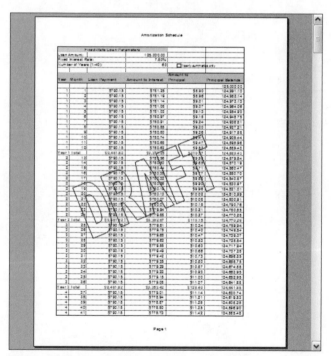

Figure 126-1: Using Word Art for a watermark.

NOTE

I should also mention that there's another, low-tech solution. Add a watermark to a blank page, print the page, and then make photocopies. Then use the copied pages in your printer.

Changing the Shape of a Cell Comment

Cell comments are useful for a variety of purposes. But sometimes, you just get tired of looking at the same old yellow rectangle. If you'd like your comment to get noticed, try changing the shape.

Figure 127-1 shows a normal cell comment. Figure 127-2 shows that same comment after it's been spiffed up a bit.

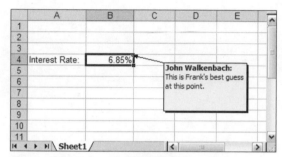

Figure 127-1: A typical cell comment.

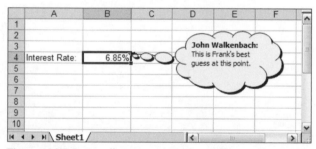

Figure 127-2: A cell comment with a different shape.

Changing the shape of a cell comment is easy. Just follow these steps:

1. Choose Insert➪Comment to add a comment to a cell.

2. Right-click the cell and choose Show Comment.

3. Make sure the Drawing toolbar is displayed. If not, right-click any toolbar and select Drawing.

4. Ctrl+click the comment to select it.

5. From the Drawing toolbar, choose Draw➪Change AutoShape and choose your desired shape.

You'll find that some of the AutoShapes can be reshaped a bit. For example, those in the Callouts category allow you to move the pointer so it points to the cell that contains the comment.

Inserting a Graphic into a Cell Comment

You probably know that you can insert graphic images on a worksheet. Just use the Insert⇨Picture⇨From File command, select your image file, and it's there. But most users don't realize that you can also display a graphic image inside a cell comment. The procedure isn't exactly intuitive, but here's how to do it:

1. Activate the cell that will hold the comment and choose Insert⇨Comment.

2. Double-click the comment's border to display the Format Comment dialog box.

3. In the Format Comment dialog box, click the Colors and Lines tab.

4. Click the Color drop-down box and select Fill Effects to display the Fill Effects dialog box.

5. In the Fill Effects dialog box, click the Picture tab.

6. Click the Select Picture button and select the image file.

7. Click OK twice to dismiss the dialog box.

8. You may want to resize the comment box to accommodate the image. Just click a border and drag it.

Figure 128-1 shows a cell with a photo displayed in the comment.

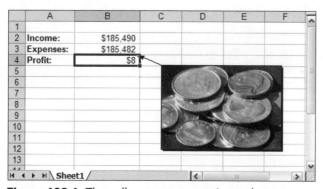

Figure 128-1: The cell comment contains a photo.

WARNING

Keep in mind that every image you add increases the size of your workbook file. In other words, don't go overboard with this technique. To help reduce the size of your workbook, you can compress the images. Display the Picture toolbar and then click the Compress Picture button.

Part VII

Data Analysis
and Lists

Much of the data contained in your worksheets is in the form of a list. In this part, you'll find tips that deal with lists and data analysis.

Tips and Where to Find Them

Tip 129 Using the List Feature in
Excel 2003   315

Tip 130 Sorting on More Than Three
Columns   319

Tip 131 Using Custom Views with
AutoFiltering   321

Tip 132 Putting Advanced Filter
Results on a Different Sheet 323

Tip 133 Comparing Two Ranges with
Conditional Formatting   325

Tip 134 Randomizing a List   329

Tip 135 Filling the Gaps in a Report 331

Tip 136 Creating a List from a
Summary Table   333

Tip 137 Finding Duplicates by Using
Conditional Formatting   337

Tip 138 Preventing Row or Column
Insertions within a Range 339

Tip 139 Creating a Quick Frequency
Tabulation   341

Tip 140 Controlling References to
Cells within a PivotTable 343

Tip 141 Grouping Items by Date in a
PivotTable   345

Tip 142 Hiding the Field Buttons in a
PivotChart   349

Using the List Feature in Excel 2003

In Excel, a list is nothing more than a contiguous range of data, usually with a row of labels at the top. Excel has always had the ability to work with lists, but with Excel 2003, Microsoft introduced a new concept that lets you designate a range of cells to be an "official" list.

To avoid confusion with a normal list, I refer to the type of list described in this tip as a *designated list*. The only difference between a designated list and a normal list is that you specifically tell Excel that you're dealing with a list. After doing so, Excel displays an outline around the list and automatically expands the list as new data is added. A worksheet can contain any number of these designated lists.

Creating a Designated List

To create a designated list, select any cell within your list and choose Data⇨List⇨Create List (or press Ctrl+L). Excel displays its Create List dialog box, which gives you the opportunity to verify the list's address and specify whether it contains headers. When you click OK, the list displays a colored border, and AutoFilter mode for the list is enabled. In addition, Excel displays its List toolbar. This toolbar contains a menu and buttons relevant to working with a list (see Figure 129-1).

	A	B	C	D	E	F	G
1							
2		Name	Annual Salary	Monthly Salary	Location	Date Hired	Exempt
3		Anthony Taylor	$55,500	$4,625	Los Angeles	5/2/1998	FALSE
4		Charles S. Billings	$39,000	$3,250	Los Angeles	11/1/2000	FALSE
5		C				6/12/1997	FALSE
6		C	List ▾ Σ Toggle Total Row			4/19/2000	TRUE
7		Douglas Williams	$89,687	$7,474	Portland	1/3/2004	TRUE
8		Ivan Silberstein	$95,000	$7,917	Los Angeles	12/1/1998	TRUE
9		James Millen	$27,690	$2,308	Los Angeles	3/16/1997	FALSE
10		Jeffrey P. Jones	$42,000	$3,500	Seattle	4/9/2000	FALSE
11		Joe Morrison	$24,000	$2,000	Seattle	3/13/2003	FALSE
12		John T. Foster	$39,500	$3,292	Seattle	10/10/1999	FALSE
13		Kurt Kamichoff	$48,000	$4,000	Los Angeles	11/5/2000	FALSE
14		Michael Hayden	$78,230	$6,519	Seattle	6/1/1999	TRUE
15		Phillip A. Todd	$29,500	$2,458	Portland	1/3/1998	FALSE
16		Richard E. Card	$43,000	$3,583	Seattle	7/2/2003	FALSE
17		Rick Fogerty	$89,873	$7,489	Portland	6/28/1998	TRUE
18		Robert H. Miller	$149,000	$12,417	Portland	5/1/1999	TRUE
19		Stephen C. Carter	$44,123	$3,677	Los Angeles	9/29/2004	FALSE
20		Steven H. Katz	$32,900	$2,742	Los Angeles	3/16/2000	FALSE
21		Thomas E. Abbott	$60,000	$5,000	Los Angeles	4/12/1997	FALSE
22		Tom Brown	$65,000	$5,417	Seattle	5/27/2000	TRUE
23		*					
24							

Sheet1

Figure 129-1: The data in range B2:G23 has been designated as a list.

Notice that the designated list includes an additional empty row at the bottom. This row is reserved for new data that is entered into the list. The first cell in this empty row contains an asterisk.

To convert a designated list back to a standard range, choose Data⇨List⇨Convert to Range.

Adding Rows or Columns to a Designated List

To add data to the end of a designated list, enter it into the empty row that contains the asterisk. A new empty row will then appear at the bottom of the list. To insert rows or columns, right-click and choose the appropriate command from the Insert menu (or use the List⇨Insert command on the List toolbar).

To delete rows or columns, right-click and choose the appropriate command from the Delete menu (or use the List⇨Delete command on the List or XML toolbar).

Adding Summary Formulas to a Designated List

A designated list can contain formulas that summarize the data in each column. Before you can add these formulas, you must insert a Total row. Do this by choosing Data⇨List⇨ Total Row or by clicking the Toggle Total Row button on the List toolbar. Either of these actions appends a new row to the end of the designated list. Cells in the total row display drop-down list arrows, which resemble AutoFilter headings. Use these drop-down lists to select the type of summary — for example, Average, Count, Sum, and so on (see Figure 129-2).

Unfortunately, you cannot create your own formulas for the total row. You are limited to the functions displayed in the drop-down list. You will find that, regardless of which formula you choose from the drop-down list, SUBTOTAL is the only function used. The first argument of the SUBTOTAL function determines the type of summary displayed. For example, if the first argument is 109, the function displays the sum.

WARNING

Workbooks that use a designated list are not backward-compatible with older versions of Excel. If you distribute your workbook to someone who uses an earlier version of Excel, the data will be intact, but it will not function as a designated list. In addition, if you used summary formulas, they will display a #VALUE! error.

Advantages of Using a Designated List

Some users may find a few advantages in using a designated list. For example, you may like the idea that the list is clearly delineated with a dark border. Or you may find that it's easier to insert summary formulas. The key advantage in using a designated list is apparent when you create a chart from data in the list. You'll find that the chart series expands as you insert new data at the end of the list.

	A	B	C	D	E	F	G
1							
2		Name ▾	**Annual** Salary ▾	**Monthly** Salary ▾	Location ▾	Date Hired ▾	Exempt ▾
3		Anthony Taylor	$55,500	$4,625	Los Angeles	5/2/1998	FALSE
4		Charles S. Billings	$39,000	$3,250	Los Angeles	11/1/2000	FALSE
5		Chris Poundsworth	$29,850	$2,488	Seattle	6/12/1997	FALSE
6		Clark Bickerson	$120,000	$10,000	Los Angeles	4/19/2000	TRUE
7		Douglas Williams	$89,687	$7,474	Portland	1/3/2004	TRUE
8		Ivan Silberstein	$95,000	$7,917	Los Angeles	12/1/1998	TRUE
9		James Millen	$27,690	$2,308	Los Angeles	3/16/1997	FALSE
10		Jeffrey P. Jones	$42,000	$3,500	Seattle	4/9/2000	FALSE
11		Joe Morrison	$24,000	$2,000	Seattle	3/13/2003	FALSE
12		John T. Foster	$39,500	$3,292	Seattle	10/10/1999	FALSE
13		Kurt Kamichoff	$48,000	$4,000	Los Angeles	11/5/2000	FALSE
14		Michael Hayden	$78,230	$6,519	Seattle	6/1/1999	TRUE
15		Phillip A. Todd	$29,500	$2,458	Portland	1/3/1998	FALSE
16		Richard E. Card	$43,000	$3,583	Seattle	7/2/2003	FALSE
17		Rick Fogerty	$89,873	$7,489	Portland	6/28/1998	TRUE
18		Robert H. Miller	$149,000	$12,417	Portland	5/1/1999	TRUE
19		Stephen C. Carter	$44,123	$3,677	Los Angeles	9/29/2004	FALSE
20		Steven H. Katz	$32,900	$2,742	Los Angeles	3/16/2000	FALSE
21		Thomas E. Abbott	$60,000	$5,000	Los Angeles	4/12/1997	FALSE
22		Tom Brown	$65,000	$5,417	Seattle	5/27/2000	TRUE
23		*					
24		Total		▾			20
25				None			
26				Average			
27				Count			
28				Count Nums			
29				Max			
30				Min			
31				Sum			
32				StdDev			
				Var			

Sheet1

Figure 129-2: It's easy to insert summary formulas in a designated list.

Part VII

Sorting on More Than Three Columns

If you have a list of data, you may need to sort it. Many users mistakenly think that Excel can sort by, at most, three different columns. After all, the Sort dialog box (shown in Figure 130-1) displays only three Sort By fields.

Figure 130-1: Despite evidence to the contrary, sorting a list is not limed to three fields.

Actually, you can sort your list using any number of columns. I generally avoid the Sort dialog box and use the Sort Ascending or Sort Descending buttons on the Standard toolbar. You just need to use those buttons multiple times.

For example, assume that you have a mailing list and you need to sort the data by four columns: Country, Region, City, and Postal Code. In other words, you want all of the Country records together. In addition, you want the Country records sorted by Region, the Region records sorted by City, and the City records sorted by Postal Code.

To accomplish this type of sorting, you need to sort the data four times. Just start with the "least significant" sort and end with the "most significant" sort. In this case, perform four sorts in this order: Postal Code, City, Region, Country.

Part VII

Using Custom Views with AutoFiltering

Excel's AutoFilter feature is handy for hiding specific items in a list. For example, if you have a mailing list, you can choose to display only the rows in which the State column contains "Montana." You can filter a list using as many columns as you need, and the Custom option provides even more flexibility.

Creating a Named View

Unfortunately, Excel does not allow you to give a name to a particular set of filters. Therefore, if you tend to use several different filtering criteria for a particular list, you can waste a lot of time setting the filters manually.

The solution: The rarely used View⇨Custom Views command. Here's how to do it:

1. Apply AutoFiltering to your list, and set the filters to your liking.

2. Select View⇨Custom Views to display the Custom View dialog box.

3. Click the Add button to display the Add View dialog box, shown in Figure 131-1.

4. Provide a name for the view, and make sure that the Hidden Rows, Columns and Filter Settings box is checked.

5. Click OK to close the Add View dialog box.

Repeat this for as many different AutoFilter settings as you like. You might also want to create a view called Unfiltered to display the list with no filtering applied.

Figure 131-1: Adding a custom view.

Then, to apply a set of AutoFilter settings, select View⇨Custom Views and select the named view from the list.

Part VII

Adding the Custom View Control to a Toolbar

To simplify things even more, you can add the Custom Views control to one of your toolbars. Select View⇨Toolbars⇨Customize. In the Customize dialog box, click the Commands tab. Select View from the Categories list and drag the Custom Views control to any toolbar. You can use this tool to quickly select a named view, and also to create new views (just type the name into the box and press Enter).

WARNING

For reasons known only to Microsoft, the View⇨Custom Views command is not available if your workbook contains a designated list (covered in Tip 129) created with the Data⇨ List command. In addition, the Custom Views tool becomes inoperable if the workbook contains a designated list.

Putting Advanced Filter Results on a Different Sheet

If you use Excel's Advanced Filter feature, you may have discovered that Excel is rather picky about where you choose to put the results.

Figure 132-1 shows an Advanced Filter operation in progress. Notice that the List Range and the Criteria Range are on the active sheet (Sheet1), but the user has specified Sheet2 as the Copy To range. Clicking the OK button results in an error message: *You can only copy filtered data to the active sheet.*

	A	B	C	D	E	F	G	H	I
1									
2		Name	Annual Salary	Monthly Salary	Location	Date Hired	Exempt		Location
3		Anthony Taylor	$55,500	$4,625	Los Angeles	5/2/1998	FALSE		Los Angeles
4		Charles S. Billings	$39,000				FALSE		
5		Chris Poundsworth	$29,850				FALSE		
6		Clark Bickerson	$120,000				TRUE		
7		Douglas Williams	$89,687				TRUE		
8		Ivan Silberstein	$95,000				TRUE		
9		James Millen	$27,690				FALSE		
10		Jeffrey P. Jones	$42,000				FALSE		
11		Joe Morrison	$24,000				FALSE		
12		John T. Foster	$39,500				FALSE		
13		Kurt Kamichoff	$48,000				FALSE		
14		Michael Hayden	$78,230				TRUE		
15		Phillip A. Todd	$29,500				FALSE		
16		Richard E. Card	$43,000				FALSE		
17		Rick Fogerty	$89,873				TRUE		
18		Robert H. Miller	$149,000				TRUE		
19		Stephen C. Carter	$44,123	$3,677	Los Angeles	9/29/2004	FALSE		
20		Steven H. Katz	$32,900	$2,742	Los Angeles	3/16/2000	FALSE		
21		Thomas E. Abbott	$60,000	$5,000	Los Angeles	4/12/1997	FALSE		
22		Tom Brown	$65,000	$5,417	Seattle	5/27/2000	TRUE		
23									

Advanced Filter dialog box overlaid:

Advanced Filter

Action
○ Filter the list, in-place
● Copy to another location

List range: $B$2:$G$22
Criteria range: $I$2:$I$3
Copy to: Sheet2!A1
☐ Unique records only

[OK] [Cancel]

Sheet1 / Sheet2 /

Figure 132-1: Specifying a different sheet as the Copy To range will cause an error.

Fortunately, there's a simple way around this meaningless limitation:

1. Start out on the sheet that will contain the results. If the List Range and Criteria Range are on Sheet1, and you want the results on Sheet2, just activate Sheet2 when you issue the Data⇨Filter⇨Advanced Filter command.

2. To specify the List Range and Criteria Range, click the sheet tab for Sheet1 and select the ranges.

3. Then, enter a range on the active sheet (Sheet2) for the Copy To range.

Comparing Two Ranges with Conditional Formatting

A common task is comparing two lists of items. Doing it manually is far too tedious and error-prone, but Excel can make it easy. This tip describes a method that uses conditional formatting.

Figure 133-1 shows an example of two multicolumn lists of words. Applying conditional formatting can make the differences in the lists become immediately apparent. These example lists contain text, but this technique also works with numeric data.

	A	B	C	D	E	F
1	Old List			New List		
2	Banish	Limber		Bemoan	Mister	
3	Bemoan	Module		Boyish	Mottos	
4	Boyish	Mottos		Chisel	Paints	
5	Coaxes	Paints		Coaxes	Plaids	
6	Covens	Plaids		Covens	Reverb	
7	Crumbs	Poison		Crumbs	Roared	
8	Dafter	Roared		Dafter	Rowels	
9	Draffy	Rowels		Eyelid	Scurvy	
10	Eyelid	Scurvy		Fixate	Sealed	
11	Fixate	Sealed		Ghetto	Smooch	
12	Friend	Smooch		Goalie	Spikes	
13	Ghetto	Thanks		Incite	Thanks	
14	Incite	Tutees		Knurly	Tutees	
15	Knurly	Upends		Lapels	Upends	
16	Lapels	Vested		Laptop	Vested	
17	Laptop	Waving		Legend	Wetter	
18	Licked	Wetter		Licked	Wished	
19	Lifer	Wishing		Limber	Wishing	
20						

Figure 133-1: You can use conditional formatting to highlight the differences in these two ranges.

The first list is in A2:B19, and this range is named OldList. The second list is in D2:E19, and the range is named NewList. The ranges were named by using the Insert➪Name➪Define command. Naming the ranges is not necessary, but it makes them easier to work with.

Start by formatting the old list:

1. Select the cells in the OldList range.
2. Choose Format➪Conditional Formatting to display the Conditional Formatting dialog box.
3. In the Conditional Formatting dialog box, use the drop-down list to choose Formula Is.
4. Enter this formula (see Figure 133-2):

   ```
   =COUNTIF(NewList,A2)=0
   ```

5. Click the Format button and specify the formatting to apply when the condition is true (a different colored background is a good choice).
6. Click OK.

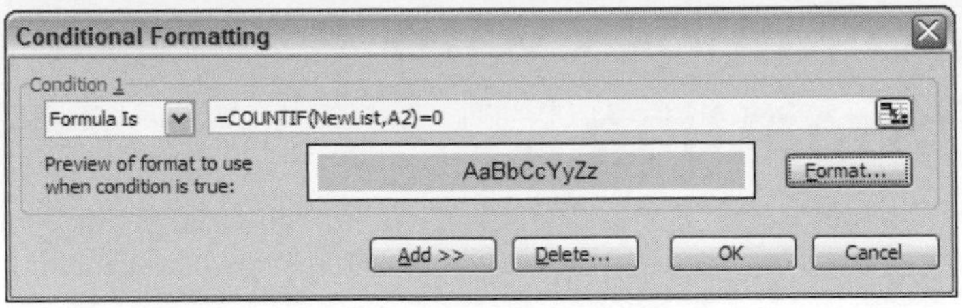

Figure 133-2: Applying conditional formatting.

The cells in the NewList range use a similar conditional formatting formula.

1. Select the cells in the NewList range.

2. Choose Format⇔Conditional Formatting.

3. In the Conditional Formatting dialog box, use the drop-down list to choose Formula Is.

4. Enter this formula:

   ```
   =COUNTIF(OldList,D2)=0
   ```

5. Click the Format button and specify the formatting to apply when the condition is true (another colored background).

6. Click OK.

Figure 133-3 shows the result. Cells that are in the old list but not in the new list are highlighted. In addition, cells in the new list that are not in the old list are highlighted in a different color.

Figure 133-3: Conditional formatting causes differences in the two lists to be highlighted.

Both of these conditional formatting formulas use the COUNTIF function. This function counts the number of times a particular value appears in a range. If the formula returns 0, it means that the item does not appear in the range. Therefore, the conditional formatting kicks in and the cell's background color is changed.

NOTE

The cell reference in the COUNTIF function should always be the upper-left cell of the selected range.

Part VII

Randomizing a List

This tip describes a quick method to randomize a list. It's like shuffling a deck of cards, and each row is a card.

Figure 134-1 shows a simple two-column list, arranged alphabetically by column A. The goal is to arrange the rows in random order.

	A	B	C	D
1	Artist	DVD		
2	Alanis Morissette	Jagged Little Pill, Live		
4	Alberta Hunter	My Castle's Rocking		
5	Animusic	Special Edition		
6	B.B. King	The Jazz Channel Presents B.B. King		
7	Blue Man Group	Audio		
8	Brian Setzer Orchestra	Live In Japan		
9	Cheryl Crow	Rockin' The Globe Live		
10	Dayna Kurtz	Postcards From Amsterdam		
11	Diana Krall	Live At The Montreal Jazz Festival		
12	Diana Krall	Live In Paris		
13	Eagles	Hell Freezes Over		
14	Eric Clapton	Live On Tour 2001		
15	Gillian Welch	The Revelator Collection		
16	J.J. Cale & Leon Russell	Sessions At The Paradise Studios		
17	James Taylor	Live At The Beacon Theatre		
18	John Prine	Live From Sessions At West 54th		
19	Joni Mitchell	Woman Of Heart And Mind		
20	Joni Mitchell	Painting With Words And Music		
21	Joni Mitchell	Shadows And Light		
22	Joni Mitchell	Refuge Of The Roads		
23	Keb' Mo'	Sessions At West 54th		
24	Keola Beamer	Ki Ho Alu		
25	King Crimson	Deja Vrooom		
26	Norah Jones	Live In 2004		
27	Norah Jones	Live In New Orleans		

Sheet1

Figure 134-1: This alphabetized list will be randomly arranged.

1. In cell C1, enter **Random**.

2. In cell C2, enter this formula:

```
=RAND()
```

3. Copy C2 down the column to accommodate the number of rows in the table.

4. Activate any cell in column C and click the Sort Ascending (or Sort Descending) button.

Now every time you sort column C, the list is randomly rearranged. Figure 134-2 shows the randomized list.

Part VII

	A	B	C	D
1	Artist	DVD	Rand	
2	Robert Earl Keen	Live From Austin TX	0.672589	
4	Blue Man Group	Audio	0.812118	
5	Keb' Mo'	Sessions At West 54th	0.22093	
6	Townes Van Zandt	Houston 1988	0.267919	
7	Eagles	Hell Freezes Over	0.178324	
8	Sting	The Brand New Day Tour	0.110535	
9	Sarah McLachlan	Mirrorball	0.046302	
10	Roger Waters	In The Flesh - Live	0.805536	
11	Joni Mitchell	Painting With Words And Music	0.993952	
12	Norah Jones	Live In New Orleans	0.163226	
13	Randy Travis	Live: It Was Just A Matter Of Time	0.851439	
14	Various	The Velvet Lounge	0.739035	
15	Dayna Kurtz	Postcards From Amsterdam	0.436699	
16	Diana Krall	Live At The Montreal Jazz Festival	0.643285	
17	Sade	Sade Live	0.083399	
18	Alanis Morissette	Jagged Little Pill, Live	0.007067	
19	Joni Mitchell	Refuge Of The Roads	0.445102	
20	Stevie Ray Vaughan	Live At The El Mocambo	0.024685	
21	John Prine	Live From Sessions At West 54th	0.454845	
22	B.B. King	The Jazz Channel Presents B.B. King	0.360979	
23	Alberta Hunter	My Castle's Rocking	0.347253	
24	Joni Mitchell	Woman Of Heart And Mind	0.540462	
25	Various	Naxos Musical Journey: Bach	0.147323	
26	J.J. Cale & Leon Russell	Sessions At The Paradise Studios	0.269819	
27	Steve Goodman	Live From Austin City Limits And More	0.835446	
28	Roy Orbison	Black & White Night	0.898032	

Figure 134-2: The list after being randomized.

Filling the Gaps in a Report

When you import data, you can end up with a worksheet that looks something like the one in Figure 135-1. This is a common type of report formatting. As you can see, an entry in column A applies to several rows of data. If you sort such a list, the missing data messes things up, and you can no longer tell who sold what.

	A	B	C	D	E
1					
2	Sales Rep	Month	Units Sold	Amount	
3	Jane	Jan	182	$15,101	
4		Feb	3350	$34,230	
5		Mar	114	$9,033	
6	George	Jan	135	$8,054	
7		Feb	401	$9,322	
8		Mar	357	$32,143	
9	Beth	Jan	509	$29,239	
10		Feb	414	$38,993	
11		Mar	53	$309	
12	Dan	Jan	323	$9,092	
13		Feb	283	$12,332	
14		Mar	401	$32,933	
15					
16					

Sheet1

Figure 135-1: This report contains gaps in the Sales Rep column.

If your list is small, you can enter the missing cell values manually or by using a series of Edit⇨Fill⇨Down operations. But if you have a large list that's in this format, you need a better way of filling in those cell values. Here's how:

1. Select the range that has the gaps (A3:A14 in this example).

2. Press Ctrl+G to display the Go To dialog box.

3. In the Go To dialog box, click Special.

4. Select the Blanks option.

5. In the formula bar, type = followed by the address of the first cell with an entry in the column (**=A3** in this example), and press Ctrl+Enter.

6. Reselect the range and choose Edit⇨Copy.

7. Select Edit⇨Paste Special, choose the Values option, and click OK.

After performing these steps, the gaps are filled in with the correct information, and your worksheet looks something like the one shown in Figure 135-2. Now it's a more traditional list, and you can do whatever you like with it — including sorting.

	A	B	C	D	E
1					
2	Sales Rep	Month	Units Sold	Amount	
3	Jane	Jan	182	$15,101	
4	Jane	Feb	3350	$34,230	
5	Jane	Mar	114	$9,033	
6	George	Jan	135	$8,054	
7	George	Feb	401	$9,322	
8	George	Mar	357	$32,143	
9	Beth	Jan	509	$29,239	
10	Beth	Feb	414	$38,993	
11	Beth	Mar	53	$309	
12	Dan	Jan	323	$9,092	
13	Dan	Feb	283	$12,332	
14	Dan	Mar	401	$32,933	
15					
16					

Sheet1

Figure 135-2: The gaps are gone, and this list can now be sorted.

Creating a List from a Summary Table

You may be familiar with Excel's PivotTable feature, which creates a summary table from a list. But what if you want to perform the opposite operation? This tip describes how to create a list from a simple two-variable summary table.

The worksheet shown in Figure 136-1 shows the type of transformation I'm talking about. Range A1:E13 contains the original summary table: 48 data points. Columns G:I show part of a 48-row database table derived from the summary table. In other words, every value in the original summary table gets converted to a row, which also contains the product name and month. This type of list is useful because it can be sorted and manipulated in other ways.

	A	B	C	D	E	F	G	H	I	J
1		Prod A	Prod B	Prod C	Prod D		Month	Product	Amount	
2	Jan	132	233	314	441		Jan	Prod A	132	
3	Feb	143	251	314	447		Jan	Prod B	233	
4	Mar	172	252	345	450		Jan	Prod C	314	
5	Apr	184	290	365	452		Jan	Prod D	441	
6	May	212	299	401	453		Feb	Prod A	143	
7	Jun	239	317	413	457		Feb	Prod B	251	
8	Jul	249	350	427	460		Feb	Prod C	314	
9	Aug	263	354	448	468		Feb	Prod D	447	
10	Sep	291	373	367	472		Mar	Prod A	172	
11	Oct	294	401	392	479		Mar	Prod B	252	
12	Nov	302	437	495	484		Mar	Prod C	345	
13	Dec	305	466	504	490		Mar	Prod D	450	
14							Apr	Prod A	184	
15							Apr	Prod B	290	
16							Apr	Prod C	365	
17							Apr	Prod D	452	
18							May	Prod A	212	

Sheet2 \ **Sheet1**

Figure 136-1: Converting a summary table to a list.

The trick to creating this "reverse PivotTable " is to *use* a PivotTable. The following steps are specific to the example data shown, but you can easily modify them to work with your data.

First, create the PivotTable as follows:

1. Activate any cell in your summary table.

2. Choose Data⇨PivotTable and PivotChart Report (the menu command may vary, depending on the version of Excel).

3. In the PivotTable and PivotChart Wizard dialog box, select the Multiple Consolidation Ranges option and click Next.

4. In Step 2 of the PivotTable and PivotChart Wizard dialog box, choose the I Will Create the Page Fields option and click Next.

5. In Step 2b, specify your summary table range in the Range field (A1:E13 for the sample data) and click Add. Click Next to move on to Step 3.

6. In Step 3, select a location for the PivotTable and click the Layout button.

7. In the Layout dialog box, you change the default layout in the diagram. Drag both the Column button and Row button away from the diagram. This leaves the diagram with only a data field: Sum of Value. The dialog box should look like Figure 136-2.

8. Click OK and then click Finish to create the PivotTable.

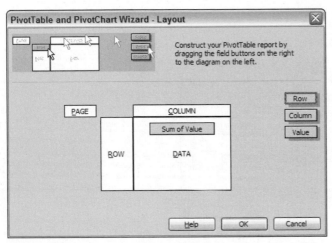

Figure 136-2: Creating a PivotTable from a summary table.

At this point, a small PivotTable shows only the sum of all values. This PivotTable is shown in Figure 136-3.

Sum of Value	Total
Total	17147

Figure 136-3: This small PivotTable can be expanded.

To finish up, double-click the cell that contains the total (17147 in this example). Excel creates a new sheet that displays the original data in the form of a much more useful list (see Figure 136-4).

The column headings display generic descriptions (Row, Column, and Value), so you probably want to change these headings to make them more descriptive.

	A	B	C	D	E
1	Row	Column	Value		
2	Jan	Prod A	132		
3	Jan	Prod B	233		
4	Jan	Prod C	314		
5	Jan	Prod D	441		
6	Feb	Prod A	143		
7	Feb	Prod B	251		
8	Feb	Prod C	314		
9	Feb	Prod D	447		
10	Mar	Prod A	172		
11	Mar	Prod B	252		
12	Mar	Prod C	345		
13	Mar	Prod D	450		
14	Apr	Prod A	184		
15	Apr	Prod B	290		
16	Apr	Prod C	365		
17	Apr	Prod D	452		
18	May	Prod A	212		
19	May	Prod B	299		
20	May	Prod C	401		
21	May	Prod D	453		

Sheet2 / Sheet1

Figure 136-4: The summary table has been successfully converted to a list.

Part VII

Finding Duplicates by Using Conditional Formatting

You might find it helpful to identify duplicate values within a range of cells. For example, take a look at Figure 137-1. Are any of the values duplicated?

One approach to identifying duplicate values is to use conditional formatting. This allows you to quickly spot the duplicated cell values.

	A	B	C	D	E	F	G
1	1,336	1,699	1,615	10	402	880	1,894
2	1,267	699	1,552	1,251	37	1,504	277
3	1,478	1,021	1,202	335	962	56	1,408
4	299	1,168	1,213	712	988	1,245	663
5	552	492	277	1,423	633	1,957	851
6	1,080	211	1,487	1,414	1,170	1,029	1,202
7	928	98	1,225	141	452	316	395
8	1,011	1,450	1,628	256	527	1,903	1,388
9	1,002	1,969	1,283	1,628	1,694	698	1,853
10	1,014	1,695	1,359	1,352	1,822	331	594
11	1,040	1,709	1,073	1,529	300	1,926	557
12	623	471	147	268	587	745	1,756
13	1,563	567	1,787	1,221	1,735	888	1,736
14	1,192	721	1,162	1,914	317	1,763	1,672
15	1,344	459	1,259	1,804	924	1,781	160
16	654	898	103	62	553	61	1,202
17	456	12	525	1,863	1,058	304	481
18	1,864	906	475	226	1,752	808	428
19	71	1,555	1,734	1,831	1,595	1,277	1,126
20	295	893	1,086	204	1,718	221	1,130
21	1,769	1,691	20	261	1,769	1,932	1,113
22	1,738	496	755	993	388	230	529
23							

◄ ◄ ► ►◄\ **Sheet1** /

Figure 137-1: You can use conditional formatting to quickly identify duplicate values in a range.

Here's how to set up the conditional formatting

1. Select the cells in the range (in this example, A1:G22).

2. Choose Format⇨Conditional Formatting to display the Conditional Formatting dialog box.

3. In the Conditional Formatting dialog box, use the drop-down list to choose Formula Is.

4. For this example, enter this formula (change the range references to correspond to your own data):

   ```
   =COUNTIF($A$1:$G$22,A1)>1
   ```

5. Click the Format button and specify the formatting to apply when the condition is true (changing the background pattern is a good choice).

6. Click OK.

Part VII

Figure 137-2 shows the result. Nine cells are highlighted. These are the duplicated values in the range.

	A	B	C	D	E	F	G
1	1,336	1,699	1,615	10	402	880	1,894
2	1,267	699	1,552	1,251	37	1,504	277
3	1,478	1,021	1,202	335	962	56	1,408
4	299	1,168	1,213	712	988	1,245	663
5	552	492	277	1,423	633	1,957	851
6	1,080	211	1,487	1,414	1,170	1,029	1,202
7	928	98	1,225	141	452	316	395
8	1,011	1,450	1,628	256	527	1,903	1,388
9	1,002	1,969	1,283	1,628	1,694	698	1,853
10	1,014	1,695	1,359	1,352	1,822	331	594
11	1,040	1,709	1,073	1,529	300	1,926	557
12	623	471	147	268	587	745	1,756
13	1,563	567	1,787	1,221	1,735	888	1,736
14	1,192	721	1,162	1,914	317	1,763	1,672
15	1,344	459	1,259	1,804	924	1,781	160
16	654	898	103	62	553	61	1,202
17	456	12	525	1,863	1,058	304	481
18	1,864	906	475	226	1,752	808	428
19	71	1,555	1,734	1,831	1,595	1,277	1,126
20	295	893	1,086	204	1,718	221	1,130
21	1,769	1,691	20	261	1,769	1,932	1,113
22	1,738	496	755	993	388	230	529
23							

Sheet1

Figure 137-2: Conditional formatting causes the duplicated cells to be highlighted.

You can extend this technique to identify entire rows within a list that are identical. The trick is to add a new column and use a formula that concatenates the data in each row. For example, if your list is in A2:G500, enter this formula in cell H2:

=A2&B2&C2&D2&E2&F2&G2

Copy the formula down the column and then apply the conditional formatting to the formulas in column H. In this case, the conditional formatting formula is

=COUNTIF($H$2:$H$500,H2)>1

Highlighted cells in column H indicate duplicated rows.

CROSS-REFERENCE

For more on conditional formatting, see Tip 133.

Preventing Row or Column Insertions within a Range

Excel is capable of recognizing lists — it just looks for a contiguous block of data. If you have a list of data, it's important that the list maintains its integrity. Inserting a blank row or column within the list can cause serious problems because Excel will no longer recognize the complete list. For example, if you attempt to sort a list after inserting a new column, not all of the columns will be sorted, and your data will be transformed into a jumbled mess.

This tip describes several ways to prevent users from inserting new rows or columns within a list. The approach you use depends on the version of Excel that you use.

Excel 2002 and Later

Beginning with Excel 2002, Microsoft made worksheet protection much more flexible. When you protect a worksheet, you can specify any of several options that determine what the user can do. Figure 138-1 shows the Protect Sheet dialog box, which is displayed when you select Tools⇨Protection⇨Protect Sheet.

Figure 138-1: In Excel 2002 and later, you can specify what can be done when the worksheet is protected.

To prevent users from inserting rows or column, you can protect the worksheet and make sure the Insert Columns and Insert Rows options are not checked. If you check all of the other options, the worksheet will work normally except for the inability to insert rows or columns.

For additional insurance, specify a password that will be required to unprotect the worksheet.

Part VII

NOTE

Keep in mind that worksheet password protection is not at all secure. Unprotecting a password-protected worksheet is simple to do in all versions of Excel.

Excel 2000 and Earlier

If you're using an earlier version of Excel, your only choice is to protect the worksheet. This, however, makes some other actions impossible because these versions do not have the protection flexibility of Excel 2002 and later.

Creating a Quick Frequency Tabulation

This tip describes a quick method for creating a frequency tabulation for a single column of data. Figure 139-1 shows a small part of a range that contains 18,000 state abbreviations. The state abbreviations occupy the range B2:B18001. The goal is to tally the number of times each item appears in the list.

Although you usually think of a PivotTable as a tool for summarizing multicolumn data, it's actually the perfect choice for this task.

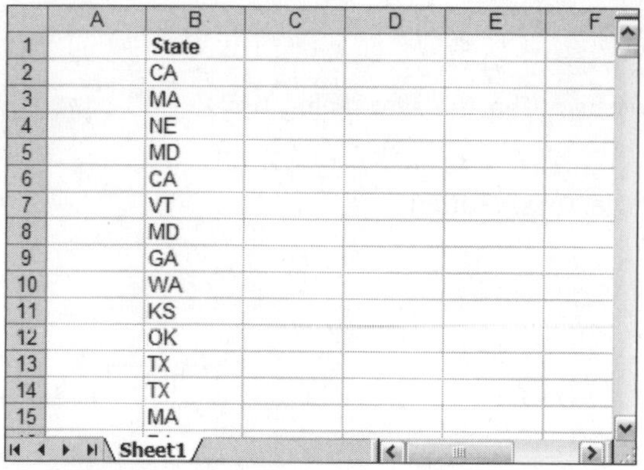

	A	B	C	D	E	F
1		State				
2		CA				
3		MA				
4		NE				
5		MD				
6		CA				
7		VT				
8		MD				
9		GA				
10		WA				
11		KS				
12		OK				
13		TX				
14		TX				
15		MA				

Figure 139-1: You can use a PivotTable to generate a frequency tabulation for these 18,000 state abbreviations.

Before you get started on this task, make sure that your data column has a heading. In this example, it's in cell B1.

Activate any cell in the data column and then follow these steps:

1. Select Data⇨PivotTable and PivotChart Report to display the PivotTable and PivotChart Wizard.
2. In Step 1, accept the defaults and click Next.
3. In Step 2, ensure that Excel has guessed the correct range and click Next.
4. In Step 3, click the Layout button to display the Layout dialog box.
5. In the Layout dialog box, drag the States button into the Row area of the diagram.
6. Drag the States button into the Data area. The dialog box should resemble Figure 139-2.
7. Click OK and then specify a location for the PivotTable.

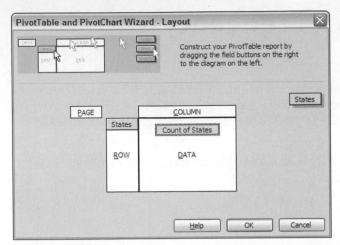

Figure 139-2: The Layout area in the PivotTable and PivotChart Wizard dialog box.

Figure 139-3 shows the result after sorting by the Total column.

	A	B	C	D	E	F
1		State		Count of State		
2		CA		State	Total	
3		MA		CA	2753	
4		NE		TX	1512	
5		MD		NY	1107	
6		CA		FL	876	
7		VT		IL	847	
8		MD		NJ	726	
9		GA		OH	650	
10		WA		PA	647	
11		KS		MI	590	
12		OK		VA	581	
13		TX		WA	579	
14		TX		MA	530	
15		MA		GA	507	
16		PA		MD	473	
17		CA		NC	460	
18		AL		CO	346	
19		MA		CT	330	

Figure 139-3: A quick PivotTable shows the frequency of each state abbreviation.

Controlling References to Cells within a PivotTable

If you work with PivotTables, you've probably noticed that if you write a formula that refers to a cell within the PivotTable, the cell reference is converted automatically to a GETPIVOTDATA function with a number of arguments. For example, a simple cell reference, such as =F32, might get converted to something like this:

```
=GETPIVOTDATA("Sales",$A$9,"SalesRep","Robinson","Month","Q1")
```

If you prefer to avoid this automatic conversion, you can use absolute references for cells within a PivotTable. Instead of =F32, use =$F$32.

You can also turn off the Generate GetPivotData option, but Excel makes this operation very difficult because the only way to do it is by using a toolbar button that's not normally displayed. The PivotTable toolbar would be the perfect place for this button, but it's not there.

To add the Generate GetPivotData toolbar button to your PivotTable toolbar, follow these steps:

1. Make sure the PivotTable toolbar is displayed.

2. Choose View⇨Toolbars⇨Customize to display the Customize dialog box.

3. In the Customize dialog box, click the Commands tab.

4. Select Data from the Categories list.

5. Locate Generate GetPivotData in the Commands list.

6. Drag the Generate GetPivotData item to your PivotTable toolbar.

7. Click Close to dismiss the Customize dialog box.

The Generate GetPivotData button is a toggle. Click it once, and Excel stops generating GETPIVOTTABLE formulas. Click it again, and Excel starts generating those formulas again.

Part VII

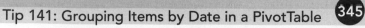

Grouping Items by Date in a PivotTable

One of the more useful features of a PivotTable is the ability to combine items into groups. Grouping items is simple: Select them, right-click, and choose Group and Outline⇨Group from the shortcut menu that appears.

You can go a step further, though. When a field contains dates, Excel can create groups automatically. This is a great feature that many users overlook. Figure 141-1 shows a portion of a simple list with two fields: Date and Sales. This list has 370 records and covers dates between June 1, 2004 and October 31, 2005. The goal is to summarize the sales information by month.

	A	B	C
1	Date	Sales	
2	6/1/2004	1,344	
3	6/2/2004	1,189	
4	6/3/2004	1,023	
5	6/4/2004	998	
6	6/7/2004	1,384	
7	6/8/2004	1,156	
8	6/9/2004	1,185	
9	6/10/2004	1,256	
10	6/11/2004	1,030	
11	6/14/2004	641	
12	6/15/2004	1,475	
13	6/16/2004	792	
14	6/17/2004	1,200	
15	6/18/2004	1,187	
16	6/21/2004	532	
17	6/22/2004	787	
18	6/23/2004	1,193	
19	6/24/2004	1,233	
20	6/25/2004	675	
21	6/28/2004	691	

Figure 141-1: You can use a PivotTable to summarize the sales data by month.

Figure 141-2 shows part of a PivotTable created from the data. Not surprisingly, it looks exactly like the input data because the dates have not been grouped. To group the items by month, right-click the Date heading and select Group and Show Detail⇨Group.

You see the Grouping dialog box shown in Figure 141-3. In the list box, select Months and Years, and verify that the starting and ending dates are correct. Click OK.

The Date items in the PivotTable are grouped by years and by months (as shown in Figure 141-4).

Figure 141-2: The PivotTable, before grouping by Months and Years.

Figure 141-3: Use the Grouping dialog box to group items in a PivotTable.

NOTE

If you select *only* Months in the Grouping list box, months in different years combine together. For example, the June item would display sales for both 2004 and 2005. Notice that the Grouping dialog box contains other time-based units. For example, you can group the data into quarters.

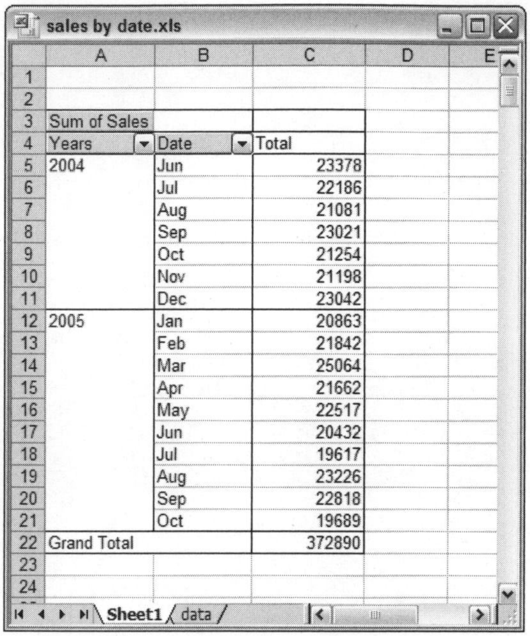

	A	B	C	D	E
	sales by date.xls				
1					
2					
3	Sum of Sales				
4	Years ▼	Date ▼	Total		
5	2004	Jun	23378		
6		Jul	22186		
7		Aug	21081		
8		Sep	23021		
9		Oct	21254		
10		Nov	21198		
11		Dec	23042		
12	2005	Jan	20863		
13		Feb	21842		
14		Mar	25064		
15		Apr	21662		
16		May	22517		
17		Jun	20432		
18		Jul	19617		
19		Aug	23226		
20		Sep	22818		
21		Oct	19689		
22	Grand Total		372890		
23					
24					

Sheet1 / data

Figure 141-4: The PivotTable, after grouping by Months and Years.

Hiding the Field Buttons in a PivotChart

If you use PivotTables, you may have experimented with PivotCharts, and you probably noticed something right away: PivotCharts are great because they're so flexible. When you rearrange your data in a PivotTable, the associated PivotChart also changes.

But there's a problem. PivotCharts are ugly! Who wants to see those field buttons, anyway? Figure 142-1 shows a typical PivotChart. It's not exactly something you want to present in the boardroom.

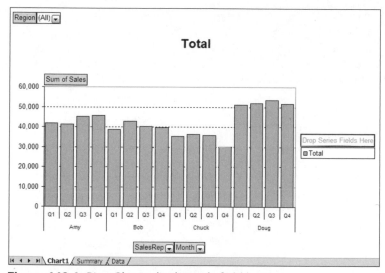

Figure 142-1: PivotCharts display ugly field buttons.

I used PivotCharts for quite a while before I figured out that you can hide those field buttons. Just right-click any of the field buttons and choose Hide PivotChart Field Buttons. Figure 142-2 shows a PivotChart that's a bit more presentable.

 WARNING

But there's one problem: After the field buttons are hidden, there's no way to get them back. So if you need to rearrange the fields, you need to do so in the original PivotTable.

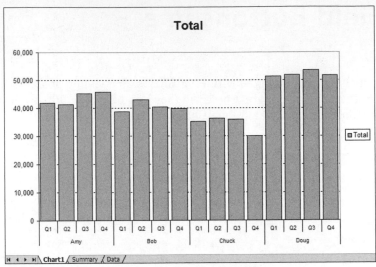

Figure 142-2: A PivotChart after hiding the field buttons.

Part VIII

Working with Files

In this part, you'll find tips that deal with files — information that every Excel user should know (but many don't).

Tips and Where to Find Them

Tip 143 Importing a Text File into a
Worksheet Range   353

Tip 144 Getting Data from a
Web Page   355

Tip 145 Displaying a Workbook's
Full Path   359

Tip 146 Saving a Preview of Your
Workbook   361

Tip 147 Using Document Properties   363

Tip 148 Learning Who Opened a
File Last   365

Tip 149 Finding the Missing
No To All Button When
Closing Files   367

Tip 150 Getting a List of Filenames   369

Tip 151 Understanding Excel's
Passwords   371

Tip 152 Using Workspace Files   373

Tip 153 Reducing the Size of a
Workbook   375

Importing a Text File into a Worksheet Range

If you need to insert a text file into a specific range in a worksheet, you might think that your only choice is to import the text (by choosing File⇨Open), and then to copy the data and paste it to the range where you want it to appear. Actually, there's a more direct way to do it.

Figure 143-1 shows a small CSV (comma separated value) file. The following instructions describe how to import this file, named `monthly.csv`, beginning at cell C4.

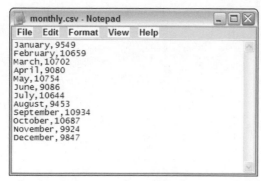

Figure 143-1: This CSV file will be imported into a range.

1. Select Data⇨Import External Data⇨Import Data to display the Select Data Source dialog box.

2. Navigate to the directory that contains the text file.

3. Select the file from the list, and then click the Open button to display the Text Import Wizard.

4. Use the Text Import Wizard to specify how the data will be imported. For a CSV file, specify Delimited, with a Comma Delimiter.

5. Click the Finish button, and Excel displays the Import Data dialog box.

6. In the Import Data dialog box, click the Properties button to display the External Data Range Properties dialog box.

7. In the External Data Range Properties dialog box, remove the check mark from Save Query Definition, and click OK to return to the Import Data dialog box.

8. In the Import Data dialog box, specify the location for the imported data (it can be a cell in an existing worksheet or a new worksheet).

9. Click OK, and Excel imports the data (see Figure 143-2).

Part VIII

NOTE

You can ignore Step 7 if the data that you're importing will be changing. By saving the query definition, you can quickly update the imported data by right-clicking any cell in the range and choosing Refresh Data.

	A	B	C	D	E	F
1						
2						
3						
4			January	9549		
5			February	10659		
6			March	10702		
7			April	9080		
8			May	10754		
9			June	9086		
10			July	10644		
11			August	9453		
12			September	10934		
13			October	10687		
14			November	9924		
15			December	9847		
16						
17						
18						
19						
20						

monthly report.xls — Sheet1

Figure 143-2: This range contains data imported directly from a CSV file.

Getting Data from a Web Page

This tip describes three ways to capture data contained on a Web page: Pasting a static copy of the information, creating a refreshable link to the site, and opening the page directly in Excel.

Pasting Static Information

One approach is to simply highlight the text in your browser, press Ctrl+C to copy it to the Clipboard, and then paste it into Excel. The results will vary, depending on what browser you use. If you use Microsoft Internet Explorer, the pasted results will probably look very similar to the original — complete with formatting, hyperlinks, and graphics.

If you use a browser other than Internet Explorer, selecting Edit⇨Paste will probably put everything you copied from the Web page into a single cell — probably not what you want. The solution is to choose Edit⇨Paste Special, and then select the Text option. The result will be plain text (no formatting, hyperlinks, or graphics).

Pasting Refreshable Information

If you need to access updated data from a Web page on a regular basis, you'll want to create a Web Query. Figure 144-1 shows a Web site that contains currency exchange rates.

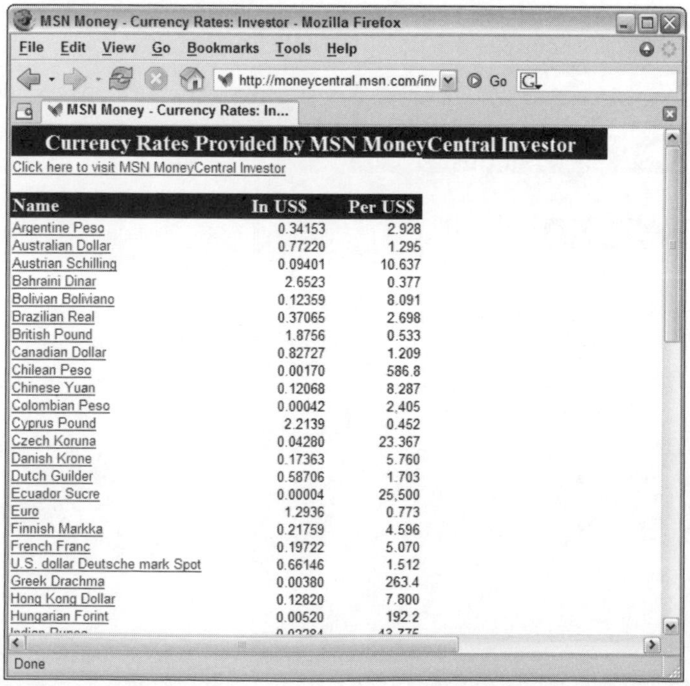

Figure 144-1: This site contains information that changes frequently.

Part VIII

The instructions that follow create a Web Query that will allow this information to be refreshed with a single mouse click:

1. Select Data⇨Import External Data⇨New Web Query to display the New Web Query dialog box.

2. In the Address field, enter the URL of the Web site. For this example, the URL for the Web page shown in Figure 144-1 is

   `http://moneycentral.msn.com/investor/external/excel/rates.asp`

   Notice that the New Web Query dialog box contains a mini-browser. You can click links and navigate the Web site until you locate the data you're interested in.

3. When a Web page is displayed in the New Web Query dialog box, you'll see one or more yellow arrows, which correspond to the tables in the Web page. Click an arrow, and it turns into a green check box, which indicates that the data in that table will be imported. You can import as many tables as you need. The example Web site has only one table (see Figure 144-2).

4. Click the Import button to display the Import Data dialog box.

5. In the Import Data dialog box, specify the location for the imported data (it can be a cell in an existing worksheet or a new worksheet).

6. Click OK, and Excel imports the data (see Figure 144-3).

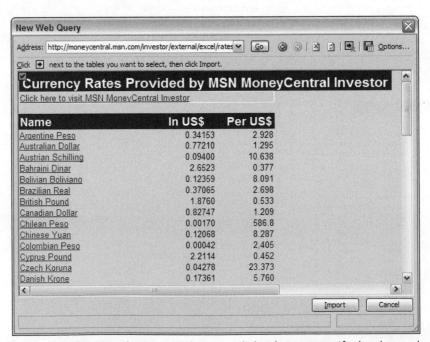

Figure 144-2: Using the New Web Query dialog box to specify the data to be imported.

	A	B	C	D
1	Currency Rates Provided by MSN MoneyCentral Investor			
2	Click here to visit MSN MoneyCentral Investor			
3				
4	Name	In US$	Per US$	
5	Argentine Peso	0.34153	2.928	
6	Australian Dollar	0.7711	1.297	
7	Austrian Schilling	0.09381	10.66	
8	Bahraini Dinar	2.6523	0.377	
9	Bolivian Boliviano	0.12359	8.091	
10	Brazilian Real	0.37065	2.698	
11	British Pound	1.8757	0.533	
12	Canadian Dollar	0.82734	1.209	
13	Chilean Peso	0.0017	586.8	
14	Chinese Yuan	0.12068	8.287	
15	Colombian Peso	0.00042	2405	
16	Cyprus Pound	2.2134	0.452	
17	Czech Koruna	0.04279	23.371	
18	Danish Krone	0.1736	5.761	
19	Dutch Guilder	0.58703	1.704	
20	Ecuador Sucre	0.00004	25500	

Figure 144-3: The data, imported from a Web page.

By default, the imported data is a Web Query. To refresh the information, right-click any cell in the imported range and choose Refresh Data from the shortcut menu. If you don't want to create a refreshable query, you specify this in Step 5 of the preceding step list. In the Import Data dialog box, click the Properties button and remove the check mark from Save Query Definition.

Opening the Web Page Directly

Yet another way to get Web page data into a worksheet is to open the URL directly, using Excel's File➪Open command. Just enter the complete URL into the File Name field and click Open. Figure 144-4 shows the MSN currency rate page opened in Excel.

	A	B	C	D	E
1	**Currency Rates Provided by MSN MoneyCentral Investor**				
2	Click here to visit MSN MoneyCentral Investor				
3					
4	**Name**	**In US$**	**Per US$**		
5	Argentine Peso	0.34188	2.925		
6	Australian Dollar	0.7733	1.293		
7	Austrian Schilling	0.09422	10.614		
8	Bahraini Dinar	2.6523	0.377		
9	Bolivian Boliviano	0.12359	8.091		
10	Brazilian Real	0.37411	2.673		
11	British Pound	1.8878	0.53		
12	Canadian Dollar	0.82645	1.21		
13	Chilean Peso	0.00171	586		
14	Chinese Yuan	0.12068	8.287		
15	Colombian Peso	0.00042	2372		
16	Cyprus Pound	2.2163	0.451		
17	Czech Koruna	0.04314	23.181		
18	Danish Krone	0.17393	5.749		
19	Dutch Guilder	0.58827	1.7		
20	Ecuador Sucre	0.00004	25500		

Figure 144-4: This Web page was opened directly in Excel.

Displaying a Workbook's Full Path

If you have lots of files open in Excel, you may have a need to know the full path of the active workbook. Oddly, Excel provides no direct way to get this information.

You can always issue the File⇨Save As command. Excel will propose that you save the file in its current directory. But even then, the Save As dialog box doesn't actually display the full path of the workbook.

The solution is simple — but certainly not very intuitive. Just display the Web toolbar. This toolbar has a control called Address, which displays the full path of the active workbook (see Figure 145-1).

Figure 145-1: The Address control in the Web toolbar displays the full path of the active workbook.

You can, of course, put that Address control on a different toolbar. Choose View⇨ Toolbars⇨Customize to display the Customize dialog box. Click the Commands tab, select Web from the Categories list, and locate the Address control in the Commands list. Then drag the control to any toolbar.

Saving a Preview of Your Workbook

When you open a workbook (using the Open dialog box), you have a number of options regarding how the files are displayed. You can change how the file display looks by clicking the arrow on the Views icon in the Open dialog box. You can choose from among the following options:

- **Thumbnails:** Shows each filename with a large icon (this option is more appropriate for graphic images).

- **Tiles:** Shows each filename with an icon, along with the file type and size.

- **Icons:** Similar to Tiles, but the file type and size are not displayed.

- **List:** Shows the filenames with no other information.

- **Details:** Shows the filenames, along with other information. You can sort the list by clicking any of the column headers.

- **Properties:** Displays information about the selected file. If you've entered any information in the Properties dialog box (displayed when you choose File⇨Properties), that information is also displayed.

- **Preview:** Displays a preview of the file (if you've specified that option in the Properties dialog box). Figure 146-1 shows an example.

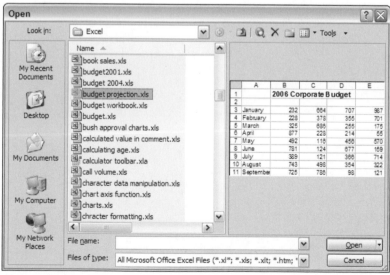

Figure 146-1: Using the Preview option can make it easier to locate workbooks.

The Preview option can be useful if you know what a workbook looks like, but you can't remember the filename. But it's not at all useful if you don't remember to save the preview picture. To save a preview picture for the active workbook, choose File⇨Properties to display the Properties dialog box. Click the Summary tab, and place a check mark next to the Save Preview Picture option.

The workbook will then contain a picture of the upper-left corner of the first sheet in the workbook. The picture is updated when the file is saved.

NOTE

If the workbook requires a password to open it, the preview is not shown.

Unfortunately, Excel offers no way to enable this feature for all of your workbooks. If you want a preview picture, you must specify it manually for each file. Or you can create a `book.xlt` template that has the Save Preview Picture setting enabled.

CROSS-REFERENCE

See Tip 12 for instructions on customizing the default workbook.

Using Document Properties

If you have many Excel files, one of the best organizational tools at your disposal is the File Properties dialog box, which contains a number of fields that help describe a particular workbook file. If you fill in the fields, you can later search for files using this information.

Figure 147-1 shows the Summary tab of the File Properties dialog box. Access this dialog box by selecting File➪Properties.

database.xls Properties

General | **Summary** | Statistics | Contents | Custom

Title: 2006 Budget

Subject: Budgeting

Author: John Walkenbach

Manager:

Company: J-Walk & Associates

Category: Accounting

Keywords: budget, 2006

Comments: Based on the budget.xlt template

Hyperlink base:

Template:

☑ Save preview picture

OK   Cancel

Figure 147-1: The Summary tab of the File Properties dialog box.

Part VIII

If you click the Custom tab in the Properties dialog box, you'll find many additional categories, and you can even create your own categories.

Using this tool takes some discipline. But if you get in the habit of entering the information when you save a workbook, it will pay off in the long run. To help you remember to use this dialog box, you can tell Excel to display it automatically when you save a workbook the first time. To do so, select Tools➪Options to display the Options dialog box. In the Options dialog box, click the General tab, and select the Prompt for Workbook Properties check box.

To search for files using the information in the file properties, select File➪File Search. Excel displays the Advanced File Search controls in the task pane (see Figure 147-2).

Figure 147-2: Excel's Advanced File Search options appear in the task pane.

Learning Who Opened a File Last

This tip is, perhaps, more interesting than useful. It describes a way to find out who was the last person to open a particular workbook file. The method works even if the person opened the workbook and closed it immediately, without making any changes or saving it. The only exception that I've found is if the file is read-only. For those types of files, this technique will not work.

The trick is to open the workbook using a text editor (or a hex editor). Figure 148-1 shows an example of a workbook file that I downloaded from the Internet and opened in Windows Notepad. It happens to be a workbook created by Jon Peltier. Notice that Jon's name is embedded in the file?

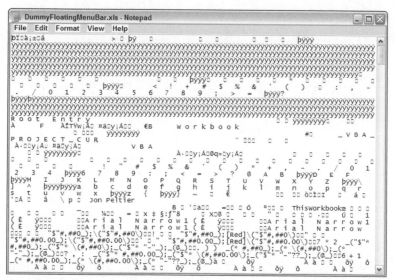

Figure 148-1: The name of the last person to open a workbook is embedded in an Excel workbook.

Next, I opened that workbook in Excel and then closed it immediately. The file's date and time did not change because I didn't save it. Figure 148-2 shows the workbook after I opened it in Notepad. As you can see, my name replaced Jon's.

The exact location of the embedded name will vary, but it's always near the top of the file. Presumably, this is how Excel keeps track of the file reservations.

The name embedded in the file is the username that appears in the General tab of the Options dialog box. So, obviously, if a person opens the file using someone else's computer, the name will not be correct.

Part VIII

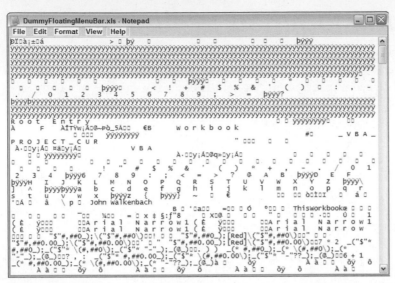

Figure 148-2: The name of the last person to open a workbook is embedded in an Excel workbook.

Finding the Missing No To All Button When Closing Files

Assume that you have a dozen or so workbooks open, and you want to close Excel without saving any of your changes. Excel will display the dialog box shown in Figure 149-1. And it does it for every changed workbook that is open.

Figure 149-1: Excel displays this prompt for every unsaved file.

As you can see, this dialog box has a Yes To All button, but it lacks a No To All button. Here's the secret: Press Shift while you click the No button. That functions exactly like clicking a No To All button — if one existed.

By the way, this tip works in many of the Windows dialog boxes as well. For example, if you're copying a group of files and some of the files already exist, Windows makes you verify your overwrite intentions. That dialog box also lacks a No To All button, but you can use the Shift+clicking the No button trick.

Part VIII

Getting a List of Filenames

Putting a list of filenames into a worksheet range should be fairly straightforward, right? Just instruct Windows to generate a list of files for a directory, and then import it into an Excel worksheet. Unfortunately, it's not that easy. Most users are surprised to discover that Windows does not provide a direct way to export a list of filenames to a file.

To generate an importable list of files, you need to go back in time and use an old-fashioned command line interface.

The following instructions assume that you want to generate a list of files contained in the `c:\my files\excel files` directory:

1. Choose Start⇨Run, type **cmd**, and click OK. This displays the Windows command shell.

2. Navigate to the directory that you're interested in by typing **cd**, followed by the full path. In this example, enter:

   ```
   cd c:\my files\excel files
   ```

3. Type the following command and press Enter:

   ```
   dir >filelist.txt
   ```

Figure 150-1 shows what the command prompt window looks like as you go through the preceding steps.

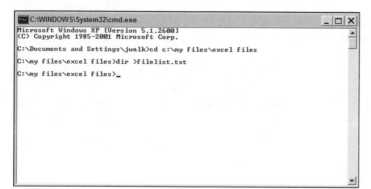

Figure 150-1: Using the Windows command prompt to generate a list of files.

Windows will create a file named `filelist.txt` in the current directory (the one you specified in Step 2). You can then use Excel's File⇨Open command to import this file, which will start the File Import Wizard (make sure that you specify fixed-width data). Figure 150-2 shows some data that I imported.

	A	B	C	D	E
	filelist.txt				
1	Volume in	drive C h	as no labe	l.	
2	Volume Se	rial Numbe	r is F08D-	900C	
3					
4	Directory	of C:\my	files\exce	l files	
5					
6	3/30/2005	2:08 PM	<DIR>		.
7	3/30/2005	2:08 PM	<DIR>		..
8	1/20/2003	3:35 PM		13,824	2003 budget.xls
9	5/12/2003	8:50 AM		92,672	addresses.xls
10	1/21/2003	4:58 PM		35,328	background.xls
11	7/21/2003	10:26 AM		56,320	bank accounts.xls
12	1/16/2003	7:27 PM		17,408	book sales.xls
13	9/12/2002	2:50 PM		14,848	brk-900.xls
14	3/25/2003	11:37 AM		29,184	budget workbook.xls
15	5/7/2003	6:21 PM		34,816	budget.xls
16	3/24/2003	5:34 PM		14,848	call volume.xls
17	12/31/2002	8:41 AM		143,360	cash accounts.xls
18	2/15/2003	11:24 AM		18,432	charts.xls
19	3/25/2003	11:37 AM		29,184	Copy of budget workbook.xls
20	6/28/2003	9:59 AM		15,360	data.xls
21	2/9/2003	7:36 AM		15,872	econ analysis.xls
22	9/9/2002	7:21 AM		17,920	file1.xls
23	9/9/2002	7:30 AM		14,336	file2.xls
24	3/30/2005	2:08 PM		0	filelist.txt
25	6/6/2003	11:40 AM		14,848	financial projects.xls
26	1/21/2003	2:04 PM		13,824	fonts.xls
27	1/21/2003	2:11 PM		14,848	frank and jill.xls
28	1/23/2003	6:34 PM		13,824	intersection.xls
29	5/30/2003	4:39 PM		15,360	map.xls

Figure 150-2: This file listing was imported from a text file.

As you can see, the listing needs to be cleaned up a bit, but all of the information is there, including the date, time, and size of each file.

NOTE

The dir command has quite a few options. For example, you can get a list of the files in all of the subdirectories as well as the current directory. Do an online search for *dos commands,* and you'll find lots of information about the dir command.

Understanding Excel's Passwords

Excel provides several ways to "protect" your work using passwords. That word is in quotation marks because using passwords offers no real protection. You can enter a password in five places in Excel:

- The Protect Sheet dialog box (accessed by choosing Tools⇨Protection⇨Protect Sheet)

- The Protect Workbook dialog box (accessed by choosing Tools⇨Protection⇨Protect Workbook)

- The Protect Shared Workbook dialog box (accessed by choosing Tools⇨Protection⇨Protect and Share Workbook)

- The Save Options dialog box (accessed by choosing File⇨Save As, and then by choosing Tools⇨General Options in the Save As dialog box)

- The Protection tab of the Project Properties dialog box (accessed in the Visual Basic Editor by choosing Tools⇨VBAProject Properties)

Many users assume that password protection is a way to make their work secure, protecting all or parts of it from those who don't know the password. The truth is that anyone who knows the secret can crack all of Excel's passwords.

The moral of this story: If you're looking for a way to keep your data secure, assigning a password in Excel is not the solution.

Using Workspace Files

If you have a project that uses multiple workbooks, you probably get tired of opening the same files every time you work on the project.

The solution? Create a workspace file:

1. Open all the files used for your project.

2. Arrange the windows the way you like them.

3. Select File⇨Save Workspace to display the Save Workspace dialog box.

4. Excel proposes the name `resume.xlw`, but you can specify any name you like.

5. Click Save, and the workspace file is created.

After creating a workspace file, you can open it by choosing File⇨Open. In the Open dialog box, specify Workspaces (*.xlw) in the Files of Type drop-down list.

NOTE

It's important to understand that a workspace file contains only the filenames and window position information. It does not contain the actual workbooks.

Part VIII

Reducing the Size of a Workbook

If you have a workbook that's been around a long time and undergoes lots of changes, you may notice that the file continues to increase in size, even though you're not adding much new information to it. This is sometimes known as *file bloat*.

In many cases, you can significantly reduce the size of a workbook file by "round-tripping" it as an HTML file. Here's how to do it:

1. Make a backup copy of your original workbook.

2. Open your workbook.

3. Choose File⇨Save as Web Page to display the Save As dialog box.

4. Select the Entire Workbook option and click Save.

5. Close your workbook.

6. Choose File⇨Open to open the HTML file you just saved. Examine it carefully to make sure that everything works properly.

If the file imported accurately, choose File⇨Save As again, and then save it as a normal workbook file. Using this technique, I've been able to reduce the size of some workbooks by more than 50 percent.

Part IX

Printing

We haven't quite reached the "paperless office" yet, so it's still important to get your work on paper in a way that looks good. The tips in this part deal with printing and previewing your work.

Tips and Where to Find Them

Tip 154   Controlling What Gets
Printed   379

Tip 155   Displaying Repeating Rows
or Columns on a Printout   381

Tip 156   Printing Noncontiguous
Ranges on a Single Page   383

Tip 157   Preventing Objects from
Printing   385

Tip 158   Page Numbering Tips   387

Tip 159   Previewing Page Breaks   389

Tip 160   Adding and Removing
Page Breaks   391

Tip 161   Printing to a PDF File   393

Tip 162   Avoiding Printing
Specific Rows   395

Tip 163   Making Your Printout Fit
on One Page   397

Tip 164   Printing Formulas   399

Tip 165   Copying Page Setup Settings
Across Sheets   401

Tip 166   Using Custom Views for
Printing   403

Controlling What Gets Printed

When you click the Print button on the Standard toolbar, Excel prints the entire contents of the active worksheet. But sometimes, you want a bit more control over what gets sent to your printer. This tip describes various ways to control how Excel prints a worksheet.

Printing All Sheets

To print all sheets (worksheets and chart sheets), select File⇨Print to display the Print dialog box. In the Print What section, select the Entire Workbook option, and then click OK.

Printing Specific Sheets

If you want to print only certain sheets in your workbook, press Ctrl, and then click the sheet tabs of the sheets to be printed. Then click the Print button on the Formatting toolbar.

Setting the Print Area for a Worksheet

To print only a specific range on a worksheet, select the range, and then choose File⇨ Print Area⇨Set Print Area.

The print area can also consist of a noncontiguous range (that is, a multiple selection). To select multiple ranges, press Ctrl while you select the range. Then choose File⇨ Print Area⇨Set Print Area. Each range will be printed beginning on a new page.

Another way to accomplish this (without changing the sheet's print area) is to select the range(s) to be printed. Then select File⇨Print, select the Selection option in the Print What section of the Print dialog box, and click OK.

Printing Specific Pages

If you're printing a lengthy report, you may discover an error on one or more pages. It's not necessary to reprint the entire report after you've corrected any errors. You can print only specific pages by following these steps:

1. Choose File⇨Print to display the Print dialog box.

2. In the Print Range section, select the Page(s) option and enter the beginning and ending page numbers. For example, to print only page 25, enter **25** in both the From field and the To field.

3. Click OK to print the specified page(s).

If you're not sure which pages you need to print, click the Print Preview button to preview the print job.

Part IX

Displaying Repeating Rows or Columns on a Printout

You may be familiar with Excel's Window⇨Freeze Panes command, which allows you to specify rows and/or columns that will remain fixed while you scroll the worksheet.

The Window⇨Freeze Panes command has no effect on printed output. If you would like your printout to display one or more fixed rows at the top and/or one or more fixed columns along the left, you need to set this up separately as follows:

1. Select File⇨Page Setup to display the Page Setup dialog box.

2. In the Page Setup dialog box, click the Sheet tab.

3. To specify one or more rows to repeat at the top, click the box in the far right of the Rows to Repeat at Top field, and then point to the rows in your worksheet.

4. To specify one or more columns to repeat at the left, click the box in the far right of the Columns to Repeat at Left field, and then point to the columns in your worksheet.

5. Click OK to close the Page Setup dialog box, and then print the worksheet.

CROSS-REFERENCE
See Tip 154 for more about printing.

Part IX

Printing Noncontiguous Ranges on a Single Page

If you need to print several different ranges, Excel will always start printing each range on a separate sheet of paper. This tip describes a technique that allows you to print multiple ranges on a single page.

The trick involves taking a picture of each of the ranges to be printed, and then arranging these pictures on a separate worksheet. Excel has a perfect tool for the job: the Camera tool. But, for some reason, Microsoft keeps it rather hidden.

Breaking Out the Camera Tool

To make the Camera tool accessible, follow these steps:

1. Select View⇨Toolbars⇨Customize to display the Customize dialog box.

2. In the Customize dialog box, click the Commands tab.

3. Select Tools from the Categories list.

4. Locate Camera in the Commands list, and drag the command to any toolbar.

5. Click Close to close the Customize dialog box.

The Camera tool creates a linked picture of a range. Therefore, if the data in the linked range changes, the picture updates automatically.

Figure 156-1 shows a worksheet. The goal is to print two ranges (A3:C10 and E13:G20) on a single page.

Shooting with the Camera

The following steps show you how to use the Camera tool to print multiple ranges on one piece of paper:

1. Make sure that the Camera tool is available on a toolbar (see the preceding steps if it's not).

2. Insert a new worksheet to hold the linked pictures (Sheet2).

3. Select A3:C10, and click the Camera tool.

4. Activate Sheet2 and click to insert the linked picture.

5. Return to the previous worksheet, select E13:G20, and click the Camera tool.

6. Activate Sheet2 and click to insert the linked picture.

7. Use your mouse to arrange the linked pictures any way you like. You might want to turn off the gridline display in the worksheet that holds the linked pictures.

	A	B	C	D	E	F	G	H
1	**Call Volume Stats**							
2								
3	Date	Calls	Weekday		235	75	7	
4	3/1	254	Tuesday		66	942	342	
5	3/2	265	Wednesday		571	57	476	
6	3/3	211	Thursday		66	630	947	
7	3/4	190	Friday		211	157	434	
8	3/5	225	Saturday		890	11	84	
9	3/6	175	Sunday		681	778	616	
10	3/7	266	Monday		658	786	982	
11								
12								
13	978	533	838		Date	Calls	Weekday	
14	894	983	308		4/1	254	Friday	
15	400	50	745		4/2	265	Saturday	
16	908	160	506		4/3	211	Sunday	
17	964	411	383		4/4	190	Monday	
18	768	230	283		4/5	225	Tuesday	
19	134	462	809		4/6	175	Wednesday	
20	163	968	491		4/7	266	Thursday	
21								

Sheet1 / Sheet2 /

Figure 156-1: It's not normally possible to print ranges A3:C10 and E13:G20 on a single page.

Figure 156-2 shows the worksheet that contains the linked pictures. If the data in Sheet1 changes, the linked pictures will update. When you print Sheet2, both of the ranges will appear on the same page.

	A	B	C	D	E
1					
2	Date	Calls	Weekday		
3	3/1	254	Tuesday		
4	3/2	265	Wednesday		
5	3/3	211	Thursday		
6	3/4	190	Friday		
7	3/5	225	Saturday		
8	3/6	175	Sunday		
9	3/7	266	Monday		
10					
11	Date	Calls	Weekday		
12	4/1	254	Friday		
13	4/2	265	Saturday		
14	4/3	211	Sunday		
15	4/4	190	Monday		
16	4/5	225	Tuesday		
17	4/6	175	Wednesday		
18	4/7	266	Thursday		
19					

Sheet1 \ Sheet2 /

Figure 156-2: Using linked pictures makes it possible to print the two ranges on a single page.

 NOTE

You can create a linked picture without using the Camera tool. Select the range and choose Edit➪Copy. Press the Shift key and choose Edit➪Paste Picture Link (this command is available only when the Shift key is pressed). The result is a linked picture of the original range. You can move this picture anywhere you like.

Preventing Objects from Printing

You can place a wide variety of objects on a worksheet — charts, Autoshapes, pictures, controls, and so on. By default, all of these objects will print when you print the worksheet.

To prevent a particular object from printing, right-click the object and choose Format *xxxx* from the shortcut menu. (The *xxxx* represents the type of object; for example, if you right-click a picture, select Format Picture from the shortcut menu.) In the Format dialog box that appears, click the Properties tab and remove the check mark from the Print Object option (see Figure 157-1).

Figure 157-1: Preventing an object from printing.

If the object is a chart, you must select the chart's container first. Do this by Ctrl+clicking the chart. Then you can right-click and choose Format Chart from the shortcut menu.

To prevent all objects on a sheet from printing, select them all before working in the Format dialog box. To select all objects on a sheet, follow these steps:

1. Choose Edit⇨Go To to display the Go To dialog box.

2. Click the Special button, and then select the Objects option.

3. Click OK, and all objects will be selected.

4. Right-click on any of the selected objects and choose Format Object from the shortcut menu.

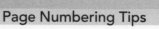

Page Numbering Tips

For lengthy printouts, you'll probably want to add page numbers to help keep the pages in order. Excel gives you a fair amount of control over page numbering, and this tip describes your options.

Basic Page Numbering

To add page numbering, follow these steps:

1. Select File⇨Page Setup to display the Page Setup dialog box.

2. In the Page Setup dialog box, click the Header/Footer tab.

3. To put page numbers at the top of the pages, click the Custom Header button. To put page numbers at the bottom of the pages, click the Custom Footer button. Excel displays either the Header or the Footer dialog box.

4. Click in one of the three sections, depending on where you want the page numbers to appear (on the left side of the page, the center of the page, or on the right side of the page).

5. Click the Page Number button (it has a single hash mark on it), and Excel inserts its page numbering code: &[Page].

6. Click OK twice to close the dialog boxes.

7. At this point, you can click the Print Preview button to make sure the page numbers appear where you want them.

The &[Page] code simply inserts a number. In Step 5, you can add additional text to the page numbering code. For example, if you'd like your page numbers to read like "Page 3," type **Page** (followed by a space) before the code. The entry would look like this:

```
Page &[Page]
```

You might prefer to include the total number of pages, so the page numbering would read something like, "Page 3 of 20." In Step 5, click the Total Pages button (the one with the two plus signs) to insert the code. You also need to enter the word **of**. The complete code would look like this:

```
Page &[Page] of &[Pages]
```

Changing the Starting Page Number

If your printout will be part of a larger report, you may want to begin page numbering with a number other than 1. To do so, follow these steps:

1. Select File⇨Page Setup to display the Page Setup dialog box.

2. In the Page Setup dialog box, click the Page tab.

3. Enter the starting page number in the field labeled First Page Number.

NOTE

If you specify a starting page number other than 1, you probably won't want to use the &[Pages] code in your header or footer. If you do, you might see page numbers such as "Page 8 of 3."

Previewing Page Breaks

You're probably familiar with Excel's Print Preview mode. Click the Print Preview button on the Standard toolbar, and you'll see a representation of how your work will look when it's printed. This mode is useful because it also displays the header and footers.

If you click the Margins button in the Preview window, Excel displays the margins and cell width indicators along the top (see Figure 159-1). You can adjust the margins and the cell widths in Print Preview mode by dragging them. For example, if you notice that a single column of data is printed separately on a page, you can tweak the column widths so that the information doesn't extend to a new page on the right. Or you can make the page margins smaller.

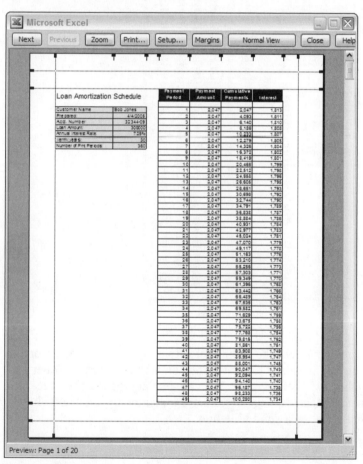

Figure 159-1: Clicking the Margins button displays the margins and cell width indicators.

Print Preview mode is useful, but it displays only one page at a time. Many users tend to overlook the equally handy Page Break Preview mode. To enter Page Break Preview mode, select View➪Page Break Preview. Excel reduces the zoom factor of the sheet and also displays the page breaks and page numbers (see Figure 159-2).

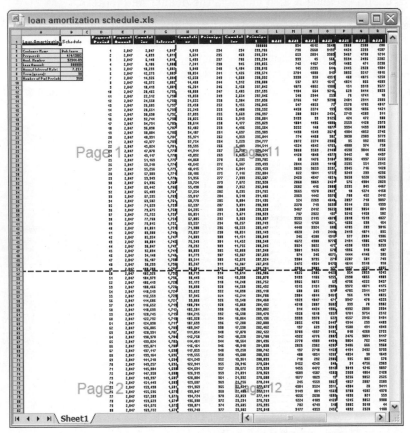

Figure 159-2: Page Break Preview mode shows multiple pages.

In Page Break Preview mode, you can adjust the zoom factor to make the text larger or smaller (use the Zoom control on the Standard toolbar). You can make the text 100 percent, and the overlaid page numbers will still appear. You can also adjust the page breaks simply by dragging the blue lines. Automatic page breaks are indicated by a dashed blue line. Manual page breaks are indicated by a solid blue line.

To get out of Page Break Preview mode, select View➪Normal.

Adding and Removing Page Breaks

Most Excel users just let page breaks fall where they may. That may be acceptable most of the time, but in some situations, it's important to have control over where the pages break. For example, you normally wouldn't want a row to print on a page by itself — especially if it's part of a report that will be viewed by others. This tip describes how to control page breaks.

As you may have discovered, Excel handles page breaks automatically. After you print or preview your worksheet, Excel displays dashed lines to indicate where page breaks occur. Sometimes, however, you want to force a page break — either a vertical or a horizontal one — so that the worksheet prints the way you want it to. For example, if your worksheet consists of several distinct sections, you may want to print each section on a separate sheet of paper.

Forcing a Page Break to Appear Where You Want It

To insert a horizontal page break line, move the cell pointer to the cell that will begin the new page, but make sure that you place the pointer in column A; otherwise, you'll insert a vertical page break and a horizontal page break. For example, if you want row 14 to be the first row of a new page, select cell A14. Then choose Insert⇨Page Break. Excel displays a dashed line to indicate the page break.

To insert a vertical page break line, move the cell pointer to the cell that will begin the new page, but in this case, make sure that you place the pointer in row 1. Select Insert⇨ Page Break to create the page break.

Removing Page Breaks You've Added

To remove a manual page break, move the cell pointer to the first row beneath (or the first column to the right) of the manual page break, and then select Insert⇨Remove Page Break. (This command appears only when you place the cell pointer adjacent to a manual page break.)

To remove all manual page breaks in the worksheet, click the Select All button (or press Ctrl+A), and then choose Insert⇨Remove Page Break.

Printing to a PDF File

Adobe's PDF (Portable Document Format) file standard has become increasingly popular for several reasons:

- These files can be read on many different platforms using Adobe Acrobat Reader.

- The information looks the same, regardless of the computer or printer used.

- The document cannot be easily modified.

Excel doesn't have a built-in option to print to a PDF file, but many free (or low-cost) alternatives are available. Do a Web search for *PDF driver*, and you'll find lots of choices. When you install such a driver, it appears in the Name drop-down list of printers displayed in the Print dialog box (see Figure 161-1). Select the printer and click OK. You'll be prompted for a filename, and then the PDF driver will create the PDF file from your Excel worksheet.

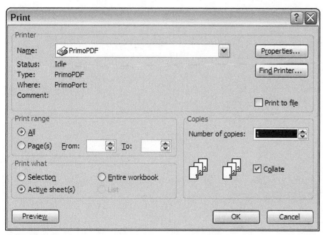

Figure 161-1: After installing a PDF driver, a new printer appears in the Name drop-down list.

Part IX

Avoiding Printing Specific Rows

Excel makes it easy to print your work, but sometimes you may not want to print everything. What if you need to avoid printing certain rows in your worksheet? For example, the rows may contain confidential information, or perhaps they contain intermediate results that need not be printed.

To avoid printing specific rows, you can hide the rows before you print, and then unhide the rows after printing. If your sheet has many rows that should not be printed, hiding and unhiding the rows may be a tedious process. This tip shows you how to use Excel's Group and Outline feature as a way to quickly toggle the hidden status of any number of rows.

Figure 162-1 shows a simple example. In this case, rows 5, 10, 15, and 20 should not be printed.

	A	B	C	D	E	F	G
1		56	-8	17	44	52	
2		-4	59	34	55	-62	
3		30	7	60	-20	76	
4		52	52	90	72	54	
5	Total	134	110	201	151	120	
6		33	-19	69	8	49	
7		-4	1	20	2	37	
8		50	70	26	89	61	
9		70	42	88	53	1	
10	Total	149	94	203	152	148	
11		35	16	49	18	26	
12		-41	18	72	-16	79	
13		66	29	98	47	43	
14		39	17	74	10	35	
15	Total	99	80	293	59	183	
16		27	68	71	19	43	
17		-19	26	30	1	16	
18		71	25	23	73	-27	
19		22	44	37	32	74	
20	Total	101	163	161	125	106	
21							

H ◄ ► H \ Sheet1 /

Figure 162-1: The goal is to prevent the Total rows from being printed.

To set up a simple worksheet outline for this example, follow these steps:

1. Select row 5.

2. Choose Data⇨Group and Outline⇨Group (or press Alt+Shift+right arrow).

3. Select row 10.

4. Press F4 (this key repeats the last command).

5. Select row 15.

6. Press F4.

7. Select row 20.

8. Press F4.

The preceding steps create an outline on the worksheet, and the outline symbols display along the left side of the sheet. You can hide all of the grouped rows by clicking the small 1 button at the top of the outline symbol area (see Figure 162-2).

After you've printed the sheet, click the 2 button to redisplay all of the rows.

1 2		A	B	C	D	E	F	G
	1		56	-8	17	44	52	
	2		-4	59	34	55	-62	
	3		30	7	60	-20	76	
	4		52	52	90	72	54	
+	6		33	-19	69	8	49	
	7		-4	1	20	2	37	
	8		50	70	26	89	61	
	9		70	42	88	53	1	
+	11		35	16	49	18	26	
	12		-41	18	72	-16	79	
	13		66	29	98	47	43	
	14		39	17	74	10	35	
+	16		27	68	71	19	43	
	17		-19	26	30	1	16	
	18		71	25	23	73	-27	
	19		22	44	37	32	74	
+	21							
	22							
	23							

Sheet1

Figure 162-2: Use the outline controls to quickly hide the rows that you don't want printed.

NOTE

If you don't like seeing those outline symbols, you can toggle them on and off by pressing Ctrl+8. The outline remains in effect even if the symbols are hidden.

Making Your Printout Fit on One Page

If you need to ensure that your printed output fits on a single page, you can spend time adjusting the font sizes — or you can let Excel do the work for you.

Figure 163-1 shows a print preview of a worksheet. The status line in the Print Preview window reports that it will use four pages.

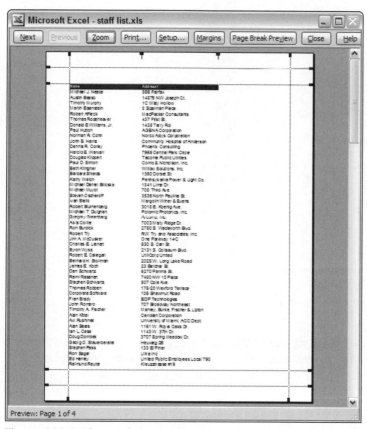

Figure 163-1: This worksheet will print on four pages.

To force Excel to print it on a single sheet, select File⇨Page Setup to display the Page Setup dialog box (if the Print Preview window is active, click the Setup button). In the Page Setup dialog box, click the Page tab, and then select the Fit To option and enter the number of pages desired. Excel will shrink the output to your specifications. Figure 163-2 shows the Print Preview window after selecting the Fit To option and entering **1**.

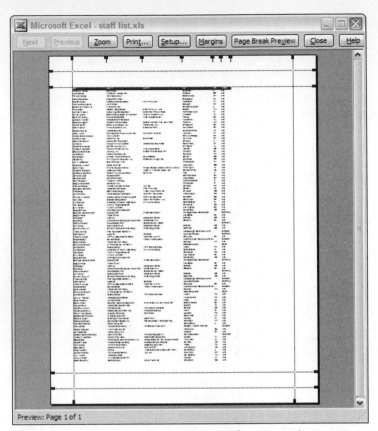

Figure 163-2: Excel shrunk the output to fit on a single page.

Obviously, you'll need to consider the legibility of the printout. If you force too much information on a single sheet, it will be printed so small that you'll need a magnifying glass to read it.

Printing Formulas

A common question about Excel is "How can I print the formulas in my worksheet?" Unfortunately, Excel doesn't provide a satisfactory answer to that question.

Printing in Formula View Mode

One solution is to use Formula View mode, and then print as usual. To view your formulas, select Tools⇨Options, click the View tab in the Options dialog box, and place a check mark next to the Formulas option.

Figure 164-1 shows a typical spreadsheet in Formula View mode. Printing this view usually isn't very helpful.

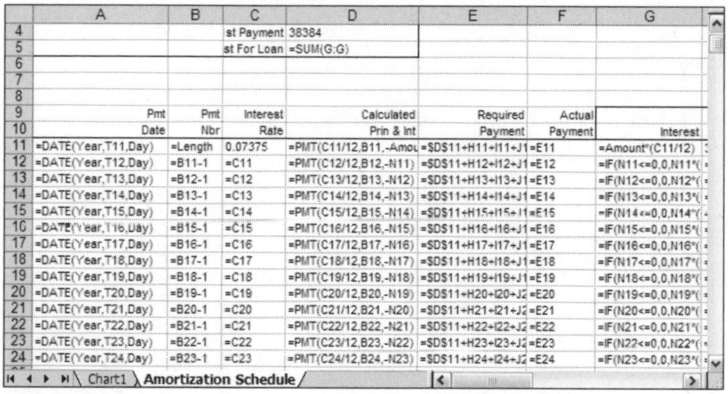

Figure 164-1: Printing formulas isn't always pretty.

Printing a Formula List with a Macro

Another option is to use a macro to print a nicely formatted list of formulas. Many such macros are available, including one that's part of my Power Utility Pak add-in. Here's a simple VBA procedure that prints a list of formulas, along with the cell address (see Figure 164-2):

```
Sub DisplayFormulas()
    Dim FormulaCells As Range
    Dim FormulaReport As Worksheet
    Dim r As Long
    Set FormulaCells = Range("A1").SpecialCells(-4123, 23)
    Set FormulaReport = Worksheets.Add
    r = 1
```

```
    For Each cell In FormulaCells
        FormulaReport.Cells(r, 1) = cell.Address
        FormulaReport.Cells(r, 2) = "'" & cell.Formula
        r = r + 1
    Next cell
End Sub
```

Enter this code into a VBA module. Select the sheet that contains the formulas, and press Alt+F8 to display the Macro dialog box. Select DisplayFormulas from the list, and then click the Run button. The macro inserts a new worksheet for the formula list.

Keep in mind that this is a very simple macro, and it doesn't even do any error checking. For example, if the active sheet contains no formulas, it will generate an error.

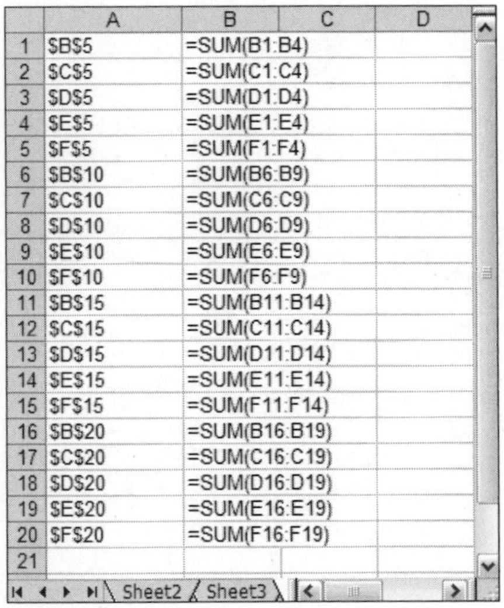

	A	B	C	D
1	$B$5	=SUM(B1:B4)		
2	$C$5	=SUM(C1:C4)		
3	$D$5	=SUM(D1:D4)		
4	$E$5	=SUM(E1:E4)		
5	$F$5	=SUM(F1:F4)		
6	$B$10	=SUM(B6:B9)		
7	$C$10	=SUM(C6:C9)		
8	$D$10	=SUM(D6:D9)		
9	$E$10	=SUM(E6:E9)		
10	$F$10	=SUM(F6:F9)		
11	$B$15	=SUM(B11:B14)		
12	$C$15	=SUM(C11:C14)		
13	$D$15	=SUM(D11:D14)		
14	$E$15	=SUM(E11:E14)		
15	$F$15	=SUM(F11:F14)		
16	$B$20	=SUM(B16:B19)		
17	$C$20	=SUM(C16:C19)		
18	$D$20	=SUM(D16:D19)		
19	$E$20	=SUM(E16:E19)		
20	$F$20	=SUM(F16:F19)		
21				

Sheet2 / Sheet3

Figure 164-2: A simple macro created this list of formulas.

Copying Page Setup Settings Across Sheets

Each Excel worksheet has its own print setup options (orientation, margins, headers and footers, and so on). These options are specified in the Page Setup dialog box, which you access by choosing File⇨Page Setup. When you add a new sheet to a workbook, it contains the default page setup settings. Here's an easy way to transfer the settings from one worksheet to additional worksheets:

1. Activate the sheet that contains the desired setup information. This is the source sheet.

2. Select the target sheets. Ctrl+click the sheet tabs of the sheets you want to update with the settings from the source sheet.

3. Select File⇨Page Setup, and click OK.

4. Ungroup the sheets by right-clicking on any selected sheet and choosing Ungroup Sheets from the shortcut menu.

The Page Setup settings of the source sheet will be transferred to all of the target sheets.

NOTE

Two settings located on the Sheet tab of the Page Setup dialog box are not transferred: Print Area and Print Titles.

Using Custom Views for Printing

Most users who need to print different sections of a large worksheet usually spend a lot of time changing the print area by using the File⇨Print Area⇨Set Print Area command. A simpler solution is to create a custom view for each print area, as follows:

1. Select the range to be printed, and then choose File⇨Print Area⇨Set Print Area.

2. Select View⇨Custom Views to display the Custom Views dialog box.

3. In the Custom Views dialog box, click the Add button to display the Add View dialog box.

4. In the Add View dialog box, enter a descriptive name for the view (see Figure 166-1).

5. Make sure that the Print Settings check box is checked, and click OK.

Repeat these steps for each additional view.

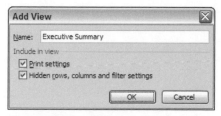

Figure 166-1: Adding a view that contains a specific print area.

After you've defined your views, you can quickly change the print area by selecting the desired view from the Custom Views dialog box.

NOTE

To simplify things even more, you can add the Custom Views control to one of your toolbars. Select View⇨Toolbars⇨Customize. In the Customize dialog box, click the Commands tab. Select View from the Categories list, and drag the Custom Views control to any toolbar. You can use this tool to quickly select a named view, and also to create new views (just type the name into the box and press Enter).

Part X

Customizing Toolbars and Menus

Excel certainly has no shortage of toolbars. The tips in this part will help you get the most out of toolbars — and even describe how to create a few custom toolbars of your own.

Tips and Where to Find Them

Tip 167 Finding the Multifunctional
Toolbar Buttons   407

Tip 168 Finding the Hidden Menu
Commands   409

Tip 169 Customizing Menus and
Toolbars   411

Tip 170 Creating a Custom Toolbar   413

Tip 171 Taming Pop-Up Toolbars   417

Tip 172 Attaching Toolbars to
Worksheets   419

Tip 173 Backing Up Your Customized
Toolbars and Menus   421

Finding the Multifunctional Toolbar Buttons

Several of Excel's toolbar buttons are multifunctional: Their behavior changes if you press the Shift key while you click the button. Generally, the toolbar will perform the "opposite" function.

What's the point? I guess these multifunctional buttons enable you to create more compact custom toolbars if you like. For example, you can eliminate the Print Preview button because Shift+clicking the Print button performs the same function.

Table 167-1 provides a list of the toolbar buttons that perform a different function if you press the Shift key while you click the button.

TABLE 167-1   MULTIFUNCTION BUTTONS

Shift+Click This Button . . .	. . . To Perform This Command
Print	Print Preview
Print Preview	Print
Open	Save As
Save	Open
Sort Ascending	Sort Descending
Sort Descending	Sort Ascending
Underline	Double Underline
Increase Decimal	Decrease Decimal
Decrease Decimal	Increase Decimal
Increase Indent	Decrease Indent
Decrease Indent	Increase Indent
Center	Center Across Columns

Part X

Finding the Hidden Menu Commands

Excel has a few hidden menu commands that are accessible only if you press the Shift key while you click the menu.

If you Shift+click the File menu, the Close All menu item appears.

If you Shift+click the Edit menu, the following menu items are available:

- Copy Picture
- Paste Picture
- Paste Picture Link

Customizing Menus and Toolbars

This tip is a crash course for those who want to customize Excel's user interface — specifically the toolbars and menus. How much customization can you do? Quite a bit. The following list also applies to menus, because menus are actually toolbars in disguise:

- **Remove buttons from built-in toolbars.** You may want to do this to eliminate buttons that you never use.

- **Add buttons to built-in toolbars.** You can add as many buttons as you want to any toolbar. Excel has many useful buttons that don't appear on any toolbar.

- **Create new toolbars.** You can create as many new toolbars as you like, with as many buttons as you like.

- **Change the functionality of a button.** You make such a change by attaching your own macro to a built-in toolbar button.

- **Change the image that appears on any toolbar button.** A rudimentary but functional toolbar-button editor is included with Excel.

To make any changes to toolbars or menus, you need to be in Customization mode (Excel is in Customization mode when the Customize dialog box is displayed). To display the Customize dialog box, select View⇨Toolbars⇨Customize (or right-click any toolbar and select Customize from the shortcut menu).

When Excel is in Customization mode, you have access to all the commands and options in the Customize dialog box. In addition, you can perform the following actions:

- Reposition a button on a toolbar by clicking and dragging it.

- Move a button to a different toolbar by clicking and dragging it to the desired location.

- Copy a button from one toolbar to another by pressing Ctrl while you click and drag.

- Add new buttons to a toolbar by using the Commands tab of the Customize dialog box by dragging an item from the Commands list to a toolbar.

- Perform other actions by right-clicking a toolbar button and using the shortcut menu (see Figure 169-1).

Part X

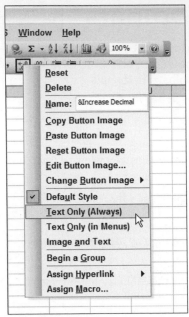

Figure 169-1: In Customization mode, right-clicking a toolbar button gives you lots of options.

Creating a Custom Toolbar

Excel has lots of toolbars, but sometimes it's better to create one that contains the tools you use most. This tip contains step-by-step instructions for creating a useful Custom Formatting toolbar.

Adding the First Button

Follow these steps to create the toolbar and add the first button:

1. Right-click any toolbar and select Customize from the shortcut menu to display the Customize dialog box.

2. In the Customize dialog box, click the Toolbars tab, and click New to display the New Toolbar dialog box.

3. In the New Toolbar dialog box, enter the name **Custom Formatting** and click OK. Excel creates an empty toolbar.

4. In the Customize dialog box, click the Commands tab.

5. In the Categories list, scroll down and select New Menu.

6. Drag the New Menu item from the Commands list to the new toolbar.

7. Right-click the New Menu button in the new toolbar and change the name to Font.

8. In the Customize dialog box, select Format from the Categories list.

9. Scroll through the Command list and drag the Bold command to the Font button in your new toolbar.

10. Repeat Step 9, adding the following buttons from the Format category: Italic, Underline, Font Size, and Font.

At this point, you may want to click the Close button in the Customize dialog box to try out the new toolbar. It contains only one button, but this button expands to show five font-related commands (see Figure 170-1).

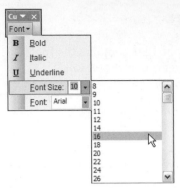

Figure 170-1: A custom toolbar after adding a menu button with five commands.

Adding More Buttons

If you followed the preceding steps, you should understand how toolbar customization works, and you can now add additional buttons to your custom toolbar. To finish the custom toolbar, get back into Customization mode and add additional tools.

Figure 170-2 shows the final version of the custom toolbar, and it includes all of the tools that are in the built-in Formatting menu, plus quite a few more (39 tools in all). But, because the Custom Formatting toolbar uses five menus (which expand to show more commands), the toolbar takes up a relatively small amount of space.

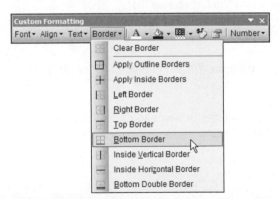

Figure 170-2: The final version of the Custom Formatting toolbar.

With two exceptions, all of the tools are found in the Formatting category. The Clear Formatting tool is in the Edit category, and the Format Cells tool is in the Built-In Menus category. Table 170-1 lists all the tools that I added to the Custom Formatting toolbar.

TABLE 170-1   TOOLS IN THE CUSTOM FORMATTING TOOLBAR

Tool	Subcommands
New Menu (renamed Font)	Bold, Italic, Underline, Font Size, Font
New Menu (renamed Align)	Align Left, Center, Align Right, Decrease Indent, Increase Indent, Merge and Center, Merge Cells, Unmerge Cells, Merge Across
New Menu (renamed Text)	Vertical Text, Rotate Text Up, Rotate Text Down, Angle Text Downward, Angle Text Upward
New Menu (renamed Border)	Clear Border, Apply Outline Borders, Apply Inside Border, Left Border, Right Border, Top Border, Bottom Border, Inside Vertical Border, Inside Horizontal Border, Bottom Double Border
Font Color	(none)
Fill Color	(none)
Pattern	(none)
Clear Formatting	(none)
Format Cells	(none)
New Menu (renamed Number)	Currency Style, Percent Style, Comma Style, Decrease Decimal, Increase Decimal

Saving the Custom Toolbar

Excel doesn't have a command to save a toolbar. Rather, the new toolbar is saved automatically when you exit Excel. Therefore, it will always be available.

Part X

Taming Pop-Up Toolbars

Normally, Excel displays a particular toolbar automatically when you change contexts; this is called *autosensing*. For example, when you activate a chart, the Chart toolbar appears. When you activate a sheet that contains a PivotTable, the Pivot416 toolbar appears.

Some people like this feature. Others find it annoying. You can easily defeat autosensing simply by hiding the toolbar. After you do so, Excel no longer displays that toolbar when you switch to its former context. You can restore this automatic behavior, however, by displaying the appropriate toolbar when you're in the appropriate context. Thereafter, Excel reverts to its normal automatic toolbar display when you switch to that context.

Attaching Toolbars to Worksheets

If you create a custom toolbar that you want to share with someone else, the only direct way to do so is to attach it to a workbook. To do so, follow these steps:

1. Choose View⇨Toolbars⇨Customize to display the Customize dialog box.

2. In the Customize dialog box, click the Attach button, which displays the Attach Toolbars dialog box. This dialog box lists all custom toolbars.

3. Select the toolbars that you want to attach to a workbook (see Figure 172-1). You can attach any number of toolbars to a workbook.

4. Click OK to attach the toolbars.

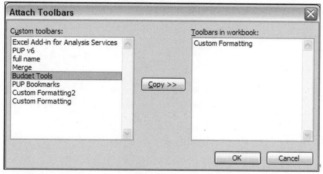

Figure 172-1: You can attach custom toolbars to a workbook in the Attach Toolbars dialog box.

A toolbar that's attached to a workbook appears automatically when the workbook is opened, unless the workspace already has a toolbar by the same name.

NOTE

The toolbar that's stored in the workbook is an exact copy of the toolbar at the time that you attach it. If you modify the toolbar after attaching it, the changed version is not stored in the workbook automatically. You must manually remove the old toolbar and then add the edited toolbar.

Part X

Backing Up Your Customized Toolbars and Menus

Many users like to customize Excel by creating custom toolbars, modifying existing toolbars, and even changing the menus. This tip describes how to make sure your customizations don't get lost.

Locating Your *.xlb File

The changes that you make to Excel's user interface are stored in a file with an .xlb extension. The name and location of that file varies, depending on the version of Excel that you use. The easiest way to locate your *.xlb file is to search for it using Windows: Choose Start⇨Search to display the Windows Search Results window. Then search your main hard drive for *.xlb.

Backing Up Your *.xlb File

If your *.xlb file gets damaged, you'll not only lose all of your toolbar and menu customizations, but the damaged file may even cause Excel to crash when it starts. Therefore, it's a good idea to make a backup copy of that file every once in a while — preferably on a different drive.

 WARNING

Also, pay attention to the size of your *.xlb file. Typically, the file will be less than 200K in size. If it gets much larger than that, it may be a sign of a problem.

Deleting Toolbar and Menu Customizations

If you would like to get rid of all of your toolbar and menu customizations, just delete the *.xlb file and restart Excel. When you close the program, Excel will create a new *.xlb file, and your toolbars and menus will be just like new.

Part X

Part XI

Spotting, Fixing, and Preventing Errors

Just because your spreadsheet doesn't display an error value doesn't mean that it's accurate. The tips in this part will help you identify, fix, and prevent errors.

Tips and Where to Find Them

Tip 174 Using Excel's Error-Checking Features 425

Tip 175 Identifying Formula Cells 427

Tip 176 Dealing with Floating-Point Number Problems 429

Tip 177 Creating a Table of Cell and Range Names 431

Tip 178 Viewing Names Graphically 433

Tip 179 Locating Phantom Links 435

Tip 180 Understanding Displayed versus Actual Values 437

Tip 181 Tracing Cell Relationships 439

Using Excel's Error-Checking Features

If your worksheets use a lot of formulas, you may find it helpful to take advantage of Excel's automatic error-checking feature. This feature is enabled in the Error Checking tab of the Options dialog box (see Figure 174-1). Error checking is turned on or off by using the Enable Background Error Checking option. In addition, you can specify which types of errors to check for by selecting check boxes in the Rules section.

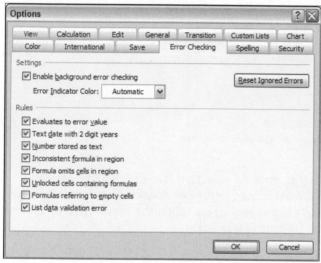

Figure 174-1: Excel can check your formulas for potential errors.

 NOTE
This feature is available in Excel 2002 and later versions.

When error checking is turned on, Excel continually evaluates your worksheet, including its formulas. If a potential error is identified, Excel places a small triangle in the upper-left corner of the cell. When the cell is activated, a Smart Tag appears. Clicking this Smart Tag provides you with some options. Figure 174-2 shows the options that appear when you click the Smart Tag in a cell that contains a #DIV/0! error. The options vary, depending on the type of error.

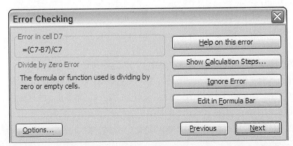

Figure 174-2: Clicking an error Smart Tag gives you a list of options.

In many cases, you will choose to ignore an error by selecting the Ignore Error option. Selecting this option eliminates the cell from subsequent error checks. However, all previously ignored errors can be reset so that they appear again (click the Reset Ignored Errors button on the Error Checking tab of the Options dialog box).

You can use the Tools⇨Error Checking command to display a dialog box that displays each potential error cell in sequence, much like using a spell-checking feature. Figure 174-3 shows the Error Checking dialog box. Note that this is a nonmodal dialog box, so you can still access your worksheet when the Error Checking dialog box is displayed.

Figure 174-3: Using the Error Checking dialog box to cycle through potential errors identified by Excel.

 WARNING

Understand that the error-checking feature is not perfect. In fact, it's not even *close* to perfect. In other words, you can't assume that you have an error-free worksheet simply because Excel does not identify any potential errors! Also, be aware that this error-checking feature won't catch a very common type of error — that of overwriting a formula cell with a value.

Identifying Formula Cells

One of the most common spreadsheet problems occurs when a formula is accidentally replaced with a value. This type of error is often difficult to locate, especially if your worksheet contains a large number of formulas. This tip describes two ways to quickly identify the formulas in a worksheet by highlighting them. Then, if you zoom out (make the cells appear very small), you might be able to spot gaps in groups of formulas.

Using Go To Special

This method of identifying formula cells is easy, but it's not dynamic. In other words, it's good for a one-time check:

1. Select any single cell in your worksheet.

2. Select Edit⇨Go To (or press Ctrl+G) to display the Go To dialog box.

3. In the Go To dialog box, click the Special button to display the Go To Special dialog box.

4. In the Go To Special dialog box, click the Formulas option, and make sure all of the check boxes below it are checked.

5. Click OK, and Excel selects all formula cells.

6. Click the Fill Color button on the formatting toolbar (select any color that's not already being used).

7. Use the Zoom control, and zoom your worksheet to a small percent (25 percent is a good choice).

8. Check the sheet carefully, looking for any unshaded cells in a group of shaded cells. That may be a formula that was overwritten by a value.

If you didn't make any edits, you can select Edit⇨Undo to remove the fill colors you applied in Step 6.

Using Conditional Formatting

This method of identifying formula cells takes a bit of setup work, but it has a distinct advantage over the previous method: It's dynamic. Formula cells are identified immediately when they are entered.

To set up the conditional formatting, follow these steps:

1. Select Insert⇨Name⇨Define to display the Define Name dialog box.

2. In the Define Name dialog box, enter the following in the Names in Workbook field:

```
CellHasFormula
```

Part XI

3. Enter the following formula in the Refers To field:

   ```
   =GET.CELL(48,INDIRECT("rc",FALSE))
   ```

4. Click Add, and then click OK to close the Define Name dialog box.

5. Select all the cells to which you want to apply the conditional formatting. Generally, this is a range from A1 down to the lower-right corner of the used area of the worksheet.

6. Select Format⇨Conditional Formatting to display the Conditional Formatting dialog box.

7. In the Conditional Formatting dialog box, select Formula Is from the drop-down list, and then enter this formula in the adjacent field (see Figure 175-1):

   ```
   =CellHasFormula
   ```

8. Click the Format button to display the Format Cells dialog box. Select the type of formatting you want for the cells that contain a formula. A yellow fill color is a good choice.

9. Click OK to close the Format Cells dialog box.

After you've completed these steps, every cell that contains a formula and is within the range you selected in Step 5 displays the formatting of your choice. In addition, if you enter a formula, it immediately displays the formatting.

Figure 175-1: Using conditional formatting to highlight formula cells.

Dealing with Floating-Point Number Problems

Excel users are often baffled by Excel's apparent inability to perform simple math. It's not Excel's fault. Computers, by their very nature, don't have infinite precision. Excel stores numbers in binary format by using 8 bytes, which can handle numbers with 15-digit accuracy. Some numbers can't be expressed precisely by using 8 bytes, so the number stores as an approximation.

To demonstrate how this may cause problems, enter the following formula into cell A1:

```
=(5.1-5.2)+1
```

The result should be 0.9. However, if you format the cell to display 15 decimal places, you'll discover that Excel calculates the formula with a result of 0.899999999999999 — close to 0.9, but certainly not 0.9. This occurs because the operation in parentheses is performed first, and this intermediate result stores in binary format by using an approximation. The formula then adds 1 to this value, and the approximation error is propagated to the final result.

In many cases, this type of error does not present a problem. However, if you need to test the result of that formula by using a logical operator, it *may* present a problem. For example, the following formula (which assumes that the previous formula is in cell A1) returns FALSE:

```
=A1=.9
```

One solution to this type of error is to use Excel's ROUND function. The following formula, for example, returns TRUE because the comparison is made by using the value in A1 rounded to one decimal place:

```
=ROUND(A1,1)=0.9
```

Here's another example of a precision problem. Try entering the following formula:

```
=(1.333-1.233)-(1.334-1.234)
```

This formula should return 0, but it actually returns −2.220441E-16 (a number very close to zero).

If that formula were in cell A1, the following formula would return *Not Zero*:

```
=IF(A1=0,"Zero","Not Zero")
```

One way to handle these "very close to zero" rounding errors is to use a formula like this:

```
=IF(ABS(A1)<1E-6,"Zero","Not Zero")
```

This formula uses the less-than operator to compare the absolute value of the number with a very small number. This formula would return *Zero*.

Creating a Table of Cell and Range Names

Providing names for cells and ranges is a handy tool, but sometimes they may get overwhelming. After you create a large number of range names, you may need to know the ranges that each name defines, particularly if you're trying to track down errors or document your work.

Excel lets you create a list of all names in the workbook and their corresponding addresses. To create a table of names, first move the cell pointer to an empty area of your worksheet — the table is created at the active cell position and will overwrite any information at that location. Choose Insert⇨Name⇨Paste (or press F3), and Excel displays the Paste Name dialog box, which lists all the defined names. To paste a list of names, click the Paste List button.

Viewing Names Graphically

If your worksheet has lots of range names, it may be helpful to identify the location of the ranges. Excel can help. Just zoom the worksheet to 39 percent or less, and the names are displayed. Figure 178-1 shows an example.

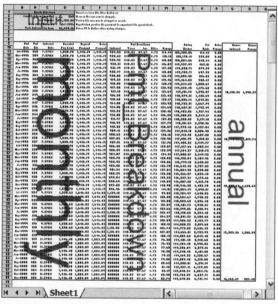

Figure 178-1: Excel displays the range names when you zoom a worksheet to 39 percent or less.

Locating Phantom Links

You may open a workbook and see a message like the one shown in Figure 179-1. If the workbook actually contains links, this is the message you expect. But sometimes this message appears even when a workbook contains no linked formulas.

Figure 179-1: Excel's way of asking you if you want to update links in a workbook.

To get rid of these phantom links, first try choosing Edit⇨Links to display the Edit Links dialog box. Then select each link and click Break Link.

If that doesn't solve the problem, the phantom link may be caused by an erroneous name (phantom links may be created when you copy a worksheet that contains names). Select Insert⇨Name⇨Define and scroll through the list of names. If you see a name that refers to #REF!, delete the name. There's an excellent chance that your phantom link will disappear.

Understanding Displayed versus Actual Values

You may encounter a situation in which values in a range don't appear to add up properly. For example, Figure 180-1 shows a worksheet with the following formula entered into each cell in the range B3:B5:

```
=1/3
```

Figure 180-1: A simple demonstration of numbers that appear to add up incorrectly.

Cell B6 contains the following formula:

```
=SUM(B3:B5)
```

All of the cells are formatted to display with two decimal places. As you can see, the formula in cell B6 appears to display an incorrect result. (You may expect it to display 0.99.) The formula, of course, *does* return the correct result. The formula uses the *actual* values in the range B3:B5, not the *displayed* values.

You may be tempted to instruct Excel to use the displayed values. You do this by checking the Precision as Displayed check box on the Calculation tab of the Options dialog box. (Choose Tools⇨Options to display this dialog box.)

Generally, using the Precision as Displayed check box is not the best way to handle this problem. Checking the Precision as Displayed check box also affects normal values (not formulas) that have been entered into cells. For example, if a cell contains the value 4.68 and is displayed with no decimal places (that is, 5), checking the Precision as Displayed check box converts 4.68 to 5.00. This change is permanent, and you can't restore the original value if you later uncheck the Precision as Displayed check box.

A better approach is to use Excel's ROUND function to round the values to the desired number of decimal places. In the example shown here, the range B3:B5 would contain this formula:

```
=ROUND(1/3,2)
```

Summing the three values results in 0.99.

Tracing Cell Relationships

In a typical worksheet, the cells contain complex interrelationships. Trying to debug a formula can be easier if you understand two key concepts: cell precedents and cell dependents. First, the definitions:

- **Cell precedents:** Applicable only to cells that contain a formula, a formula cell's precedents are all the cells that contribute to the formula's result. A *direct precedent* is a cell that you use directly in the formula. An *indirect precedent* is a cell that is not used directly in the formula, but is used by a cell that you refer to in the formula.

- **Cell dependents:** These are formula cells that depend on a particular cell. A cell's dependents consist of all formula cells that use the cell. Again, the formula cell can be a direct dependent or an indirect dependent.

Identifying cell precedents for a formula cell often sheds light on why the formula is not working correctly. Conversely, knowing which formula cells depend on a particular cell is also helpful. For example, if you're about to delete a formula, you may want to check whether it has any dependents.

Identifying Precedents

You can identify cells used by a formula in the active cell in a number of ways:

- **Press F2.** The cells that are used directly by the formula are outlined in color, and the color corresponds to the cell reference in the formula. This technique is limited to identifying cells on the same sheet as the formula.

- **Select Edit⇨Go To (or press F5) to display the Go To dialog box.** Then click the Special button to display the Go To Special dialog box. Select the Precedents option, and then select either Direct Only (for direct precedents only) or All Levels (for direct and indirect precedents). Click OK, and Excel highlights the precedent cells for the formula. This technique is limited to identifying cells on the same sheet as the formula.

- **Press Ctrl+[to select all direct precedent cells on the active sheet.**

- **Press Ctrl+Shift+[to select all precedent cells (direct and indirect) on the active sheet.**

- **Display the Formula Auditing toolbar by selecting Tools⇨Formula Auditing⇨ Show Formula Auditing Toolbar.** Click the Trace Precedents button to draw arrows to indicate a cell's precedents. Click this button multiple times to see additional levels of precedents. Figure 181-1 shows a worksheet with precedent arrows drawn to indicate the precedents for the formula in cell C13.

	A	B	C	D	E	F	G	H
1	Commission Rate	5.50%	Normal commission rate					
2	Sales Goal	15%	Improvement from prior month					
3	Bonus Rate	6.50%	Paid if Sales Goal is attained					
4								
5	Sales Rep	Last Month	This Month	Change	Pct. Change	Met Goal?	Commission	
6	Murray	101,233	108,444	7,211	7.1%	TRUE	7,049	
7	Knuckles	120,933	108,434	-12,499	-10.3%	FALSE	5,964	
8	Lefty	139,832	165,901	26,069	18.6%	TRUE	10,784	
9	Lucky	98,323	100,083	1,760	1.8%	FALSE	5,505	
10	Scarface	78,322	79,923	1,601	2.0%	FALSE	4,396	
11	Total	538,643	562,785	24,142	4.5%		33,697	
12								
13	Average Commission Rate:		5.99%					
14								
15								

Figure 181-1: This worksheet displays lines that indicate cell precedents for the formula in cell C13.

Identifying Dependents

You can identify formula cells that use a particular cell in a number of ways:

- **Select Edit➪Go To (or press Ctrl+G) to display the Go To dialog box.** Then click the Special button to display the Go To Special dialog box. Select the Dependents option, and then select either Direct Only (for direct dependents only) or All Levels (for direct and indirect dependents). Click OK; Excel highlights the cells that depend on the active cell. This technique is limited to identifying cells on the active sheet only.

- **Press Ctrl+] to select all direct dependent cells on the active sheet.**

- **Press Ctrl+Shift+] to select all dependent cells (direct and indirect) on the active sheet.**

- **Display the Formula Auditing toolbar by selecting Tools➪Formula Auditing➪ Show Formula Auditing Toolbar.** Click the Trace Dependents button to draw arrows to indicate a cell's dependents. Click this button multiple times to see additional levels of dependents. Figure 181-2 shows a worksheet with dependent arrows pointing to all formula cells that depend on cell B6.

	A	B	C	D	E	F	G	H
1	Commission Rate	5.50%	Normal commission rate					
2	Sales Goal	15%	Improvement from prior month					
3	Bonus Rate	6.50%	Paid if Sales Goal is attained					
4								
5	Sales Rep	Last Month	This Month	Change	Pct. Change	Met Goal?	Commission	
6	Murray	101,233	108,444	7,211	7.1%	TRUE	7,049	
7	Knuckles	120,933	108,434	-12,499	-10.3%	FALSE	5,964	
8	Lefty	139,832	165,901	26,069	18.6%	TRUE	10,784	
9	Lucky	98,323	100,083	1,760	1.8%	FALSE	5,505	
10	Scarface	78,322	79,923	1,601	2.0%	FALSE	4,396	
11	Total	530,643	562,705	24,142	4.5%		33,697	
12								
13	Average Commission Rate:		5.99%					
14								
15								

Figure 181-2: This worksheet displays lines that indicate cells that depend on cell B6.

Part XII

Basic VBA and Macros

Even if you know nothing about VBA and macros, you may find that some of the tips in this section will whet your appetite to learn more. And if you're just starting out with macros, you'll find some useful tips in this part.

Tips and Where to Find Them

Tip 182 Learning about Macros
and VBA 445

Tip 183 Recording a Macro 447

Tip 184 Understanding Security
Issues Related to Macros 451

Tip 185 Using a Personal Macro
Workbook 453

Tip 186 Understanding Functions
versus Subs 455

Tip 187 Displaying Pop-Up
Messages 457

Tip 188 Getting Information from
the User 461

Tip 189 Running a Macro When a
Workbook Is Opened 463

Tip 190 Creating Simple Worksheet
Functions 467

Tip 191 Making Excel Talk 471

Tip 192 Understanding Custom
Function Limitations 473

Tip 193 Executing a Menu Item
with a Macro 475

Tip 194 Storing Custom Functions
in an Add-In 477

Tip 195 Displaying a Pop-Up
Linked Calendar 479

Tip 196 Using Add-Ins 481

Learning about Macros and VBA

The terms *macro* and *VBA* remain a mystery to most Excel users. This tip provides a broad overview to help you decide if creating Excel macros would be useful.

What Is a Macro?

A *macro* is a sequence of instructions that automates some aspect of Excel so that you can work more efficiently and with fewer errors. You use a scripting language called VBA (Visual Basic for Applications) to create macros. You may create a macro, for example, to format and print your month-end sales report. After the macro is developed, you can then execute the macro to perform many time-consuming procedures automatically.

You need not be a power user to create and use simple VBA macros. Casual users can simply turn on Excel's macro recorder: Excel records your actions and converts them into a VBA macro. When you execute this macro, Excel performs the actions again.

More advanced users can write code that tells Excel to perform tasks that can't be recorded. For example, you can write procedures that display custom dialog boxes, add new commands to Excel's menus, or process data in a series of workbooks.

What Can a Macro Do?

VBA is an extremely rich programming language with thousands of uses. The following list contains just a few things that you can do with VBA macros:

- **Insert a text string or formula:** If you need to enter your company name into worksheets frequently, you can create a macro to do the typing for you. The AutoCorrect feature can also do this.

- **Automate a procedure that you perform frequently:** For example, you may need to prepare a month-end summary. If the task is straightforward, you can develop a macro to do it for you.

- **Automate repetitive operations:** If you need to perform the same action in 12 different workbooks, you can record a macro while you perform the task once — and then let the macro repeat your action in the other workbooks.

- **Create a custom command:** For example, you can combine several of Excel's menu commands so that they are executed from a single keystroke or from a single mouse click.

- **Create a custom toolbar button:** You can customize Excel's toolbars with your own buttons to execute macros that you write.

- **Create a simplified "front end" for users who don't know much about Excel:** For example, you can set up a foolproof data entry template.

- **Develop a new worksheet function:** Although Excel includes a wide assortment of built-in functions, you can create custom functions that greatly simplify your formulas.

- **Create complete, macro-driven applications:** Excel macros can display custom dialog boxes and add new commands to the menu bar.

- **Create custom add-ins for Excel:** Most of the add-ins that are shipped with Excel were created with Excel macros.

Recording a Macro

The easiest way to get started learning about Excel macros is to use the macro recorder to record a sequence of actions. Then, you can play back the sequence (or run the macro).

Following is a hands-on demonstration to give newcomers a feel for how macros work. This example demonstrates how to record a macro that changes the alignment of text in the cells in the current range selection. Specifically, this macro makes the text display vertically in the cell.

Creating the Macro

To create the macro, follow these steps:

1. Enter a value or text into a cell — anything is okay. This gives you something to start with.

2. Select the cell that contains the value or text that you entered in the preceding step.

3. Choose Tools⇨Macro⇨Record New Macro. Excel displays the Record Macro dialog box.

4. Enter a new name for the macro to replace the default Macro1 name. For this example, enter **VerticalText**.

5. Assign this macro to the shortcut key Ctrl+Shift+V by entering an uppercase **V** in the Shortcut Key field.

6. Click OK. This closes the Record Macro dialog box. Excel displays a small two-button toolbar called Stop Recording.

7. Choose Format⇨Cells and then click the Alignment tab. Select Center from the Horizontal drop-down list and select Center from the Vertical drop-down list. Change the orientation to 90 Degrees. Click OK to close the Format Cells dialog box.

8. The macro is finished, so click the Stop Recording button on the Stop Recording toolbar (or select Tools⇨Macro⇨Stop Recording).

This macro is very simple. Most of the time, you'll record more actions than this.

Examining the Macro

The macro was recorded in a new VBA module named Module1. If you're interested, you can take a look at the instructions that were recorded. To view the code in this module, you must activate the Visual Basic Editor (VBE). You can activate the VBE in either of two ways:

- Press Alt+F11.

- Select Tools⇨Macro⇨Visual Basic Editor.

The Project window displays a list of all open workbooks and add-ins. This list is displayed as a tree diagram, which can be expanded or collapsed. The code that you recorded previously is stored in Module1 in the current workbook. When you double-click Module1, the code in the module is displayed in a Code window.

Figure 183-1 shows the recorded macro, as displayed in the Code window.

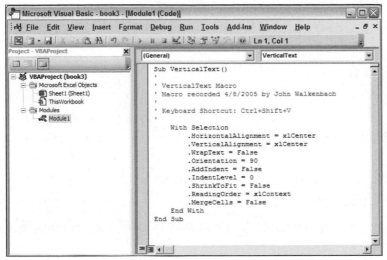

Figure 183-1: The VerticalText procedure was generated by Excel's macro recorder.

The macro recorded is a Sub procedure that is named VerticalText. The statements tell Excel what to do when the macro is executed.

Notice that Excel inserted some comments at the top of the procedure. This is some of the information that appeared in the Record Macro dialog box. These comment lines (which begin with an apostrophe) aren't really necessary, and deleting them has no effect on how the macro runs.

NOTE

You may notice that the macro recorded some actions that you didn't take. For example, it sets the WrapText, AddIndent, and other properties. This is just a byproduct of the method that Excel uses to translate actions into code. Excel sets the properties for every option in the Alignment tab of the Format Cells dialog box, even though you didn't change all of them.

Testing the Macro

Before you recorded this macro, you set an option that assigned the macro to the Ctrl+Shift+V shortcut key combination. To test the macro, return to Excel by using either of the following methods:

- Press Alt+F11.
- Click the View Microsoft Excel button on the VBE toolbar.

When Excel is active, activate a worksheet. (It can be in the workbook that contains the VBA module or in any other workbook.) Select a cell or range and press Ctrl+Shift+V. The macro immediately changes the alignment of the text in the selected cell(s).

Continue testing the macro with other selections consisting of one or more cells. You find that the macro always applies exactly the same formatting.

NOTE

In the preceding example, notice that you selected the cell to be formatted *before* you started recording your macro. This is important. If you select a cell while the macro recorder is turned on, the actual cell that you selected will be recorded into the macro. In such a case, the macro would always format that particular cell, and the macro would not be a "general-purpose" macro.

Understanding Security Issues Related to Macros

When you open a workbook that contains macros, Excel may display the Security Warning dialog box, like the one shown in Figure 184-1. This dialog box lets you disable or enable the macros in the workbook.

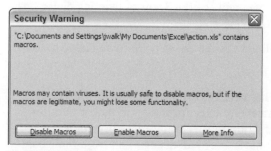

Figure 184-1: Excel's Security Warning dialog box may appear when you open a workbook that contains macros.

Depending on your macro security settings, you may not see the Security Warning dialog box. By selecting Tools⇨Macro⇨Security, you can change your macro security settings in the Security dialog box, shown in Figure 184-2.

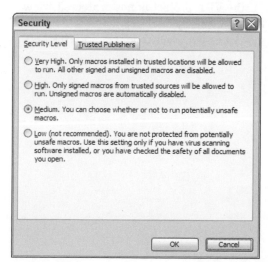

Figure 184-2: Use the Security dialog box to change your security setting for macros.

The different security levels you can choose from in the Security dialog box are as follows:

- **Very High:** If your security level is Very High, macros will be disabled and you won't even be informed about it — unless the workbook is located in a trusted location.

- **High:** If your security level is High, you will get a different dialog box informing you that macros are disabled (and you can't override that). Only signed macros from trusted sources will be enabled.

- **Medium:** If your security level is Medium, you will see the Security Warning dialog box every time you open a workbook that contains macros.

- **Low:** If your security level is Low, you will not see the Security Warning dialog box. The workbook will open with macros enabled.

Why all this fuss about macros and security? The main reason is that VBA is a powerful language — so powerful that it can do some extremely harmful things to your computer and even other computers on your network. Unfortunately, there are lots of people in the world who find it entertaining to see how much harm they can accomplish from their computer desks. In addition, VBA macros can carry computer viruses that spread to other files.

Bottom line: Never enable macros on a workbook that comes from someone you don't know. Better yet, be extra cautious and disable macros in workbooks from people that you do know. It's possible that the workbook can be carrying a virus and the owner doesn't even know it.

If you have any doubts, check the VBA code for the workbook. If the VBA project is protected with a password, don't enable the macros. If the VBA project is not protected, view the VBA code. If anything looks suspicious, don't take a risk by enabling macros. Also, consider installing virus-scanning software that examines your workbooks before they are opened.

Using a Personal Macro Workbook

When you start recording a macro, the Record Macro dialog box prompts you for a location to store the macro (see Figure 185-1). Your choices are

- Personal Macro Workbook
- New Workbook
- This Workbook

Part XII

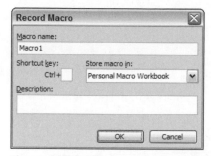

Figure 185-1: The Record Macro dialog box lets you choose where to store the recorded macro.

Most user-created macros are designed for use in a specific workbook, but you may want to use some macros in all of your work. You can store these general-purpose macros in the Personal Macro Workbook, so that they are always available to you.

The Personal Macro Workbook is loaded whenever you start Excel. The file, `personal.xls`, is stored in the XlStart folder, which is in your Excel folder. This file doesn't exist until you record a macro using Personal Macro Workbook as the destination.

 NOTE

The Personal Macro Workbook normally is in a hidden window (to keep it out of the way).

To record the macro in your Personal Macro Workbook, select the Personal Macro Workbook option in the Record Macro dialog box before you start recording. This is one of the options in the Store Macro In drop-down list.

If you store macros in the Personal Macro Workbook, you don't have to remember to open the Personal Macro Workbook when you load a workbook that uses macros. Excel automatically opens the Personal Macro Workbook.

If you've made any changes to your Personal Macro Workbook, you will be prompted to save the file when you close Excel.

Understanding Functions versus Subs

Excel VBA macros come in two distinct varieties: *Sub procedures* and *Function procedures*. This tip describes how they differ.

VBA Sub Procedures

You can think of a *Sub procedure* as a new command. You can have any number of Sub procedures in an Excel workbook. Figure 186-1 shows a simple VBA Sub procedure. When this code is executed, VBA inserts the current date into the active cell, formats it, makes the cell bold, and then adjusts the column width.

Figure 186-1: A simple VBA procedure.

Sub procedures always start with the keyword Sub, the macro's name, and then a pair of parentheses. The End Sub statement signals the end of the procedure. The lines in between comprise the procedure's code.

You execute a VBA Sub procedure in any of the following ways:

- Choose Tools⇨Macro and select the procedure's name from the list.

- Press the procedure's shortcut key combination (if it has one).

- If the Visual Basic Editor is active, move the cursor anywhere within the code and press F5.

- Refer to the procedure in another VBA procedure.

NOTE

When you record a macro, it is always a Sub procedure.

VBA Functions

The second type of VBA procedure is a Function procedure. A *Function procedure* always returns a single value (just as a worksheet function always returns a single value). A VBA Function procedure can be executed by other VBA procedures or used in worksheet formulas, just as you would use Excel's built-in worksheet functions.

Figure 186-2 shows the listing of a custom worksheet function and shows the Function procedure in use in a worksheet. This Function procedure is named CubeRoot, and it requires a single argument. CubeRoot calculates the cube root of its argument. A Function procedure looks much like a Sub procedure. Notice, however, that Function procedures begin with the keyword Function and end with an End Function statement.

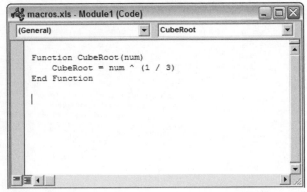

Figure 186-2: A Function procedure that calculates a cube root.

Displaying Pop-Up Messages

It's very easy to display pop-up messages using VBA, thanks to its handy MsgBox function. MsgBox is thoroughly described in the VBA Help system. This tip just provides a few examples of the versatility of this function.

Displaying the Time

The macro listed below, when executed, displays the current time, as shown in Figure 187-1:

```
Sub ShowTheTime()
    MsgBox "It's now " & Time
End Sub
```

Figure 187-1: Using MsgBox to display the time.

By using optional arguments for MsgBox, you can display custom text in the title bar and even add an icon. Figure 187-2 shows the result of executing the following macro:

```
Sub ShowTheTime2()
    MsgBox "It's now " & Time, vbInformation, "Wake up!"
End Sub
```

Figure 187-2: Using MsgBox to display the time, along with custom title bar text and an icon.

In this example, vbInformation is one of several built-in constants that you can use in the second argument of the MsgBox function. Table 187-1 lists all of the MsgBox constants, along with brief descriptions.

TABLE 187-1   CONSTANTS USED FOR BUTTONS IN THE MSGBOX FUNCTION

Constant	Value	Description
vbOKOnly	0	Display OK button only.
vbOKCancel	1	Display OK and Cancel buttons.
vbAbortRetryIgnore	2	Display Abort, Retry, and Ignore buttons.
vbYesNoCancel	3	Display Yes, No, and Cancel buttons.
vbYesNo	4	Display Yes and No buttons.
vbRetryCancel	5	Display Retry and Cancel buttons.
vbCritical	16	Display Critical Message icon.
vbQuestion	32	Display Warning Query icon.
vbExclamation	48	Display Warning Message icon.
vbInformation	64	Display Information Message icon.
vbDefaultButton1	0	First button is default.
vbDefaultButton2	256	Second button is default.
vbDefaultButton3	512	Third button is default.
vbDefaultButton4	768	Fourth button is default.
vbSystemModal	4096	All applications are suspended until the user responds to the message box (this may not work under all conditions).

Asking a Question

The following macro displays the message shown in Figure 187-3. Notice that the message box has two buttons, which result from using the vbYesNo constant.

This macro uses a variable, Ans, to store the user's response (that is, clicking the Yes button or clicking the No button). It also uses an If statement to determine if the Ans is Yes (represented as vbYes). If so, then the workbook is saved. If Ans is not equal to vbYes, nothing happens.

```
Sub AskQuestion()
    Ans = MsgBox("Do you want to save the workbook?", vbYesNo)
    If Ans = vbYes Then ActiveWorkbook.Save
End Sub
```

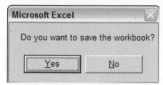

Figure 187-3: Using MsgBox to get a response from the user.

Combining Buttons and Icons

The following example below demonstrates how to combine the MsgBox constants by using the + operator. This message box, shown in Figure 187-4, displays two buttons and an icon. If the user clicks Yes, then the procedure named ReformatHardDrive (not shown here) will be executed.

```
Sub WarnUser()
  Ans = MsgBox("Your drive will be reformatted. Continue?", vbYesNo + vbCritical)
  If Ans = vbYes Then ReformatHardDrive
End Sub
```

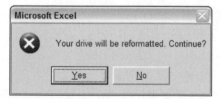

Figure 187-4: Using MsgBox to display buttons and an icon.

Getting Information from the User

Tip 187 presents a few MsgBox examples. This tip demonstrates other ways to get information from the user.

VBA's InputBox Function

VBA's InputBox function displays a field into which the user can enter information.

The following macro displays the dialog box shown in Figure 188-1. The user is prompted for a report title, and the macro then puts the text into cell A1 on the active sheet.

```
Sub GetTitle()
    Title = InputBox("Enter a title for the report.")
    Range("A1") = Title
End Sub
```

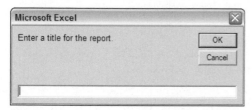

Figure 188-1: Using InputBox to get text.

The InputBox Method

The previous example used VBA's InputBox function. In addition, you can make use of Excel's InputBox method — which is similar to the InputBox function.

One advantage in using the InputBox method is that your macro can prompt for a range of cells. The user can then select the range, and the macro can work with those cells.

The following macro, when executed, displays the dialog box shown in Figure 188-2. When the user specifies a range and clicks OK, the VBA code erases the information in the range.

```
Sub EraseRange()
    Dim UserRange As Range
    DefaultRange = Selection.Address
    On Error GoTo Canceled
    Set UserRange = Application.InputBox _
        (Prompt:="Range to erase:", _
        Title:="Range Erase", _
        Default:=DefaultRange, _
        Type:=8)
    UserRange.Clear
    UserRange.Select
Canceled:
End Sub
```

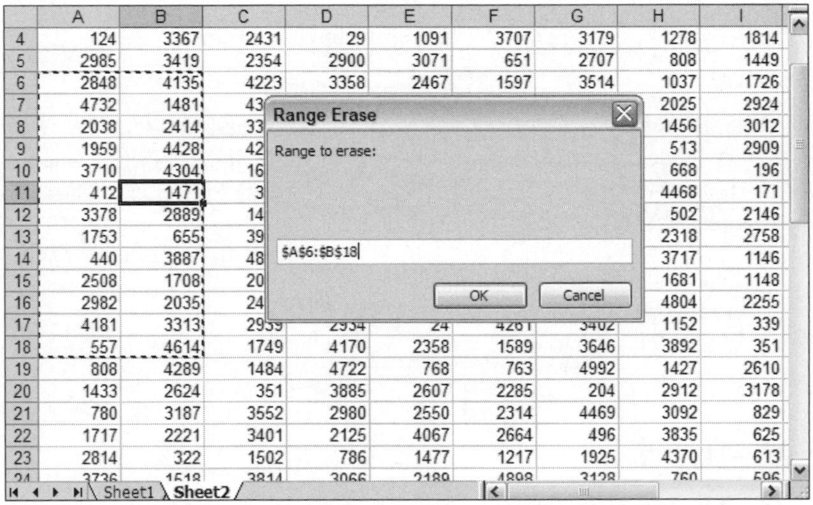

	A	B	C	D	E	F	G	H	I
4	124	3367	2431	29	1091	3707	3179	1278	1814
5	2985	3419	2354	2900	3071	651	2707	808	1449
6	2848	4135	4223	3358	2467	1597	3514	1037	1726
7	4732	1481	43					2025	2924
8	2038	2414	33					1456	3012
9	1959	4428	42					513	2909
10	3710	4304	16					668	196
11	412	1471	3					4468	171
12	3378	2889	14					502	2146
13	1753	655	39					2318	2758
14	440	3887	48					3717	1146
15	2508	1708	20					1681	1148
16	2982	2035	24					4804	2255
17	4181	3313	2959	2934	24	4261	3402	1152	339
18	557	4614	1749	4170	2358	1589	3646	3892	351
19	808	4289	1484	4722	768	763	4992	1427	2610
20	1433	2624	351	3885	2607	2285	204	2912	3178
21	780	3187	3552	2980	2550	2314	4469	3092	829
22	1717	2221	3401	2125	4067	2664	496	3835	625
23	2814	322	1502	786	1477	1217	1925	4370	613
24	3736	1518	3814	3066	2189	4898	3128	760	596

Range Erase

Range to erase:

$A$6:$B$18

OK   Cancel

Figure 188-2: Using the InputBox method to get a range selection.

Running a Macro When a Workbook Is Opened

Excel is capable of monitoring a wide variety of events and executing a VBA macro when a particular event occurs. Here are just a few of the many events Excel can recognize:

- The workbook is opened.
- The workbook is saved.
- A new worksheet is added.
- A cell has been modified.

This tip focuses on one very useful event: the workbook open event. In many cases, it's useful to execute a macro as soon as a workbook is opened. That's the purpose of a workbook open event-handler macro.

The workbook open event-handler macro must be located in a very specific place: the code module for the ThisWorkbook object. The easiest way to get to the code module for the ThisWorkbook object is to right-click the Excel icon directly to the left of the File menu. Then select View Code from the shortcut menu (see Figure 189-1).

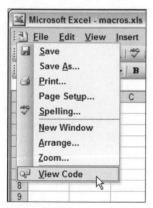

Figure 189-1: Using a shortcut menu to jump to the code module for the ThisWorkbook object.

In addition to being located in the proper place, a workbook open macro must have a specific name: It must be named Workbook_Open.

Greeting the User by Name

The following macro runs when the workbook is opened. It simply displays a message box that greets the user by name (see Figure 189-2).

```
Private Sub Workbook_Open()
    MsgBox "Hello " & Application.UserName
End Sub
```

Figure 189-2: Greeting the user when the workbook is opened.

Keeping Track of the Number of Times a Workbook Is Opened

The following Workbook_Open macro uses the Windows registry to keep track of the number of times the workbook has been opened. Every time the macro runs, it updates the number and displays that number in a message box (see Figure 189-3).

```
Private Sub Workbook_Open()
'   Get setting from registry
    Counter = GetSetting("XYZ Corp", "Budget", "Count", 0)
    LastOpen = GetSetting("XYZ Corp", "Budget", "Opened", "")

'   Display the information
    Msg = "This file has been opened " & Counter & " times."
    Msg = Msg & vbCrLf & "Last opened: " & LastOpen
    MsgBox Msg, vbInformation, ThisWorkbook.Name

'   Update the information and store it
    Counter = Counter + 1
    LastOpen = Date & " " & Time
    SaveSetting "XYZ Corp", "Budget", "Count", Counter
    SaveSetting "XYZ Corp", "Budget", "Opened", LastOpen
End Sub
```

Figure 189-3: Displaying the number of times a workbook has been opened.

Part XII

Creating a Usage Log

If you would like to keep track of who opens a workbook, and at what time, add the following procedure to the ThisWorkbook code module:

```
Private Sub Workbook_Open()
    Open ThisWorkbook.Path & "\usage.log" For Append As #1
    Print #1, Application.UserName, Now
    Close #1
End Sub
```

When this procedure is executed, it appends the user's name and the current date and time to a text file. The file is stored in the workbook's directory, and is named usage.log. If the text file does not exist, it is created. You can, of course, change the code so that the text file is written to a different directory.

NOTE

Keep in mind that this procedure is not executed if the workbook is opened with macros disabled.

Creating Simple Worksheet Functions

Excel provides many worksheet functions, but sometimes you need something other than what's available by default. This tip provides a few examples of custom functions that can be used in worksheet formulas.

NOTE

Function procedures should be placed in a normal VBA module. If your workbook doesn't have any VBA modules, activate the Visual Basic Editor, select your workbook from the Project list, and choose Insert⇨Module.

Returning the User Name

The following USERNAME function simply displays the name of the user — the name listed in the General tab of the Options dialog box:

```
Function USERNAME()
    USERNAME = Application.USERNAME
End Function
```

Here's a worksheet formula that uses this function:

```
=USERNAME()
```

Does a Cell Contain a Formula?

The following CELLHASFORMULA function accepts a single-cell argument and returns TRUE if the cell has a formula:

```
Function CELLHASFORMULA(cell) As Boolean
'   Returns TRUE if cell has a formula
    CELLHASFORMULA = cell.Range("A1").HasFormula
End Function
```

If a multicell range argument is passed to the function, the function works with the upper-left cell in the range.

Returning a Worksheet Name

The following SHEETNAME function accepts a single argument (a range) and returns the name of the worksheet that contains the range:

```
Function SHEETNAME(rng) As String
'   Returns the sheet name for rng
    SHEETNAME = rng.Parent.Name
End Function
```

Returning a Workbook Name

The following function, WORKBOOKNAME, returns the name of the workbook:

```
Function WORKBOOKNAME() As String
'   Returns the workbook name of the cell
'   that contains the function
    WORKBOOKNAME = Application.Caller.Parent.Parent.Name
End Function
```

Reversing a String

The following REVERSETEXT function returns the text in a cell backwards:

```
Function REVERSETEXT(text) As String
'   Returns its argument, reversed
    REVERSETEXT = StrReverse(text)
End Function
```

Extracting the Nth Element from a String

The EXTRACTELEMENT function extracts an element from a text string based on a specified separator character. Assume that cell A1 contains the following text:

```
123-456-789-9133-8844
```

The following formula returns the string *9133*, which is the fourth element in the string. The string uses a hyphen (-) as the separator.

```
=EXTRACTELEMENT(A1,4,"-")
```

The EXTRACTELEMENT function uses three arguments:

- **Txt:** The text string from which you're extracting. This can be a literal string or a cell reference.

- **n:** An integer that represents the element to extract.

- **Separator:** A single character used as the separator.

The VBA code for the EXTRACTELEMENT function follows:

```
Function EXTRACTELEMENT(Txt, n, Separator) As String
'   Returns the nth element of a text string, where the
'   elements are separated by a specified separator character
    Dim AllElements As Variant
    AllElements = Split(Txt, Separator)
    EXTRACTELEMENT = AllElements(n - 1)
End Function
```

Making Excel Talk

This tip describes how to make Excel monitor a particular cell and give a verbal report using the text-to-speech feature when the value changes. It uses an event-handler macro — specifically, a macro named Worksheet_Calculate.

NOTE

This technique works only with Excel 2002 and later.

CROSS-REFERENCE

See Tip 32 for more about using the Text To Speech options in Excel.

The Worksheet_Calculate macro must be placed in the code module for the worksheet that contains the cell that's being monitored. The easiest way to activate that code module is to right-click the sheet tab and choose View Code from the shortcut menu.

The following listing assumes that cell A1 contains a total and is the cell that's being monitored. The listing uses a different phrase for each of six conditions. For example, if cell A1 contains the value 1,050, Excel will say, "You are over the budget."

You can, of course, add as many conditions as you like and adjust the ranges for the conditions.

```
Private Sub Worksheet_Calculate()
    With Application.Speech
    Select Case Range("A1")
        Case Is < 600: .Speak "Way below the budget"
        Case 601 To 900: .Speak "Within the budget"
        Case 901 To 999: .Speak "Getting close to the budget"
        Case 1000: .Speak "You are exactly at the budget"
        Case 1001 To 1100: .Speak "You are over the budget"
        Case Is > 1100: .Speak "You are going to get fired"
    End Select
    End With
End Sub
```

Understanding Custom Function Limitations

Almost all users who start creating custom worksheet functions using VBA make a fatal mistake: They try to get the function to do more than what is possible.

A worksheet function returns a value, and the function must be completely *passive:* In other words, the function cannot change anything on the worksheet.

For example, you may write a function like the following. This function takes one argument (a cell reference) and attempts to change the formatting of the cell. Although the following function contains perfectly valid VBA code, it will not make the reference cell bold. The only tangible effect is that the cell that contains this function will display the #VALUE! error.

```
Function MakeBold(cell)
    If cell.Value > 100 Then
        cell.Font.Bold = True
    Else
        cell.Font.Bold = False
    End If
End Function
```

In many cases, you can use an event macro instead of a custom function. The following macro is located in the module for a worksheet. It is executed whenever the sheet is calculated. If cell A1 contains a value greater than 100, then the cell is made bold. Otherwise, it is not bold.

```
Private Sub Worksheet_Calculate()
    If Range("A1").Value > 100 Then
        Range("A1").Font.Bold = True
    Else
        Range("A1").Font.Bold = False
    End If
End Sub
```

NOTE

This simple example is for illustration only. A more efficient solution is to use Excel's conditional formatting feature.

Executing a Menu Item with a Macro

This tip describes how to write VBA code that will mimic selecting any of Excel's menu items. For example, you can write a macro that executes the Format⇨Cells command, which displays the Format Cells dialog box. This tip applies to all menu items, regardless of whether or not they open a dialog box.

First, remember that Excel has two menus: One is displayed when a worksheet is active, and another is displayed when a chart sheet is active (or when an embedded chart is activated). The worksheet menu is referred to as CommandBars(1), and the chart menu is referred to as CommandBars(2).

You need to construct a VBA statement that drills down to the desired menu item. The following examples demonstrate how to go through a menu sequence to select the desired menu item.

To display the Format Cells dialog box, use this VBA statement:

```
Application.CommandBars(1).Controls("Format").Controls("Cells...").Execute
```

Notice that the Cells menu item uses an ellipses (three periods). That's because the text must match the menu display exactly.

To insert a new row at the active cell, use this VBA statement:

```
Application.CommandBars(1).Controls("Insert").Controls("Rows").Execute
```

To clear the formatting in the selected range, use this VBA statement:

```
Application.CommandBars(1).Controls("Edit").Controls("Clear").
Controls("Formats").Execute
```

To display the Chart Type dialog box, use this VBA statement:

```
Application.CommandBars(2).Controls("Chart").Controls("Chart Type...").Execute
```

Note that the preceding example uses CommandBars(2) for the Chart menu. Also, this statement will generate an error if a chart sheet is not active, or if an embedded chart is not selected.

NOTE

Generally, it's preferable to use other methods to perform these actions. But these will do in a pinch — especially if you haven't yet learned the VBA commands.

Storing Custom Functions in an Add-In

If you create custom worksheet functions using VBA, you have three choices regarding where to store the functions:

- **In the workbook in which you use them.** This is the best choice for functions that are used in only one workbook.

- **In your Personal Macro Workbook.** This is a good choice for functions that are used in multiple workbooks. The problem, however, is that the function name must be preceded by the name of the Personal Macro Workbook, as in this example:

  ```
  =PERSONAL.XLS!MYFUNCTION(C16)
  ```

- **In an add-in.** If your functions will be used in multiple workbooks, this is the best choice because you need not precede the function name with the name of the add-in, as shown in this example:

  ```
  =MYFUNCTION(C16)
  ```

Follow these steps to create an add-in that contains your custom VBA functions:

1. Open a new workbook.

2. Copy all of your functions to a VBA module in the new workbook.

3. Select File⇨Save As to display the Save As dialog box.

4. In the Save As dialog box, select Microsoft Office Excel Add-In (*.xla) from the Save as Type drop-down list.

5. Enter a name for the add-in in the File Name field and specify a folder where you want to save the add-in.

6. Click Save.

7. Close the workbook.

Next, install the add-in you just saved by selecting Tools⇨Add-Ins. In the Add-Ins dialog box, click the Browse button and locate your new add-in. When the add-in is installed, you can use the Insert⇨Function command to insert your custom function when you create a formula. The custom functions appear in the User Defined category.

Displaying a Pop-Up Linked Calendar

This tip describes how to add a pop-up calendar control to a worksheet. If you like, you can even link the calendar to a cell in the worksheet so that you can select a date from the calendar and it will be entered into the linked cell. Follow these steps:

1. Right-click any toolbar and select Control Toolbox to display the Control Toolbox toolbar.

2. In the Control Toolbox toolbar, click the More Controls button to display a list of additional controls.

    (Note that not all of these extra controls will function properly when inserted on a worksheet.)

3. Scroll through the list and click Microsoft Date and Time Picker Control. This selects the control and also puts Excel into Design Mode.

4. Use your mouse to draw the control on your worksheet (see Figure 195-1).

5. Click the Exit Design Mode button on the Control Toolbox toolbar.

Figure 195-1: Inserting a calendar control on a worksheet.

Figure 195-2 shows this control in action.

If you would like to link the data displayed in this calendar to a cell, follow these steps:

1. Click the Design Mode button on the Control Toolbox toolbar.

2. Click the Calendar control to select it.

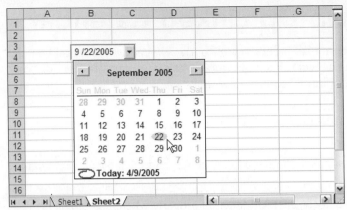

Figure 195-2: Displaying a calendar from within a worksheet.

3. Click the Properties button in the Control Toolbox toolbar to display the Properties dialog box.

4. Locate the LinkedCell property and enter a cell reference (for example, type **A1**). See Figure 195-3.

5. Click the Exit Design Mode button on the Control Toolbox toolbar.

When you select a date from the calendar, Excel enters the date into cell A1.

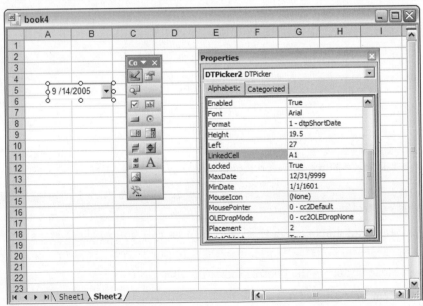

Figure 195-3: Linking a calendar control to a cell.

Using Add-Ins

Excel is a great program, but let's face it: Sometimes it just doesn't have the features that you would like. Fortunately, Excel's design allows you to use add-ins to enhance its capabilities and add new features.

Add-Ins That Ship with Excel

The following is a list of the add-ins that are included with Excel 2003. Some of these add-ins may not have been installed by default when you installed Excel. If you try to use one of these add-ins and it's not installed, you receive a prompt asking whether you want to install it.

- **Analysis ToolPak:** Contains statistical and engineering tools, plus new worksheet functions.

- **Analysis ToolPak — VBA:** Adds VBA functions for the Analysis ToolPak.

- **Conditional Sum Wizard:** Helps you to create formulas that add values based on a condition.

- **Euro Currency Tools:** Contains tools for converting and formatting the Euro currency.

- **Lookup Wizard:** Helps you to create formulas that look up data in a list.

- **Solver Add-In:** Adds a tool that helps you to use a variety of numeric methods for equation solving and optimization.

NOTE

You can download additional Excel add-ins from `http://office.microsoft.com`.

Installing Add-Ins

Most Excel add-ins are contained in an `*.xla` file. To install an `*.xla` add-in, select Tools⇨Add-Ins. Then, in the Add-Ins dialog box, click the Browse button and locate the `*.xla` file on your hard drive. The add-in name will then appear in the list (make sure it's checked).

The Add-Ins dialog box lists all add-ins that Excel knows about. The add-ins in the list with check marks are currently installed. To uninstall an add-in, just remove the check mark.

Part XII

NOTE

Most add-in files can also be opened by selecting File⇨Open. You'll find that after an add-in is opened, however, you can't choose File⇨Close to close it. The only way to remove the add-in is to exit and restart Excel or to write a macro to close the add-in.

When an add-in is opened, you may or may not notice anything different. In nearly every case, however, some change is made to the menu bar — the add-in either adds a new menu to the menu bar or adds one or more new menu items to an existing menu. For example, when you open the Analysis ToolPak add-in, a new menu item appears on the Tools menu: Data Analysis. When you open my Power Utility Pak add-in, you get a new Utilities menu, which is located between the Data and Window menus.

Finding Add-Ins

The best way to find Excel add-ins that are suitable for a particular task is to search the Web, including the Excel newsgroups (available through www.groups.google.com). If you still can't find what you're looking for, try posting a question in one of the Excel newsgroups. Describe what functionality you're looking for. If such an add-in exists, someone will know about it and respond.

Part XIII

Conversions and Mathematical Calculations

This part provides you with a variety of handy measurement conversion tables and several calculations you might find useful as you work away in Excel.

Tips and Where to Find Them

Tip 197 Converting Between
Measurement Systems   485

Tip 198 Converting Temperatures   493

Tip 199 Solving Right Triangles   495

Tip 200 Calculating Area, Surface,
Circumference, and Volume   497

Tip 201 Solving Simultaneous
Equations   501

Tip 202 Generating Unique Random
Integers   503

Tip 203 Generating Random
Numbers   505

Tip 204 Calculating Roots and a
Remainder   507

Tip 205 Calculating a Conditional
Average   509

Converting Between Measurement Systems

You know the distance from New York to London in miles, but your European office needs the numbers in kilometers. What's the conversion factor?

Using the CONVERT Function

If you've installed Excel's Analysis ToolPak add-in, you can use the CONVERT function. The CONVERT function takes three arguments:

- The value to be converted
- The abbreviation for the current measurement system (the "from" unit)
- The abbreviation for the desired measurement system (the "to" unit)

For example, to convert 550 miles to kilometers, use this formula:

```
=CONVERT(550,"mi", "km")
```

It's important that you use the correct abbreviation, of course. The abbreviations that CONVERT recognizes are listed in Excel's Help system.

Converting Units without the CONVERT Function

In some cases, you may find it more efficient to create your own conversion formulas so that you don't need to rely on the Analysis ToolPak. To create your own conversion formula, you need to know the specific conversion factor for the measurement units.

For example, if you need to convert from inches to feet, the conversion factor is 12. Create a formula to multiply the number of inches by 12, and the result will be in feet.

Tables 197-1 through 197-9 contain conversion factors for common units of measurement in the following categories:

- Distance conversions
- Weight conversions
- Liquid measurement conversions
- Surface conversions
- Volume conversions
- Force conversions
- Energy conversions

- Mass conversions
- Time conversions

Unit conversion factors for other units are readily available on the Internet (do a Web search for *unit conversion*, and you'll find what you need).

TABLE 197-1 DISTANCE CONVERSION FACTORS

	Foot	Inch	Meter	Nautical Mile	Statute Mile	Yard
Foot	1	12	0.3048	0.000164579	0.000189394	0.333333333
Inch	0.083333333	1	0.0254	1.37149E-05	1.57828E-05	0.027777778
Meter	3.280839895	39.37007874	1	0.000539957	0.000621371	1.093613298
Nautical mile	6076.115486	72913.38583	1852	1	1.150779448	2025.371828
Statute mile	5280	63360	1609.344	0.868976242	1	1759.999999
Yard	3	36	0.9144	0.000493737	0.000568182	1

TABLE 197-2 WEIGHT CONVERSION FACTORS

	Gram	Ounce	Pound
Gram	1	0.035274	0.002205
Ounce	28.34952	1	0.0625
Pound	453.5923	16	1

TABLE 197-3   LIQUID MEASUREMENT CONVERSION FACTORS

	Cup	Fluid Ounce	Gallon	Liter	Pint	Quart	Tablespoon	Teaspoon
Cup	1	8	0.0625	0.23664	0.5	0.25	16	48
Fluid ounce	0.125	1	0.007813	0.02958	0.0625	0.03125	2	6
Gallon	16	128	1	3.786235	8	4	256	768
Liter	4.225833	33.80667	0.264115	1	2.112917	1.056458	67.61333	202.84
Pint	2	16	0.125	0.473279	1	0.5	32	96
Quart	4	32	0.25	0.946559	2	1	64	192
Tablespoon	0.0625	0.5	0.003906	0.01479	0.03125	0.015625	1	3
Teaspoon	0.020833	0.166667	0.001302	0.00493	0.010417	0.005208	0.333333	1

Part XIII

TABLE 197-4   SURFACE MEASUREMENT CONVERSION FACTORS

	Acre	Hectare	Square Foot	Square Inch	Square Meter	Square Mile	Square Yard
Acre	1	0.404685642	43560	6272640	4046.856422	0.0015625	4839.999997
Hectare	2.471053815	1	107639.1042	15500031	10000	0.003861022	11959.90046
Square Foot	2.29568E-05	9.2903E-06	1	144	0.09290304	3.58701E-08	0.111111111
Square Inch	1.59423E-07	6.4516E-08	0.006944444	1	0.00064516	2.49098E-10	0.000771605
Square Meter	0.000247105	1E-04	10.76391042	1550.0031	1	3.86102E-07	1.195990046
Square Mile	640	258.998811	27878400	4014489600	2589988.11	1	3097599.998
Square Yard	0.000206612	8.36127E-05	9	1296	0.836127361	3.22831E-07	1

TABLE 197-5 ENERGY CONVERSION FACTORS

	BTU	Calorie (IT)	Calorie (Th'mic)	Electron Volt	Erg	Foot-pound	Horsepower-hour	Joule	Watt-hour
BTU	1	251.9966	252.1655	6.59E+21	1.06E+10	25036.98	0.000393	1055.058	0.293072
Calorie (IT)	0.003968	1	1.00067	2.61E+19	41867928	99.35441	1.56E-06	4.186795	0.001163
Calorie (Th'mic)	0.003966	0.99933	1	2.61E+19	41839890	99.28787	1.56E-06	4.183991	0.001162
Electron volt	1.52E-22	3.83E-20	3.83E-20	1	1.6E-12	3.8E-18	5.97E-26	1.6E-19	4.45E-23
Erg	9.48E-11	2.39E-08	2.39E-08	6.24E+11	1	2.37E-06	3.73E-14	1E-07	2.78E-11
Foot-pound	3.99E-05	0.010065	0.010072	2.63E+17	421399.8	1	1.57E-08	0.04214	1.17E-05
Horsepower-hour	2544.426	641186.8	641616.4	1.68E+25	2.68E+13	63704732	1	2684517	745.6997
Joule	0.000948	0.238846	0.239006	6.24E+18	9999995	23.73042	3.73E-07	1	0.000278
Watt-hour	3.412133	859.8459	860.4221	2.25E+22	3.6E+10	85429.48	0.001341	3599.998	1

Part XIII

TABLE 197-6 MASS CONVERSION FACTORS

	Caret	Grain	Gram	Ounce (Avdp)	Ounce (Troy)	Pound (Avdp)	Pound (Troy)	Stone	Ton
Caret	1	3.086472147	0.2	0.007054793	0.006430149	0.000440924	0.000535846	3.14946E-05	2.2E-07
Grain	0.3239945	1	0.0647989	0.002285714	0.002083333	0.000142857	0.000173611	1.02041E-05	7.14E-08
Gram	5	15.43236073	1	0.035273966	0.032150743	0.002204622	0.002679228	0.000157473	1.1E-06
Ounce (Avdp)	141.7476	437.5000193	28.34952	1	0.911458139	0.062499989	0.075954837	0.004464285	3.12E-05
Ounce (Troy)	155.5174	480.0001235	31.10348	1.097143091	1	0.068571431	0.083333324	0.004897959	3.43E-05
Pound (Avdp)	2267.962	7000.001543	453.5924	16.00000282	14.5833328	1	1.215277603	0.071428567	0.0005
Pound (Troy)	1866.209	5760.002099	373.2418	13.1657185	12.00000129	0.822857261	1	0.058775515	0.000411
Stone	31751.47	98000.02778	6350.294	224.0000536	204.166672	14.00000088	17.01388751	1	0.007
Ton	4535924	14000003.09	907184.8	32000.00564	29166.66559	2000	2430.555206	142.8571339	1

TABLE 197-7 VOLUME MEASUREMENT CONVERSION FACTORS

	Cubic Foot	Cubic Inch	Cubic Meter	Cubic Yard
Cubic Foot	1	1728	0.028316847	0.037037037
Cubic Inch	0.000578704	1	1.63871E-05	2.14335E-05
Cubic Meter	35.31466672	61023.74409	1	1.307950618
Cubic Yard	27	46656	0.764554859	1

TABLE 197-8 FORCE CONVERSION FACTORS

	Dyne	Newton	Pound Force
Dyne	1	0.00001	2.25E-06
Newton	100000	1	0.224809
Pound Force	444822.2	4.448222	1

TABLE 197-9 TIME CONVERSION FACTORS

	Day	Hour	Minute	Second	Year
Day	1	24	1440	86400	0.002738
Hour	0.041667	1	60	3600	0.000114
Minute	0.000694	0.016667	1	60	1.9E-06
Second	1.16E-05	0.000278	0.016667	1	3.17E-08
Year	365.25	8766	525960	31557600	1

Converting Temperatures

The previous tip provided conversion factors for common measurement units. This tip presents formulas for conversion among three units of temperature: Fahrenheit, Celsius, and Kelvin. Temperature conversions, unlike the unit conversions discussed previously, do not use a simple conversion factor. Rather, you need to use a formula to calculate the conversion.

Table 198-1 assumes that the temperature for conversion is in a cell named temp.

TABLE 198-1   TEMPERATURE CONVERSION FORMULAS

Type of Conversion	Formula
Fahrenheit to Celsius	=(temp-32)*(5/9)
Fahrenheit to Kelvin	=(temp-32)*(5/9)+273
Celsius to Fahrenheit	=(temp*1.8)+32
Celsius to Kelvin	=temp+273
Kelvin to Celsius	=temp-273
Kelvin to Fahrenheit	=((temp-273)*1.8)+32

Part XIII

Solving Right Triangles

This tip is provided for those who may be a bit rusty on their trigonometry skills.

A right triangle has six components: three sides and three angles. Figure 199-1 shows a right triangle with its various parts labeled. Angles arc labeled A, B, and C; sides are labeled Hypotenuse, Base, and Height. Angle C is always 90 degrees (or PI/2 radians). If you know any two of these components (excluding Angle C, which is always known), you can use formulas to solve for the others.

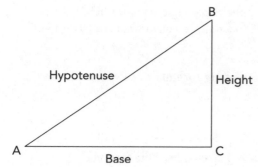

Figure 199-1: A right triangle's components.

The Pythagorean theorem states that

```
Height^2 + Base^2 = Hypotenuse^2
```

Therefore, if you know two sides of a right triangle, you can calculate the remaining side. The formula to calculate a right triangle's height (given the length of the hypotenuse and base) is as follows:

```
=SQRT((hypotenuse^2)-(base^2))
```

The formula to calculate a right triangle's base (given the length of the hypotenuse and height) is as follows:

```
=SQRT((hypotenuse^2)-(height^2))
```

The formula to calculate a right triangle's hypotenuse (given the length of the base and height) is as follows:

```
=SQRT((height^2)+(base^2))
```

Part XIII

Other useful trigonometric identities are

```
SIN(A) = Height/Hypotenuse
SIN(B) = Base/Hypotenuse
COS(A) = Base/Hypotenuse
COS(B) = Height/Hypotenuse
TAN(A) = Height/Base
SIN(A) = Base/Height
```

 NOTE

Excel's trigonometric functions all assume that the angle arguments are in radians. To convert degrees to radians, use the RADIANS function. To convert radians to degrees, use the DEGREES function.

If you know the height and base, you can use the following formula to calculate the angle formed by the hypotenuse and base (Angle A).

```
=ATAN(height/base)
```

The preceding formula returns radians. To convert to degrees, use this formula:

```
=DEGREES(ATAN(height/base))
```

If you know the height and base, you can use the following formula to calculate the angle formed by the hypotenuse and height (Angle B):

```
=PI()/2-ATAN(height/base)
```

The preceding formula returns radians. To convert to degrees, use this formula:

```
=90-DEGREES(ATAN(height/base))
```

Calculating Area, Surface, Circumference, and Volume

This tip contains formulas for calculating the area, surface, circumference, and volume for common two- and three-dimensional shapes.

Calculating the Area and Perimeter of a Square

To calculate the area of a square, square the length of one side. The following formula calculates the area of a square for a cell named side:

```
=side^2
```

To calculate the perimeter of a square, multiply one side by 4. The following formula uses a cell named side to calculate the perimeter of a square:

```
=side*4
```

Calculating the Area and Perimeter of a Rectangle

To calculate the area of a rectangle, multiply its height by its base. The following formula returns the area of a rectangle, using cells named height and base:

```
=height*base
```

To calculate the perimeter of a rectangle, multiply the height by 2 and add it to the width multiplied by 2. The following formula returns the perimeter of a rectangle, using cells named height and width:

```
=(height*2)+(width*2)
```

Calculating the Area and Perimeter of a Circle

To calculate the area of a circle, multiply the square of the radius by π. The following formula returns the area of a circle. It assumes that a cell named radius contains the circle's radius:

```
=PI()*(radius^2)
```

The radius of a circle is equal to one-half of the diameter.

To calculate the circumference of a circle, multiply the diameter of the circle by π. The following formula calculates the circumference of a circle using a cell named diameter:

```
=diameter*PI()
```

The diameter of a circle is the radius times 2.

Calculating the Area of a Trapezoid

To calculate the area of a trapezoid, add the two parallel sides, multiply by the height, and then divide by 2. The following formula calculates the area of a trapezoid, using cells named side and height:

```
=((side*2)*height)/2
```

Calculating the Area of a Triangle

To calculate the area of a triangle, multiply the base by the height, and then divide by 2. The following formula calculates the area of a triangle, using cells named base and height:

```
=(base*height)/2
```

Calculating the Surface and Volume of a Sphere

To calculate the surface of a sphere, multiply the square of the radius by π, and then multiply by 4. The following formula returns the surface of a sphere, the radius of which is in a cell named radius:

```
=PI()*(radius^2)*4
```

To calculate the volume of a sphere, multiply the cube of the radius by 4 times π, and then divide by 3. The following formula calculates the volume of a sphere. The cell named radius contains the sphere's radius.

```
=((radius^3)*(4*PI()))/3
```

Calculating the Surface and Volume of a Cube

To calculate the surface area of a cube, square one side and multiply by 6. The following formula calculates the surface of a cube using a cell named side, which contains the length of a side of the cube:

```
=(side^2)*6
```

To calculate the volume of a cube, raise the length of one side to the third power. The following formula returns the volume of a cube, using a cell named side:

```
=side^3
```

Calculating the Surface and Volume of a Cone

The following formula calculates the surface of a cone (including the surface of the base). This formula uses cells named radius and height:

```
=PI()*radius*(SQRT(height^2+radius^2)+radius))
```

To calculate the volume of a cone, multiply the square of the radius of the base by π, multiply by the height, and then divide by 3. The following formula returns the volume of a cone, using cells named radius and height:

```
=(PI()*(radius^2)*height)/3
```

Calculating the Volume of a Cylinder

To calculate the volume of a cylinder, multiply the square of the radius of the base by π, and then multiply by the height. The following formula calculates the volume of a cylinder, using cells named radius and height:

```
=(PI()*(radius^2)*height)
```

Calculating the Volume of a Pyramid

Calculate the area of the base, and then multiply by the height and divide by 3. This next formula calculates the volume of a pyramid. It assumes cells named width (the width of the base), length (the length of the base), and height (the height of the pyramid).

```
=(width*length*height)/3
```

Part XIII

Solving Simultaneous Equations

This tip describes how to use formulas to solve simultaneous linear equations. The following is an example of a set of simultaneous linear equations:

```
3x + 4y = 8
4x + 8y = 1
```

Solving a set of simultaneous equations involves finding the values for x and y that satisfy both equations. For this set of equations, the solution is as follows:

```
x = 7.5
y = -3.625
```

The number of variables in the set of equations must be equal to the number of equations. The preceding example uses two equations with two variables. Three equations are required to solve for three variables (x, y, and z).

The general steps for solving a set of simultaneous equations follow. See Figure 201-1, which uses the equations presented at the beginning of this section.

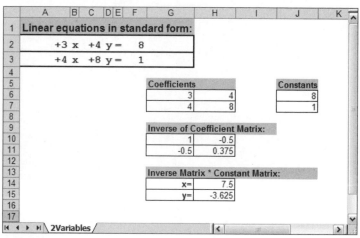

Figure 201-1: Using formulas to solve simultaneous equations.

1. Express the equations in standard form. If necessary, use simple algebra to rewrite the equations such that the variables all appear on the left side of the equal sign. The two equations that follow are identical, but the second one is in standard form:

```
3x -8 = -4y
3x + 4y = 8
```

2. Place the coefficients in an n-by-n range of cells, where n represents the number of equations. In Figure 201-1, the coefficients are in the range G6:H7.

3. Place the constants (the numbers on the right side of the equal sign) in a vertical range of cells. In Figure 201-1, the constants are in the range J6:J7.

4. Use an array formula to calculate the inverse of the coefficient matrix. In Figure 201-1, the following array formula is entered into the range G10:H11 (remember to press Ctrl+Shift+Enter to enter an array formula).

```
=MINVERSE(G6:H7)
```

5. Use an array formula to multiply the inverse of the coefficient matrix by the constant matrix. In Figure 201-1, the following array formula is entered into the range H14:H15. This range holds the solution (x = 7.5, and y = −3.625).

```
=MMULT(G10:H11,J6:J7)
```

Generating Unique Random Integers

When most spreadsheet users hear the term *circular reference,* they immediately think of an error condition. Generally, a circular reference represents an accident — something that you need to correct. Sometimes, however, a circular reference can be a good thing. This tip describes a method that uses circular references to generate a set of unique random integers.

The worksheet in Figure 202-1 generates 15 random integers between 1 and 30 in column A. The integers are generated such that they produce unique numbers (that is, not duplicated). You may want to use this technique to generate random lottery number picks.

	A	B	C	D	E
1	5	1		SOLUTION FOUND	
2	9	1			
3	8	1			
4	29	1			
5	18	1			
6	13	1			
7	23	1			
8	12	1			
9	25	1			
10	20	1			
11	22	1			
12	10	1			
13	19	1			
14	27	1			
15	11	1			
16					

Figure 202-1: Using circular reference formulas to generate unique random integers in column A.

NOTE

For this technique to work, you'll need to make a change in Excel's iteration setting. Select Tools ⇨ Options, and click the Calculation tab in the Options dialog box. Place a check mark next to the Iteration check box. This setting forces Excel to perform iterative calculations — which is necessary for this technique.

Column B contains formulas that count the number of times a particular number appears in the range A1:A15. For example, the formula in cell B1 follows. This formula displays the number of times the value in cell A1 appears in the range A1:A15:

```
=COUNTIF($A$1:$A$15,A1)
```

Each formula in column A contains a circular reference. The formula examines the sum of the cells in column B. If this sum does not equal 15, a new random integer generates. When the sum of the cells in column B equals 15, the values in column A are all unique. The formula in cell A1 is

```
=IF(SUM($B$1:$B$15)<>15,INT(RAND()*30+1),A1)
```

Cell D1, which follows, contains a formula that displays the status. If the sum of the cells in column B does not equal 15, the formula displays the text CALC AGAIN (press F9 to perform more iterations). When column B contains all ones, the formula displays *SOLUTION FOUND*.

```
=IF(SUM(B1:B15)<>15,"CALC AGAIN","SOLUTION FOUND")
```

To generate a new set of random integers, select any cell in column B. Then press F2 to edit the cell, and press Enter to reenter it. The number of calculations required depends on:

- The Iteration setting on the Calculation tab of the Options dialog box. If you specify a higher number of iterations, you have a better chance of finding 15 unique values.

- The number of values requested, compared to the number of possible values. This example seeks 15 unique integers from a pool of 30. Fewer calculations are required if, for example, you request 15 unique values from a pool of 100.

Generating Random Numbers

Excel's RAND function generates a random number between 0 and 1. If you need larger random numbers, just use a simple multiplication formula. The following formula, for example, generates a random number between 0 and 1000:

```
=RAND()*1000
```

To limit the random number to whole numbers, use the ROUND function:

```
=ROUND((RAND()*1000),0)
```

To generate random numbers between any two numbers, you can use the RANDBETWEEN function, which is available only when the Analysis ToolPak add-in is installed. The following formula, for example, generates a random number between 100 and 200:

```
=RANDBETWEEN(100,200)
```

You can avoid the RANDBETWEEN function, and use a formula like this, where *a* represents the lower limit and *b* represents the upper limit:

```
=RAND()*(b-a)+a
```

To generate a random number between 40 and 50, use this formula:

```
=RAND()*(50-40)+40
```

Part XIII

Calculating Roots and a Remainder

Sometimes you might need to figure out a complicated root of a value or you might want to know a nondecimal remainder of a division. Excel can do that for you.

Calculating Roots

If you need to calculate the square root of a value, use Excel's SQRT function. The following formula, for example, calculates the square root of the value in cell A1:

```
=SQRT(A1)
```

But what about other roots? You won't find a CUBEROOT function, and there's certainly isn't a FOURTHROOT function. The trick is to raise the number to the (1/root power) power. For example, to calculate the cube root of the value in cell A1, use this formula:

```
=A1^(1/3)
```

To calculate the fourth root, use this formula:

```
=A1^(1/4)
```

Calculating a Remainder

When you divide two numbers, if the result isn't a whole number, you end up with a remainder. When Excel performs division, the result is a decimal value. How can you determine the remainder (if any) that results from a division?

The solution is to use the MOD function, which takes two arguments: the number and the divisor. The MOD function returns the remainder.

For example, if you have 187 books to be divided equally among 5 offices, how many will be left over? To get the answer (2), use this formula:

```
=MOD(187,5)
```

Calculating a Conditional Average

Excel makes it easy to calculate the average of a range of cells by using the AVERAGE function. But in the real world, a simple average often isn't adequate for your needs.

For example, an instructor might calculate student grades by averaging a series of test scores but omitting the two lowest scores. Or you might want to compute an average that ignores both the highest and lowest values.

In cases such as these, the AVERAGE function won't do, so you must create a more complex formula. The following formula computes the average of the values contained in a range named scores, but excludes the highest and lowest values:

```
=(SUM(scores)-MIN(scores)-MAX(scores))/(COUNT(scores)-2)
```

Here's an example that calculates an average excluding the two lowest scores:

```
=(SUM(scores)-MIN(scores)-SMALL(scores,2))/(COUNT(scores)-2)
```

Part XIII

Part XIV

Sources for Excel Information

The book contains lots of information, but it certainly doesn't cover everything. In this part, you'll find some helpful tips on where to find more information about Excel.

Tips and Where to Find Them

Tip 206 Using Excel's Help System 513

Tip 207 Searching the Internet
for Help 515

Tip 208 Using Excel Newsgroups 517

Tip 209 Browsing Excel-Related
Web Sites 519

Using Excel's Help System

Many users tend to forget one good source of information about using Excel: Excel's Help system. You access Excel's Help system

- By choosing Help⇨Microsoft Excel Help.

- By pressing F1.

- By typing a question in the Type a Question for Help field. This field is located on the right side of the menu bar.

Using any of these methods displays the task pane.

If you're using Excel 2003, you can take advantage of a new feature that provides updated help information from Microsoft's Web site. To control what is searched when you are seeking help, use the controls at the bottom of the task pane. For example, if you're creating a budget, try searching for *budget* and select the Templates option (see Figure 206-1).

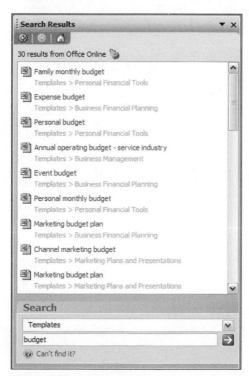

Figure 206-1: The Help system in Excel 2003 can access information on the Web.

The Help system certainly isn't perfect — you'll find that it often provides only superficial help, and that it ignores some topics altogether. But if you're stuck, using Excel's Help system is worth a try.

Searching the Internet for Help

This is probably the best tip in the book. If you have a question about Excel, there's a 90 percent chance that you can find the answer by searching the Internet. The Web has dozens of excellent sites about Excel that provide tips, advice, examples, and downloads.

Many good search engine sites are available. My favorites are

- **Google:** www.google.com
- **A9:** www.a9.com
- **MSN:** search.msn.com

The key to a successful search is composing a good search phrase. Make sure that the phrase includes *Excel*, and then add other keywords that are likely to be present in the answer to your question. Enclose common phrases in quotes. For example, if you're having a problem with formatting in a PivotTable, use a search string like *Excel "pivot table" formatting*.

The more you use the search sites, the better you'll get in composing effective search strings.

Part XIV

Using Excel Newsgroups

What if you had access to hundreds of thousands of answers to specific questions about Excel? Well, guess what? You do — all you need is an Internet connection, and you can find hundreds of thousands of answers in Usenet newsgroups. *Usenet* is an Internet service that provides access to several thousand special interest groups that enable you to communicate with people who share common interests. A newsgroup works like a public bulletin board: You can post a message with your questions, and (usually) others reply to your message.

Thousands of newsgroups cover virtually every topic you can think of (and many that you haven't thought of). Typically, questions posted on a newsgroup are answered within 24 hours — assuming, of course, that you ask the questions in a manner that makes others want to reply.

The best way to read newsgroups is to use special newsreader software designed for that purpose. Microsoft Outlook Express is a good choice, but many others are available. You can also read the newsgroups using your Web browser by visiting the following URLs:

```
http://communities.microsoft.com/newsgroups
http://groups.google.com
```

Table 208-1 lists the key English language Excel newsgroups.

Part XIV

TABLE 208-1   THE EXCEL-RELATED NEWSGROUPS

Newsgroup	Topic
microsoft.public.excel.123quattro	Converting 1-2-3 or Quattro Pro sheets into Excel sheets
microsoft.public.excel.charting	Building charts with Excel
microsoft.public.excel.crashesGPFs	Help with General Protection Faults or system failures
microsoft.public.excel.interopoledde	OLE, DDE, and other cross-application issues
microsoft.public.excel.links	Using links in Excel
microsoft.public.excel.macintosh	Excel issues on the Macintosh operating system
microsoft.public.excel.misc	General topics that do not fit one of the other categories
microsoft.public.excel.newusers	Help for newcomers to Excel

continued

TABLE 208-1   THE EXCEL-RELATED NEWSGROUPS *(continued)*

Newsgroup	Topic
`microsoft.public.excel.printing`	Printing with Excel
`microsoft.public.excel.programming`	Programming Excel with VBA or XLM macros
`microsoft.public.excel.querydao`	Using Microsoft Query and Data Access Objects (DAO) in Excel
`microsoft.public.excel.sdk`	Issues regarding the Excel Software Development Kit
`microsoft.public.excel.setup`	Setting up and installing Excel
`microsoft.public.excel.templates`	Spreadsheet Solutions templates and other XLT files
`microsoft.public.excel.worksheet.functions`	Worksheet functions

You can perform a keyword search on past newsgroup postings. Often, this is an excellent alternative to posting a question to the newsgroup because you may find the answer immediately. Regardless of the question you have, there's an excellent chance that it's already been asked and answered.

The best source for searching newsgroup postings is `http://groups.google.com`.

Browsing Excel-Related Web Sites

If you know where to look, you can find some very useful Web sites devoted to Excel. In this tip, I list a few of my favorites.

Allen Wyatt's Excel Tips

This site features hundreds of Excel tips, as well as a free newsletter. The URL is

```
http://exceltips.vitalnews.com
```

Daily Dose of Excel

This is a Weblog (or blog), maintained by Dick Kusleika, an Excel MVP. He and about a dozen others post new material at this site on a daily basis. The URL is

```
www.dicks-blog.com
```

David McRitchie's Excel Pages

David's site is jam-packed with useful Excel information and is updated frequently. The URL is

```
www.mvps.org/dmcritchie/excel
```

Jon Peltier's Excel Page

Those who frequent the `microsoft.public.excel.charting` newsgroup are familiar with Jon Peltier. Jon has an uncanny ability to solve practically any chart-related problem. His Web site contains many Excel tips and an extensive collection of charting examples. The URL is

```
www.peltiertech.com
```

Mr. Excel

Run by Bill Jelen, this site has lots of tips, downloads, and a very active user forum. The URL is

```
www.mrexcel.com
```

Pearson Software Consulting

This site, maintained by Chip Pearson, contains dozens of useful examples of VBA and clever formula techniques. The URL is

www.cpearson.com/excel.htm

The Spreadsheet Page

This is my own Web site, which contains files to download, developer tips, instructions for accessing Excel Easter eggs, spreadsheet jokes, an extensive list of links to other Excel sites, and information about my books. The URL is

www.j-walk.com/ss

Stephen Bullen's Excel Page

Stephen's Web site contains some fascinating examples of Excel code, including a section titled "They Said It Couldn't Be Done." The URL is

www.bmsltd.ie/Excel

Index

Symbols and Numerics

- (negative sign), 69

% (percent sign), 69

+ (plus sign), 69

3D formatting effects, 137–138

56-color palette. *See also* colors

    color change, 147, 148

    color duplication, 147

    default, 148

    defined, 147

    exceptions to, 148–149

    rows, 147

1904 date system, 206

A

absolute references. *See also* references

    defined, 159

    entering, 163

    mixed cell references versus, 161

    name definition with, 196

    when to use, 159–160

actual values, 437

Add View dialog box, 403

add-ins

    custom, creating, 446

    Excel 2003, 481

    files, opening, 482

    finding, 482

    installing, 481–482

    storing custom functions in, 477

    using, 481–482

Add-Ins dialog box, 477, 481

Advanced Appearance dialog box, 37, 38

Advanced File Search controls, 363–364

Advanced Filter feature, 323

age calculations, 215–216

alignment

    cell content, 49

    chart, 301–302

alternate column shading, 152

alternate row shading

    Conditional Formatting formula, 152

    inserting/deleting rows and, 152

    setting up, 151–153

    steps, 151–152

Analysis ToolPak, 481, 482

Analysis ToolPak - VBA, 481

"and" criteria, 247–248, 249

arguments, 177–178

array formulas. *See also* formulas

    for coefficient matrix inverse, 502

    defined, 217

    entering, 235, 243, 251

    ranking values with, 217

arrays

    converting range references into, 305–306

    lookups with, 263

Attach Toolbars dialog box, 419

audience, assumptions, 1

AutoComplete, 77

AutoCorrect

    dialog box, 89

    settings, customizing, 95

    shortcuts, 95–96

    using, 95

Autofill feature

    controlling, 83

    with dates, 82

    lists, 82

    for series of dates, 229

    shortcut menu, 83

    using, 81

AutoFiltering, 321–322

AutoFormat dialog box, 133, 134

AutoFormats

    accessing, 133

    applying, 134

    defined, 133

    elements, 134

    with PivotTables, 134

    types of, 133

    using, 133–134

automatic hyperlinks. *See also* hyperlinks

    controlling, 89–90

    overriding, 89

    turning off, 89

autosensing, 417

Autoshapes
    formatting, 297–298
    in picture charts, 291, 292
    Rectangle, 297
AutoSum, 165–166
AVERAGE function, 213, 509

B

background images, adding, 155
borders, 135
buttons. *See also* toolbars
    adding, 411, 413–414
    copying, 411
    deleting, 411
    repositioning, 411

C

calculations. *See also* formulas
    age, 215–216
    circle, area and perimeter, 497
    conditional average, 509
    cone, surface and volume, 499
    cube, surface and volume, 498
    cylinder, volume, 499
    holiday, 209–211
    multiple-criterion conditional sum, 255–256
    pyramid, volume, 499
    rectangle, area and perimeter, 497
    remainders, 507
    roots, 507
    single-criterion conditional sum, 253–254
    sphere, surface and volume, 498
    square, area and perimeter, 497
    trapezoid, area, 498
    triangle, area, 498
    weighted average, 213
calendars
    controls, linking to cells, 480
    displaying in range, 235
    pop-up linked, displaying, 479–480
    within worksheets, 480
Camera tool, 383–384
CEILING function, 237
CELLHASFORMULA function, 467
cells. *See also* ranges
    borders, 135
    comments, 55, 309–310
    content, aligning, 49

content, hiding, 43
counting, 247–249
counting characters in, 219
dependents, 439, 440–441
drop-down lists in, 101–102
fill handle, 81
formatted, deleting, 29
formula, 97, 183
formula, determining, 467
formula, identifying, 427–428
input, 97–98
last nonblank, 243–244
line breaks, 139
lock status, changing, 43
lower-right, activating, 29
merging, 125
name table, 431
named, 191–192
naming, 163, 191
next, determination, 75
precedents, 439–440
relationships, tracing, 439–440
selecting, 13–15
text wrapping, 139
text/value display in, 123–124
underlining, 135–136
unlocked, 53
unmerging, 125
characters. *See also* text
    counting, 219
    font, viewing, 141–142
    formatting, 127
    formatting examples, 127
    special, 143–144
Chart Location dialog box, 303
Chart menu
    Chart Options command, 288
    Chart Type command, 281
    Location command, 303
    Source Data command, 278
Chart Options dialog box, 288
Chart sheets, 303–304
Chart Type dialog box, 281, 475
Chart Wizard
    in combination chart creation, 281
    in Gantt chart creation, 285–286
    illustrated, 281
    in thermometer-style chart creation, 287

charts
    aligning, 301–302
    annotating, 275
    automatic-adjusting, 200
    combination, 281–282
    converting to pictures, 305
    fill colors, 147
    free-floating text, adding, 275
    freezing, 305–306
    Gantt, 285–286
    line, 283–284
    line colors, 147
    multiple, displaying, 303
    pasting, into graphics programs, 299
    picture, 291–292
    saving, as graphics files, 299–300
    semi-transparent, 297–298
    single-variable mathematical functions, 293–294
    sizing, 301–302, 303
    text, in range, 273–274
    text box, 275
    thermometer-style, 287–289
    two-variable mathematical functions, 295–296
checkerboard shading, 152–153
Christmas Day calculations, 211
circle, area and perimeter calculation, 497
circular references, 503
Code window, 448
colors
    changing, 148
    chart fill, 147
    chart line, 147
    Excel and, 147–149
    formatting, 107
    palette exceptions, 148–149
    sheet tab, 37
    standard, 147
    values, 121–122
Columbus Day calculations, 210–211
column headers
    hiding, 40
    numbers in, 65
columns. *See also* rows
    adding, to designated lists, 316
    alternate shading, 152
    freezing, 79
    hiding, 41
    insertions, preventing, 339–340

    limitation, 49, 50
    number, increasing, 49–50
    repeating, on printout, 381
    selecting, 14–15
    widths, changing, 35
combination charts, 281–282
comments
    adding, 179
    alternative, 55
    annotating formulas without, 179
    annotating with, 179
    graphics, inserting, 311
    hiding, 40
    shapes, changing, 309–310
concatenation, 123
conditional average, calculating, 509
conditional formatting
    applying, 325, 326
    for checkerboard shading, 152–153
    defined, 121, 151
    duplicates search with, 337–338
    list comparisons with, 325–327
    setting up, 151–152, 337
Conditional Formatting dialog box, 152, 325, 428
cone, surface and volume calculations, 499
constants
    MsgBox, 458, 459
    named, 193–194
    values, changing, 194
Control Toolbox toolbar
    Design Mode button, 479
    Exit Design Mode button, 479, 480
    More Controls button, 479
    Properties button, 51, 59, 480
conventions, this book, 2–4
conversion
    with CONVERT function, 485
    without CONVERT function, 485–492
    distance factors, 486
    energy factors, 490
    force factors, 489
    liquid measurement factors, 487
    mass factors, 491
    between measurement systems, 485–492
    surface measurement factors, 488
    temperature, 493
    time factors, 492

continued

conversion *continued*
    volume measurement factors, 489
    weight factors, 486
CONVERT function, 485
Convert Text to Columns Wizard, 226
Copy Picture dialog box, 305
copying
    buttons, 411
    formulas, 268
    formulas with relative references, 159
    range of formulas, 181
COUNTA function, 243, 278
COUNTIF function, 245–246, 247, 248, 327
counting
    cells (multiple criteria), 247–249
    characters, 219
    distinct entries in range, 251
    substring occurrences, 219
Create List dialog box, 315
credit card numbers, entering, 91
criteria
    "and," 247–248, 255
    "and"/"or," 249, 256
    counting cells, 247–249
    "or," 248–249, 256
Ctrl+End, 29
cube, surface and volume calculations, 498
CUBEROOT function, 507
currency
    format shortcut, 105
    symbol, 69
    values, rounding, 238
cursor, restricting to input cells, 97–98
Custom Views dialog box, 403
Customization mode, 411, 412
Customize dialog box
    Attach button, 419
    Commands tab, 322, 343, 403
    Options tab, 62
    Toolbars tab, 62, 413
cylinder, volume calculations, 499

D

data
    editing, 94
    missing, line chart, 283–284
    proofing, 87
    transforming, with formulas, 173–174

transforming, without formulas, 171
    types, 69–72
    Web page, 355–357
data entry
    automation, 77
    credit card numbers, 91
    dates, 69–71
    formulas, 72
    moving cell pointer after, 73
    text, 72
    times, 71
    values, 69
Data Entry Form, 93–94
Data menu
    Filter submenu, 323
    Form command, 93
    Import External Data submenu, 353, 356
    List submenu, 277, 315
    PivotChart Report command, 333, 341
    PivotTable command, 333, 341
    Text to Columns command, 226
    Validation command, 55, 101
data series
    automatic-adjusting, 200
    converting to picture charts, 291
    formatting, 281, 288
Data Validation dialog box, 55, 101–102
date determination
    day of week, 231
    day of year, 231
    first day of week after date, 232
    last day of month, 233
    most recent Sunday, 232
    nth occurrence of day of week in month, 232–233
    quarter, 233
DATE function, 254
DATEDIF function, 215–216
dates
    Autofill feature with, 82
    custom formatting, 117
    entering, 69–71
    Excel recognition, 70
    format shortcut, 105
    grouping items by, 345–347
    number format, 105, 112
    pre-1900, 203–204
    series, generating, 229–230
    specific, determining, 231–233

default workbook, 35–36
Define Name dialog box
    accessing, 175
    Names in Workbook field, 191, 201, 278, 427
    Refers To field, 194
    working with, 191
dependents. *See also* cells
    defined, 439
    identifying, 440–441
designated lists. *See also* lists
    creating, 315–316
    defined, 315
    normal lists versus, 315
    rows/columns, adding, 316
    summary formulas, adding, 316–317
Display Properties dialog box, 37
displayed values, 437
distance conversion factors, 486
DOLLARDE function, 237
DOLLARFR function, 237
Drawing toolbar, 107, 309
drop-down lists, 101–102
duplicates, finding, 337–338
dynamic named formulas
    common uses, 200
    creating, 199–200
    defined, 199
    in sales data representation, 199
    using, 199–200

E

Easter calculations, 210
Edit menu
    Clear submenu, 11
    Copy command, 131, 169, 171, 173, 384
    Cut command, 181
    Delete command, 29
    Fill submenu, 181, 331
    Find command, 45
    Go To command, 17, 385, 427, 439, 440
    Links command, 435
    Paste command, 292, 298, 305, 355
    Paste Picture Link command, 384
    Paste Special command, 11, 90, 131, 169, 171
    Redo command, 21
    Repeat command, 21
    Replace command, 45
        Shift+click, 409
        Undo command, 21
energy conversion factors, 490
Error Checking dialog box, 426
errors
    checking, 425–426
    formula, avoiding, 187–188
    values, hiding, 188
Euro Currency Tools, 481
EVEN function, 237
Excel
    crash at start, 61
    information sources, 511–520
    newsgroups, 517–518
    reinstalling, 65
    versions, 9–10
Excel-related Web sites, 519–520
    Allen Wyatt's Excel tips, 519
    daily dose of Excel, 519
    David McRitchie's Excel pages, 519
    Jon Peltier's Excel page, 519
    Mr. Excel, 519
    Pearson Software consulting, 520
    spreadsheet page, 520
    Stephen Bullen's Excel page, 520
Exponential Number format, 105
External Data Range Properties dialog box, 353
EXTRACTELEMENT function, 468–469

F

feedback, this book, 6
file bloat, 375
File Import Wizard, 369
File menu
    File Search command, 363
    Open command, 357, 369, 375
    Page Setup command, 35, 381, 387, 388, 397, 401
    Print Area submenu, 379
    Print command, 379
    Properties command, 362, 363
    Save As command, 10, 35, 299, 359, 371
    Save as Web Page command, 375
    Save Workspace command, 373
    Shift+click, 409
    View Code command, 52
File Properties dialog box, 362, 363

files
add-in, 482
closing, No to All button, 367
CSV, 353, 354
filenames list, getting, 369–370
importable list, generating, 369
last opened, 365–366
list of, 370
PDF, 393
text, importing into worksheet range, 353–354
username, 365
working with, 351–375
workspace, 373
.xlb, 421
Fill Effects dialog box, 311
Find and Replace dialog box
accessing, 45
Format button, 47
illustrated, 45
matching cell list, 48
options, 46
Replace All button, 47
Replace tab, 48
wildcard character support, 45–46
Find Format dialog box, 47
floating-point number problems, 429–430
FLOOR function, 237
fonts
Arial, 143
Bookshelf Symbol 7, 141
changing, 35
characters, viewing, 141–142
default, changing, 146
Unicode, 142
Wingdings, 274
workbook sharing and, 142
Footer dialog box, 387
force conversion factors, 489
Format AutoShape dialog box, 297–298
Format Axis dialog box, 286, 289
Format Cells dialog box, 22
Alignment tab, 139, 447, 448
Font tab, 127
Number tab, 43, 85, 91, 105, 109–110, 113
Protection tab, 43, 53, 97
Format Comment dialog box, 311
Format Data Series dialog box, 281, 288

Format menu
Cells command, 43, 53, 85, 97, 105, 109
Column submenu, 41
Conditional Formatting command, 151, 325, 428
Row submenu, 41
Sheet submenu, 59, 155, 307
Style command, 35, 146
Format Object dialog box, 301, 385
formatted cells. *See also* cells
currency, 105
deleting, 29
formatting
3D effects, 137–138
AutoShapes, 297–298
based on cell value, 121
characters, 127
color, 107
conditional, 121, 325
date, 47, 105, 117
number, 105
percentages, 119–120
replacing, 47–48
reports, 331
for suppressing entries, 122
time, 105
toolbar buttons, 107
Formatting toolbar
Borders button, 107
custom, 414–415
Fill Color button, 107, 427
Font Color button, 107
Font drop-down list, 141
Merge and Center button, 235
tools, 415
Underline button, 136
Formula Auditing toolbar, 439, 440
Formula Bar, 40
formula cells. *See also* cells
defined, 97
identifying, 427–428
monitoring, 183
formula view mode, 185, 399
formulas
annotating, no comments, 179
area calculations, 497–498
array, 217
Christmas Day, 211

circular reference, 503–504
Columbus Day, 210–211
conditional formatting, 152
converting, to values, 169
copying, 159–160
copying/pasting, 268
COUNTIF, 245–246
counting cells (multiple criteria), 247–249
counting entries in range, 251
date's quarter, 233
day of week, 231
day of year, 231
deleting values while keeping, 175
displaying, 185
dynamic named, 199–200
Easter, 210
elements, 72
entering, 72
error displays, avoiding, 187–188
evaluation, 192
exact copy of, 181
first day of week after date, 232
hiding, 40
Indcpcndence Day, 210
with INDIRECT function, 265–266
intermediate, 267
Labor Day, 210
last day of month, 233
list randomization, 329
listings, this book, 2
lookup, 257–258
lookup with array, 263
Martin Luther King Jr. Day, 209
megaformulas, 267–269
Memorial Day, 210
most recent Sunday, 232
multiple-criterion conditional sum, 255–256
nth occurrence of day of week in month, 232–233
name title removal, 227
named, 191
New Year's Day, 209
ordinal number conversion, 221
parsing names, 225
percentage, 287
President's Day, 209
printing, 185
range, exact copy, 181

with relative references, copying, 159
returning last nonblank cells, 243–244
right triangle, 495–496
rounding numbers, 237–239
rounding time values, 241
self-expanding chart, 277–279
series of dates generation, 229–230
for simultaneous equations, 501–502
single-criterion conditional sum, 253–254
SUBTOTAL, 165
SUM, 131, 165, 166
summary, 316–317
surface calculations, 498–499
temperature conversion, 493
temporary, deleting, 174
text chart, 273–274
Thanksgiving Day, 211
transforming data using, 173–174
two-column lookup, 261–262
two-way lookup, 259–260
Veterans Day, 211
volume calculations, 498–499
word extraction, 223–224
with worksheet-level names, 201
FOURTHROOT function, 507
fraction formats, 85, 120
fractions
    built-in number formats, 85, 120
    displaying, 120
    displaying values as, 86
    entering, 85
    working with, 85–86
freezing panes, 79
Function Arguments dialog box, 178
function procedures, 456
functions
    arguments, 177–178
    AVERAGE, 213, 509
    CEILING, 237
    CELLHASFORMULA, 467
    CONVERT, 485
    COUNTA, 243, 278
    COUNTIF, 245–246, 247, 248, 327
    CUBEROOT, 507
    custom, creating, 467–469
    custom, limitations, 473

continued

functions *continued*
    custom, storing in add-in, 477
    DATE, 254
    DATEDIF, 215–216
    developing, 446
    DOLLARDE, 237
    DOLLARFR, 237
    entering manually, 177
    EVEN, 237
    EXTRACTELEMENT, 468–469
    FLOOR, 237
    FOURTHROOT, 507
    GETPIVOTDATA, 343
    HLOOKUP, 257
    IF, 187, 188
    INDIRECT, 265–266
    INT, 215, 237, 239
    ISERROR, 187, 188
    LOOKUP, 263
    MATCH, 259–260
    mathematical, 293–296
    MOD, 507
    MONTH, 195
    MROUND, 237, 238
    N, 179
    in names, 195–196
    ODD, 237
    OFFSET, 278
    for pre-1900 dates, 204
    RADIANS, 496
    RAND, 505
    RANDBETWEEN, 505
    RANK, 217
    REVERSETEXT, 468
    ROUND, 237, 241, 273, 429, 437
    ROUNDDOWN, 237
    rounding, 237
    ROUNDUP, 237
    ROW, 152
    SHEETNAME, 467–468
    SIN, 293, 295
    SQRT, 507
    SUBSTITUTE, 219
    SUBTOTAL, 165, 316
    SUM, 213, 253, 265
    SUMIF, 254, 255
    TEXT, 123
    this book, 3

TODAY, 195
TRUNC, 237, 239
USERNAME, 467
VLOOKUP, 257, 263
WEEKDAY, 231
WORKBOOKNAME, 468
YEARFRAC, 215

G

Gantt charts. *See also* charts
    creating, 285–286
    defined, 285
    illustrated, 285
    steps, 285–286
General number format, 105, 111, 119, 120
GETPIVOTDATA function, 343
Go To dialog box
    accessing, 175, 385
    Special button, 175, 331, 385, 427
Go To Special dialog box
    Constants option, 175
    Dependents option, 440
    Formulas option, 427
    illustrated, 17
    option selection, 19
    options, 18
    Precedents option, 439
    using, 17–19
Goal Seek dialog box, 189–190
Goal Seek Status dialog box, 190
goal seeking
    accessing, 189
    information, entering, 190
    power, 190
    using, 189–190
graphics
    inserting, 35
    inserting into cell comments, 311
    saving charts as, 299–300
gridlines, 40, 135
Grouping dialog box, 345, 346

H

Header dialog box, 387
help
    file, 33–34
    Internet, 515, 517–520
    newsgroup, 517–518

system, 33, 513
topics, 33
Web pages, 519–520
window, 33, 57, 513
Help menu
About Microsoft Excel command, 9
Detect and Repair menu, 65
Microsoft Excel Help command, 513
hiding
cell contents, 43
comments, 40
error values, 188
Formula Bar, 40
formulas, 40
gridlines, 40
objects, 40
outline symbols, 40
page breaks, 40
row/column headers, 40
scroll bars, 40
sheet tabs, 40
status bar, 40
task pane, 40
toolbars, 39
user interface elements, 39–40
windows in Taskbar, 40
zero values, 40
HLOOKUP function, 257
holiday calculations
Christmas Day, 211
Columbus Day, 210–211
difficulties, 209
Easter, 210
Independence Day, 210
Labor Day, 210
Martin Luther King Jr. Day, 209
Memorial Day, 210
New Year's Day, 209
President's Day, 209
Thanksgiving Day, 211
Veterans Day, 211
HTML files, 299
hyperlinks
automatic, overriding, 89
automatic, turning off, 89
multiple, removing, 90

removing, 90
removing with VBA, 90

I

icons, this book, 4
IF function
for error checking, 187
for hiding error values, 188
images, background, 155
Import Data dialog box, 353, 356, 357
Independence Day calculations, 210
INDIRECT function
to create references, 266
defined, 265
to sum user-supplied rows, 265
using, 265–266
input cells. *See also* cells
cursor movement restriction to, 97–98
defined, 97
naming, 175
placement, 98
unlocked, 97, 98
InputBox function, 461
InputBox method, 461–462
Insert Function dialog box, 177
Insert menu
Chart command, 281
Comment command, 179, 309
Function command, 177, 477
Module command, 300
Name submenu, 94, 101, 175, 191, 201, 260, 431
Page Break command, 391
Picture submenu, 307, 311
Remove Page Break command, 391
Symbol command, 143
Worksheet command, 22
INT function, 215, 237, 239
intermediate formulas, 267
Internet help, 515, 517–520
ISERROR function, 187, 188

K

key names, this book, 3
keyboard shortcuts
list of, 25
menus, 12
number formatting, 105
sheet activation, 28

L

Labor Day calculations, 210
Layout dialog box, 334, 341
line breaks, forcing, 139
line charts, missing data, 283–284
links, phantom, 435
liquid measurement conversion factors, 487
List menu, 316
lists
    AutoFiltering, applying, 321
    comparing, 325–327
    conditional formatting and, 325–327
    creating, from summary table, 333–335
    defined, 315
    designated, 315–317
    filenames, 369–370
    randomizing, 329–330
    sorting, 339
LOOKUP function, 263
Lookup Wizard, 260, 481
lookups
    with arrays, 263
    exact value, 257–258
    table, 258
    two-column, 261–262
    two-way, 259–260

M

Macro dialog box, 300, 400
macros. *See also* VBA
    asking questions, 458–459
    creating, 447
    defined, 445
    drop-down lists and, 101
    examining, 447–448
    execution, 445
    function procedures, 456
    functions, 445–446
    menu item execution, 475
    pop-up message display, 457–459
    in Power Utility Pak add-in, 399
    recording, 447–449
    recording, in Personal Macro Workbook, 453
    running, with open workbook, 463–465
    for saving charts as graphics files, 299–300
    security issues, 451–452
    storage location, 453
    sub procedures, 455
    testing, 449
    time display, 457–458
    UnhideSheet, 60
    Workbook_Open, 464
    Worksheet_Calculate, 471
Martin Luther King Jr. Day calculations, 209
mass conversion factors, 491
MATCH function, 259–260
math operations, 171
mathematical functions. *See also* functions
    plotting, 293–296
    SIN, 293, 295
    single-variable, 293–294
    two-variable, 295–296
measurement systems, converting, 485–492
megaformulas. *See also* formulas
    calculation speed, 269
    creating, 267–269
    defined, 267
    intermediate formulas, 267
    step-by-step procedure, 268–269
Memorial Day calculations, 210
menus
    commands missing from, 62
    custom, backing up, 421
    custom, deleting, 421
    customizing, 411–412
    efficiency, maximizing, 11–12
    extraneous commands, 62–63
    full, displaying, 11
    hidden commands, 409
    keyboard use, 11–12
    messed up, 62
    right-click, 12
    shortcuts, 12
    this book, 3
Merge Across button, 125
merging cells, 125
missing data, line chart, 283–284
mixed references. *See also* references
    defined, 161
    entering, 163
    when to use, 161–162
MOD function, 507
MONTH function, 195
mouse conventions, this book, 4

MROUND function, 237, 238

MsgBox. *See also* VBA

  arguments, 457

  for button and icon display, 459

  button constants, 458

  constants, combining, 459

  defined, 457

  for time display, 457

  for user response, 459

multifunctional buttons, finding, 407

multiple-criterion conditional sums

  with "and" criteria, 255

  with "and"/"or" criteria, 256

  calculating, 255–256

  with "or" criteria, 256

multisheet ranges, selecting, 15

N

N function, 179

named constants

  defined, 193

  defining, 193

  text, 194

  using, 193–194

  values, changing, 194

named formulas. *See also* formulas

  defined, 191

  defining, 195

  evaluation, 192

  example, 195

  in Source Data dialog box, 279

  using, 191

named ranges. *See also* ranges

  defined, 191

  formula use of, 191

  this book, 3

  understanding, 191–192

named styles. *See also* styles

  attributes, 145

  defined, 145

  using, 145–146

names

  constant, 193–194

  defined, using, 191

  dynamic, 199–200

  functions in, 195–196

  list, pasting, 431

parsing, 225–226

references, editing, 197

removing titles from, 227

understanding, 191–192

user, returning, 467

viewing, graphically, 433

workbook, returning, 468

worksheet, returning, 467–468

worksheet-level, 201

negative sign (-), 69, 120

negative time values, 205–206

New Toolbar dialog box, 413

New Web Query dialog box, 356

New Year's Day calculations, 209

newsgroups

  defined, 517

  list of, 517–518

  postings search, 518

  reading, 517

No To All button, 367

noncontiguous ranges. *See also* ranges

  printing, 383–384

  selecting, 14

non-numeric numbers, fixing, 131

number formats

  codes, 110–111

  Currency, 105

  custom, creating, 109–112

  Date, 105, 112

  Exponential Number, 105

  General, 105, 111

  Number, 105

  Percentage, 105

  to scale values, 113–115

  section determination guidelines, 110

  string parts, 110

  for text/value display, 123–124

  Time, 105, 112

  useful, 119–122

numbers

  in column header, 65

  credit card, 91

  custom formats, 109–112

  entered with wrong decimals, 64

  floating-point, 429–430

  formatting, 105

continued

numbers *continued*
    non-numeric, fixing, 131–132
    ordinal expression, 221
    random, generating, 505
    rounding, 237–239
    scaled, displaying, 113–115

O

objects
    formatting, 301, 385
    hiding, 40
    printing prevention, 385
    selecting, 385
ODD function, 237
Office Clipboard, 99–100
OFFSET function, 278
Open dialog box, 361
Options dialog box
    Calculation tab, 206, 437, 504
    Chart tab, 283
    Color tab, 148
    Custom Lists tab, 82
    Edit tab, 64, 73, 77, 81
    Error Checking tab, 425, 426
    General tab, 35, 36, 61, 65, 363
    View tab, 39, 55, 185
"or" criteria, 249
organization, this book, 5
outline symbols, 40
outlines, worksheet, 395–396

P

Page Break Preview mode, 390
page breaks
    adding, 391
    automatic, 390
    dashed line indication, 391
    forcing, 391
    hiding, 40
    previewing, 389–390
    removing, 391
page numbering
    basic, 387
    code insertion, 387
    starting, changing, 387–388
    tips, 387–388

Page Setup dialog box
    Header/Footer tab, 387
    Page tab, 388, 397
    Sheet tab, 135, 381
parsing names, 225–226
passwords
    enter locations, 371
    limitations, 371
    understanding, 371
    worksheet, 53
Paste Name dialog box, 431
Paste Special dialog box
    Add operation, 131
    displaying, 90
    Multiply option, 90, 171
    Value option, 12, 169, 173
pasting
    refreshable information, 355–357
    static information, 355
PDF drivers, 393
PDF files, 393
percent sign (%), 69
Percentage format, 105, 120
percentages
    formatting, 119–120
    formula, 287
person age calculations, 215–216
Personal Macro Workbook, 453
phantom links, locating, 435
picture charts. *See also* charts
    creating, 291
    data series conversion to, 291
    illustrated, 291, 292
Picture toolbar, 311
PivotCharts
    flexibility, 349
    hiding field buttons in, 349–350
    illustrated, 349, 350
    uses, 349
PivotTable and PivotChart Wizard dialog box, 333–334, 341–342
PivotTable toolbar, 343, 417
PivotTables
    AutoFormatting with, 134
    creating, 333–334
    creating, from summary tables, 334

for frequency tabulation, 341–342
grouping and, 347
grouping items by date in, 345–347
location, 334
quick, 341–342
reference control within, 343
for sales data summary, 345
plus sign (+), 69
pop-up linked calendars, 479–480
pop-up toolbars, 417
Power Utility Pak
character formatting, 127
macros, 399
offer, 6
opening, 482
pre-1900 dates. *See also* dates
functions, 204
sorting, 203
working with, 203
precedents. *See also* cells
defined, 439
direct, 439
identifying, 439–440
indirect, 439
President's Day calculations, 209
Preview window, 389
previews
page breaks, 389–390
workbook, saving, 361–362
Print dialog box, 379, 393
Print Preview mode, 389–390, 397
printing
all sheets, 379
background images and, 155
controlling, 379
custom views for, 403
fitting on one page, 397–398
formula list with macro, 399–400
in Formula View mode, 399
formulas, 185
gridlines, 135
noncontiguous ranges, 383–384
objects, preventing, 385
PDF files, 393
specific pages, 379
specific rows, avoiding, 395–396
specific sheets, 379

problems, troubleshooting
commands are missing, 62
"Compile Error in Hidden Module" error message, 63
documents open automatically, 61
double-clicking doesn't work, 63
erroneous "File is Being Edited By" message, 64
Excel crashes at start, 61
Excel not working right, 65
extraneous menu commands, 62–63
macro warning, 64
menus are messed up, 62
numbers in column header, 65
workbook with multiple windows, 64–65
wrong number of decimal places, 64
procedures, this book, 3
Project Properties dialog box, 371
Properties window
controlling properties in, 52
displaying, 51, 59
in hiding worksheets, 59
Protect Sheet dialog box, 43, 53, 339, 371
Protect Workbook dialog box, 371
pyramid, volume calculations, 499
Pythagorean theorem, 495

Q

questions, asking, 458–459
quick frequency tabulation, 341–342

R

RADIANS function, 496
RAND function, 505
RANDBETWEEN function, 505
random integers, generating, 503–504
random numbers, generating, 505
randomizing lists, 329–330
ranges. *See also* cells
calendar display in, 235
checkerboard shading, 152–153
converting references into arrays, 305–306
counting entries in, 251
filling with series, 81–83
formulas, exact copy, 181
importing text file into, 353–354
input cells before entry, 75
multisheet, selecting, 15

continued

ranges *continued*
    name table, 431
    named, 191–192
    naming, 163, 191
    noncontiguous, 14, 383–384
    preventing row/column insertions, 339–340
    selecting, Shift+clicking, 13
    selecting, Shift/Arrow keys, 13
    selecting, special, 17–19
    statistics, 167
    text charts in, 273–274
RANK function, 217
ranking values, 217
Record Macro dialog box, 447, 448, 453
rectangle, area and perimeter calculation, 497
redoing, 21
references
    absolute, 159–160
    circular, 503
    converting into arrays, 305–306
    creating, with INDIRECT function, 266
    mixed, 161–162
    name, editing, 197
    nonrelative, entering, 163
    relative, 159
    type, changing, 163
Registry Editor, 23
relative references. *See also* references
    copying formulas with, 159
    defined, 159
    mixed references and, 161
    uses, 159
remainders, calculating, 507
repeating
    command, 21–22
    levels and, 22
    text, 120
reports
    formatting, 331
    gaps, filling, 331–332
REVERSETEXT function, 468
right triangles, solving, 495–496
right-click menus, 12
roots, calculating, 507
ROUND function, 237, 241, 273, 429, 437
ROUNDDOWN function, 237

rounding
    currency values, 238
    functions, 237
    with INT/TRUNC functions, 239
    to *n* significant digits, 239
    to nearest multiple, 238
    numbers, 237–239
    time values, 241
ROUNDUP function, 237
ROW function, 152
row headers, 40
rows. *See also* columns
    adding, to designated lists, 316
    alternate shading, 151–153
    freezing, 79
    grouped, hiding, 396
    hiding, 41
    insertions, preventing, 339–340
    number, increasing, 49–50
    repeating, displaying on printout, 381
    selecting, 14
    specific, avoiding printing, 395–396

S

sales tax rate, storing, 193
Save As dialog box, 477
Save Options dialog box, 371
Save Workspace dialog box, 373
scientific notation, 69
scroll bars, hiding, 40
ScrollArea property, 51–52
searches, inexact, 45–46
Security dialog box
    accessing, 451
    illustrated, 451
    security levels, 452
Security Warning dialog box, 451
selecting cells. *See also* cells
    columns, 14–15
    current region, 13
    ranges, multisheet, 15
    ranges, noncontiguous, 14
    ranges, Shift+clicking, 13
    ranges, Shift/Arrow keys, 13
    rows, 14
    specific types, 17–19

self-expanding charts. *See also* charts
    creating, 277–279
    for Excel 2003, 277
    for versions prior to Excel 2003, 278–279
semi-transparent charts. *See also* charts
    creating, 297–298
    illustrated, 297
series of dates, 229–230
setup problem, troubleshooting, 61–65
shading
    alternate column, 152
    alternate row, 151–153
    checkerboard, 152–153
sheet tabs. *See also* worksheets
    appearance, changing, 37–38
    colors, 37
    hiding, 40
    revealing, 27
    scrolling, 27
    text size, 37–38
SHEETNAME function, 467–468
Shift+Enter, 75
shortcut keys, 12, 25
SIN function, 293
single-criterion conditional sums, 253–254
Smart Tags, 425, 426
Solver Add-In, 481
Sort dialog box, 319
sorting
    lists, 339
    on more than three columns, 319
    pre-1900 dates, 203
Source Data dialog box, 278–279
special characters
    entering, 143–144
    locating, 143
Speech Properties dialog box, 87
sphere, surface and volume calculations, 498
SQRT function, 507
square, area and perimeter calculation, 497
Standard toolbar
    Print Preview button, 389
    Sort Ascending button, 319
    Sort Descending button, 319
    Undo button, 21
startup
    documents open automatically, 61
    Excel crash, 61

statistics, 167–168
status bar
    hiding, 40
    selection statistics feature, 167–168
strings
    extracting *n*th element from, 468–469
    reversing, 468
    word extraction from, 223–224
Style button, 146
Style dialog box, 35, 145
styles
    attributes, 145
    creating, 146
    named, 145–146
    power of, 145
    using, 146
sub procedures, 455
subscripts, 127
SUBSTITUTE function, 219
substrings, counting occurrences, 219
SUBTOTAL formula, 165
SUBTOTAL function, 165, 316
SUM formula, 131, 165, 166
SUM function, 213, 253, 265
SUMIF function, 254, 255
summary formulas. *See also* formulas
    adding, to designated lists, 316–317
    defined, 316
summary tables
    creating lists from, 333–335
    illustrated, 335
summing
    negative values, 253
    values based on date comparison, 254
    values based on difference range, 253–254
    values based on text comparison, 254
superscripts, 127
suppressing entries, 122
surface measurement conversion factors, 488
Symbol dialog box, 143

T

task pane
    help topics and, 33
    hiding, 40
    Options button, 100
temperatures, converting, 493

text
  boxes, 275
  entering, 72
  in named constants, 194
  repeating, 120
  sheet tab, 37–38
  single cell limit, 72
  size, changing, 57
  value display with, 123–124
  wrapping, 139
text charts, 273–274
text files, importing, 353–354
TEXT function, 123
Text Import Wizard, 353
text-to-speech feature, 87, 471
Thanksgiving Day calculations, 211
thermometer-style charts. *See also* charts
  creating, 287–289
  defined, 287
  illustrated, 289
  percentage formula, 287
  thermometer setup, 288–289
thousands separator, 69
time conversion factors, 492
times
  displaying, with VBA macro, 457
  entering, 71
  exceeding 24 hours, 129–130
  format shortcut, 105
  negative values, 205–206
  number format, 105, 112
  values, rounding, 241
  values, summing, 129
titles (name), removing, 227
TODAY function, 195
toolbars. *See also* buttons; *specific toolbars*
  attaching, to worksheets, 419
  button actions, 411
  button elimination, 411
  button images, 411
  creating, 411
  custom, backing up, 421
  custom, creating, 413–415
  custom, deleting, 421
  customizing, 411–412
  hiding, 39
  mini, 107

  multifunctional buttons, 407
  pop-up, 417
  removing, 419
  saving, 415
  "tear off," 107
Tools menu
  Add-Ins command, 63, 477
  AutoCorrect Options command, 89, 95, 143
  Error Checking command, 426
  Formula Auditing command, 439, 440
  Goal Seek command, 189
  Macro submenu, 447, 451
  Options command, 35, 36, 39, 61, 64, 65, 73
  Protection submenu, 43, 53, 97, 339
  Sheet submenu, 98
  Speech submenu, 87
transforming data
  with formulas, 173–174
  without formulas, 171
trapezoid, area calculations, 498
triangles
  area calculations, 498
  right, solving, 495–497
TRUNC function, 237, 239
two-column lookups. *See also* lookups
  formula, 261–262
  table, 261
two-way lookups. *See also* lookups
  with formula, 259–260
  with implicit intersection, 260
  table, 259

U

underlining
  accessing, 136
  examples, 136
  types of, 135–136
undo
  levels, changing, 23
  process, 21
USERNAME function, 467
users
  getting information from, 461–462
  greeting, by name, 463–464
  name, returning, 467

V

values
actual, 437
coloring, 121–122
data entry, 69
deleting, keeping formulas, 175
displayed, 437
exact, looking up, 257–258
formatting based on, 121
formulas conversion to, 169
as fractions, 86
in hundreds, 114–115
in millions, 113–114
named constant, 194
negative time, 205–206
ranking, 217
rounding, 437
scaling, 113–115
summing, 253–254
text display with, 123–124
in thousands, 114
time, rounding, 241
time, summing, 129
zero, hiding, 40
VBA. *See also* macros
defined, 445
functions, 456
Help system, 457
InputBox function, 461
MsgBox function, 457–459
pop-up message display, 457–459
removing hyperlinks with, 90
sub procedures, 455
USERNAME function, 467
VBA code
CELLHASFORMULA function, 467
entering, 4, 400
EXTRACTELEMENT function, 469
listings, this book, 3
REVERSETEXT function, 468
security and, 452
SHEETNAME function, 468
WORKBOOKNAME function, 468
VBA modules
deleting, 64
entering code into, 400
VBE toolbar, 449

versions
current usage, 9
list of, 10
use, 9
Veterans Day calculations, 211
View menu
Custom Views command, 321, 322, 403
Sized with Window command, 303
Text Size command, 57
Toolbars submenu, Customize command, 11, 39, 62,
125, 146, 322, 343
VBA Editor, 90
views
adding, 403
custom, for printing, 403
custom, with AutoFiltering, 321–322
named, creating, 321
named, selecting, 403
Visual Basic Editor, 64, 90, 300, 447
VLOOKUP function, 257, 263
volume measurement conversion factors, 489

W

Watch Window, 183
watermarks, 307
Web pages
getting data from, 355–357
imported data, 357
opening directly, 357
WEEKDAY function, 231
weight conversion factors, 486
weighted average calculations, 213
wildcard characters, 45–46
Window menu
Compare Side By Side With command, 31
Freeze Panes command, 79, 381
New Window command, 31, 64
Unfreeze Panes command, 79
windows
closing, 65
multiple, displaying, 31
multiple, illustrated, 32
multiple, use, 31
removing, 31
Windows Clipboard, 99
Windows registry, editing, 23
Word Art, 307

words
    all but first, extracting, 223–224
    first, extracting, 223
    last, extracting, 223
WORKBOOKNAME function, 468
workbooks
    default, customizing, 35–36
    display, 31
    full path, displaying, 359
    name, returning, 468
    number of times opened, 464
    Personal Macro, 453
    preview, saving, 361–362
    Preview option, 361–362
    running macros and, 463–465
    saving, 29
    sharing, fonts and, 142
    size, reducing, 375
    usage log, 465
    view options, 361
worksheet-level names, 201
worksheets. *See also* sheet tabs; workbooks
    activating, 27, 28
    attaching toolbars to, 419
    background images, 155
    contiguous, selecting, 15
    evaluating, 425
    functions, creating, 467–469
    grouping, 181
    name, returning, 467–468
    navigating, 27–28
    number of, 35
    outline, 395–396
    page setup settings across, 401
    passwords, 53
    pop-up list, 27
    print area, setting, 379
    print preview, 397
    printing, 379
    protecting, 53, 339
    ranges, selecting, 15
    ungrouping, 181, 401
    unhiding, 59
    unprotecting, 340
    used area, limiting, 51–52
    used area, resetting, 29

    very hidden, 59–60
    watermarks, 307
    zooming, 427
workspace files, 373
Wrap Text option, 139

X

.xlb file, 421
XLStart directory, 35, 36, 61

Y

YEARFRAC function, 215

Z

zeros
    hiding, 40, 119
    leading, displaying, 119
zooming, 427